Ways

of the

Hand

Ways
of the
Hand

A Photographer's Memoir

Bruce Jackson

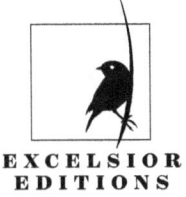

**EXCELSIOR
EDITIONS**

Cover photograph: Patti Smith in Just Buffalo's "Babel" series, 2015.

Published by State University of New York Press, Albany

Excelsior Editions is an imprint of State University of New York Press

For information, contact State University of New York Press, Albany, NY
www.sunypress.edu

Library of Congress Cataloging-in-Publication Data

Name: Jackson, Bruce, 1936– author.
Title: Ways of the hand / Bruce Jackson.
Description: Albany : State University of New York Press, [2022] | Includes index.
Identifiers: LCCN 2021045776 | ISBN 9781438488745 (pbk. : alk. paper) | ISBN
    9781438488752 (ebook)
Subjects: LCSH: Jackson, Bruce, 1936– | Photographers—United States—Biography. | Folklorists—
    United States—Biography. | Photography—United States.
Classification: LCC TR140.J26 A3 2022 | DDC 770.92 [B]—dc23/eng/20211029
LC record available at https://lccn.loc.gov/2021045776

10 9 8 7 6 5 4 3 2 1

Thanks to Diane Christian, for her help with this book, and for everything else.

This is for all my pals, here and gone. As the lads said:
"Good night and joy be to you all."

Contents

Photographs, Pictures, and Stories

The hands. "Brucie, don't talk with your hands!" My mother said that to me again and again when I was growing up in the Bedford-Stuyvesant section of Brooklyn. Our block—Vernon Avenue between Nostrand and Marcy—was second-generation Italians and Jews. My father had been born on that street. How could I not talk with my hands? Hands were the way you punctuated sounds; hands were how you said things for which words weren't on their own adequate.

I thought to do a book of photos of friends, family, and people I encountered while working on various projects. I culled thousands of photos I thought might work. The photographs surprised me: I'd planned to do faces, but the images I liked best were those in which the face and the hands were both up to something. They drove the others out.

Most of my photography has been while I was hanging out or while I was working on something else. They are the sort of pictures we all do now with our smart phones: pictures taken not as *photographs*—but rather markers of a moment. I've done only a small number of projects as pure photo projects from start to finish.

All photographs stop time. But there is more to them to that. Many of those caught moments take on—because of what was going on in them, or who was in them, or because of what happened later—a meaning we couldn't consciously sense in the moment. As with many of the images here.

I'm a photographer, so even in the hanging-out pictures I sometimes took photographs, images with their own logic, their own coherence. If you're a dancer, you can't not dance when the music plays.

Diane Christian, who appears frequently in these pages, and I have long collaborated on books, documentary films, and other projects; we have taught in the same University at Buffalo department for fifty years; we're married. Anyone you encounter here with the name Jackson is a parent or a child; anyone with the name Caico or Von Essen is a grandchild. Bill and Margaret Kunstler, Bob and Penelope Creeley, Michel Foucault, Warren Bennis, Allen Ginsberg, and many others were, and some still are, friends. The others are people I encountered while doing other things.

- The photograph of the two men playing dominoes in the Texas Death Row recreation yard was taken when Diane and I were there in 1979 working on a book and a film about what daily life was like for men waiting to be executed. One of the men in that photo was executed; the other had his sentence reversed in spring 2021.

- The 1968 photo of Janis Joplin onstage at Newport was taken when I was a director of the Newport Folk Festival.

- The 1978 photo of a prison captain punching the head of a stuffed hog at Coffield prison farm was taken when I was visiting Texas prisons preparing to testify in a civil rights case in federal court, *Ruiz v. Estelle*.

- The 1964 photo of the policeman in a garage playing a twelve-string guitar was taken when my car was getting an oil change during a visit to Hobart Smith, a musician in Saltville, Virginia, a stop-off en route to my first work in Texas prisons. Some of the recordings from that 1964 Texas visit form the basis of a 2018 play by New York's Wooster Group, *The B-Side: "Negro Folklore from Texas State Prisons": A Record Album Interpretation*. Three photos from that play are here, too.

I love Rod Stewart's 1971 rock album, *Every Picture Tells a Story*. But I always thought the title nonsense, and still do. Pictures don't tell stories. As photographer Gary Winogrand said to Bill Moyers in 1982, "Photographs—they're mute, they don't have any narrative ability at all. You know what something looks like, but you don't know what's happening, you don't know whether the hat's being held or is it being put on her head or taken off her head. From the photograph, you don't know that. A piece of time and space is well described . . . But not what is happening."

But photographs may imply stories; they may invoke them; there may be stories about the making of them. All photographs have contexts for the photographer who made them and, sometimes, for the viewer who sees them.

The images in *Ways of the Hand* mark specific moments in continuing relationships and random encounters; my comments on them are the same. Some of the photos here need no more than a who, what, and when. Some need more: how they came to be made, or stories they invoke. That is what the six "Words" sections are about. Life and memory are like that. Photographs are our markers of the fragments that remain.

B.J.
Buffalo, November 1, 2021

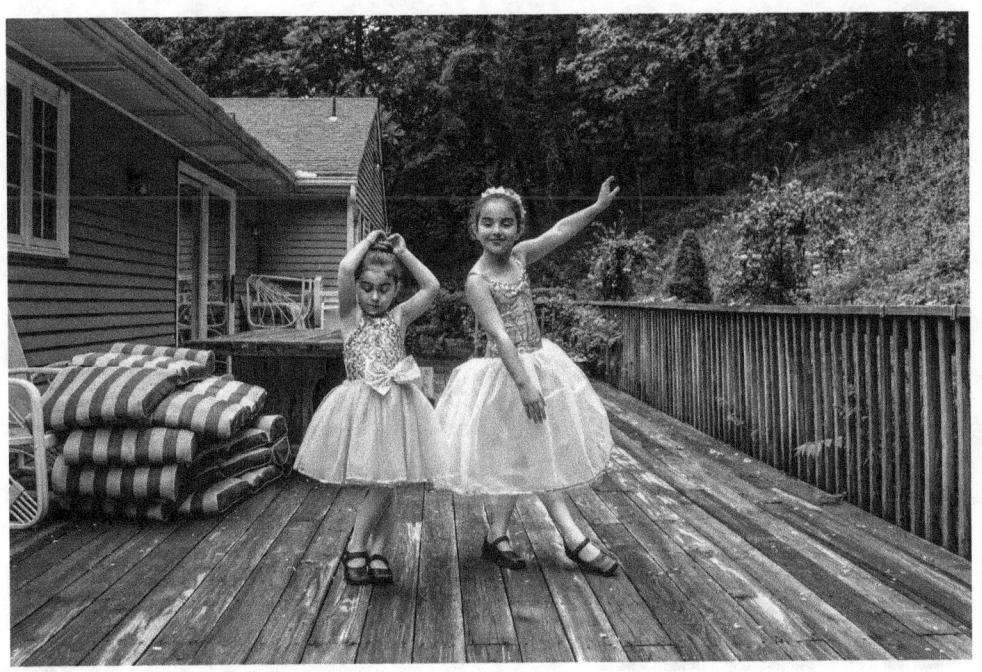

1. Alexa and Leah Von Essen. Holmdel, New Jersey, 2003.

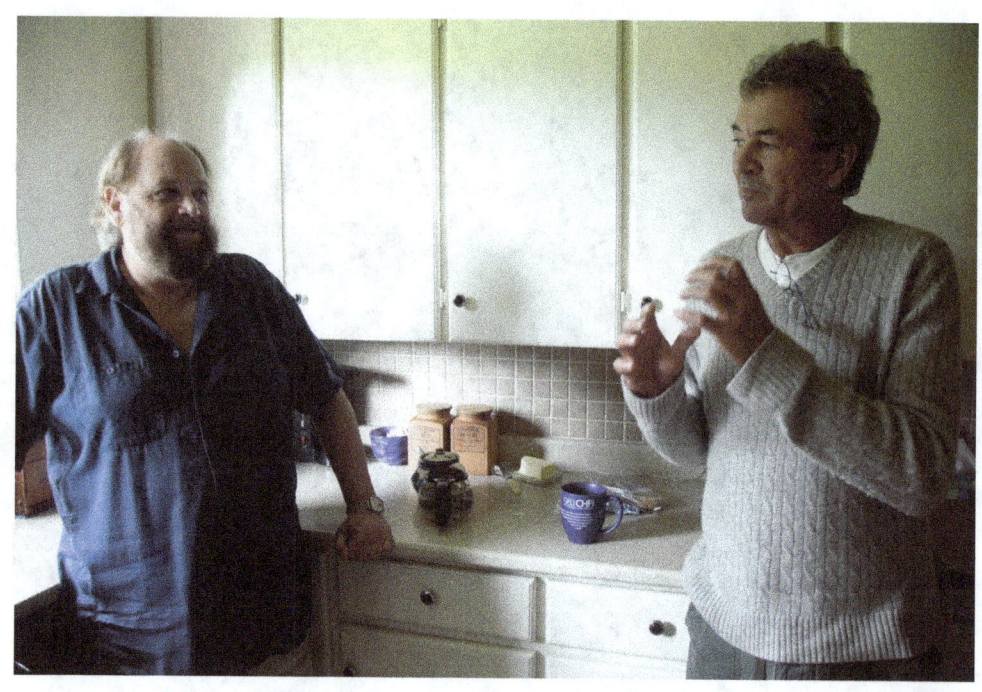

2. Nick Blagona (audio engineer) and Ian Gillan (musician). Dundas, Ontario, 2008.

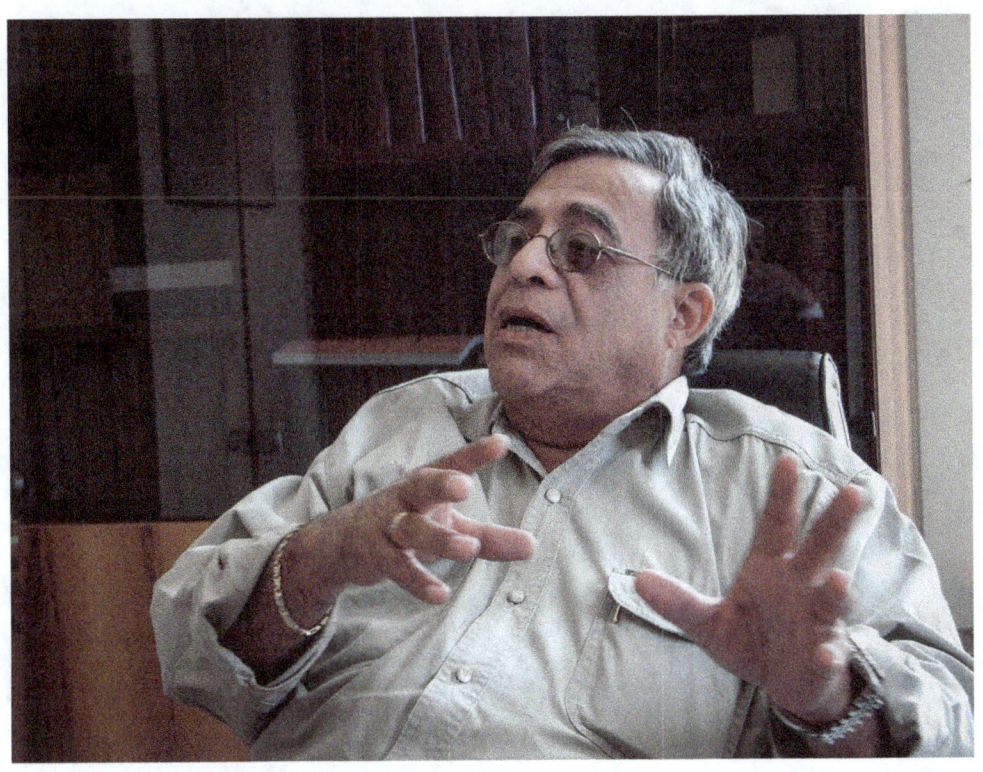
3. Percy Francisco Alvarado Godoy (spy). Rome, Italy, 2005.

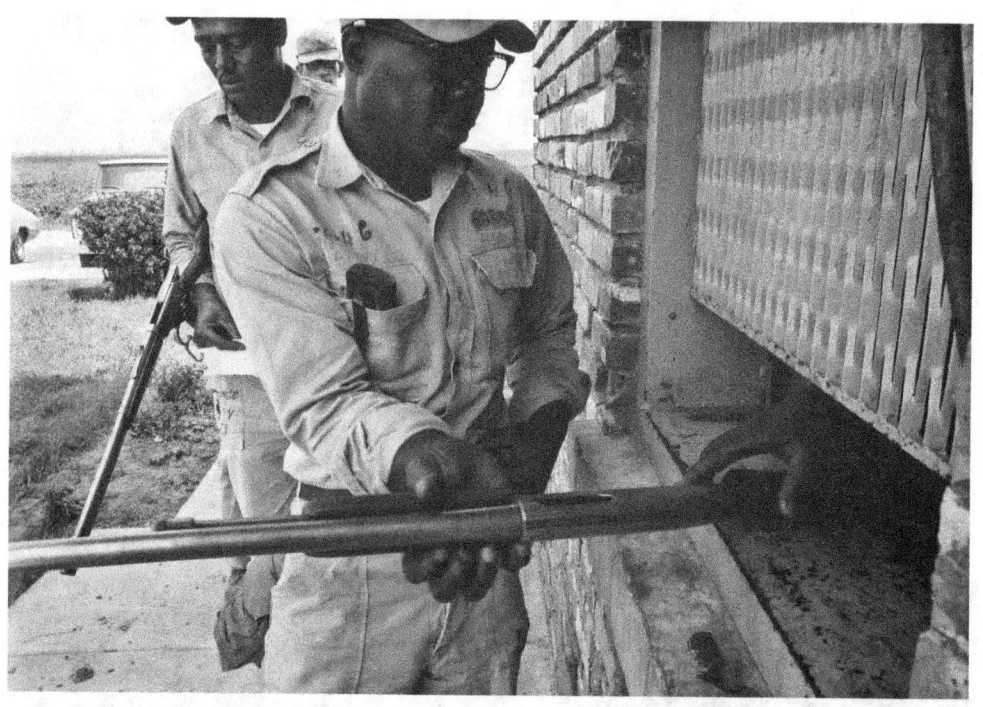

4. Convict guards returning weapons to armory. Cummins prison farm, Varner, Arkansas, 1971.

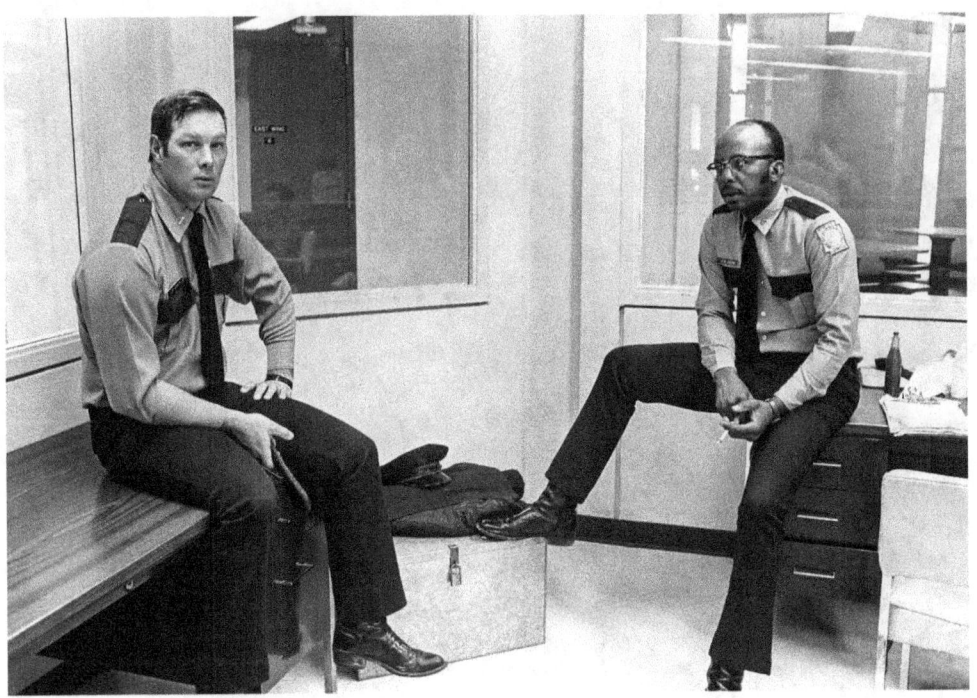

5. Lieutenant (with blackjack) and sergeant (with cigarette) in control picket, Maximum Security building. Cummins prison farm, Varner, Arkansas, 1974.

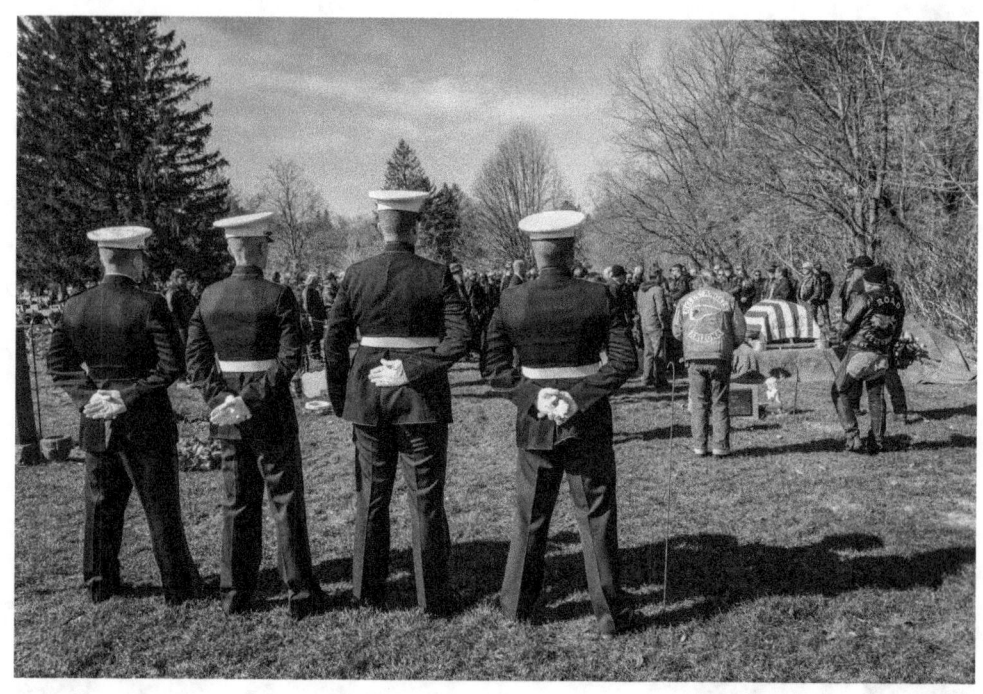

6. Marine honor guard. Funeral of James Boyer, former president, Road Vultures Motorcycle Club. Lockport, New York, 2010.

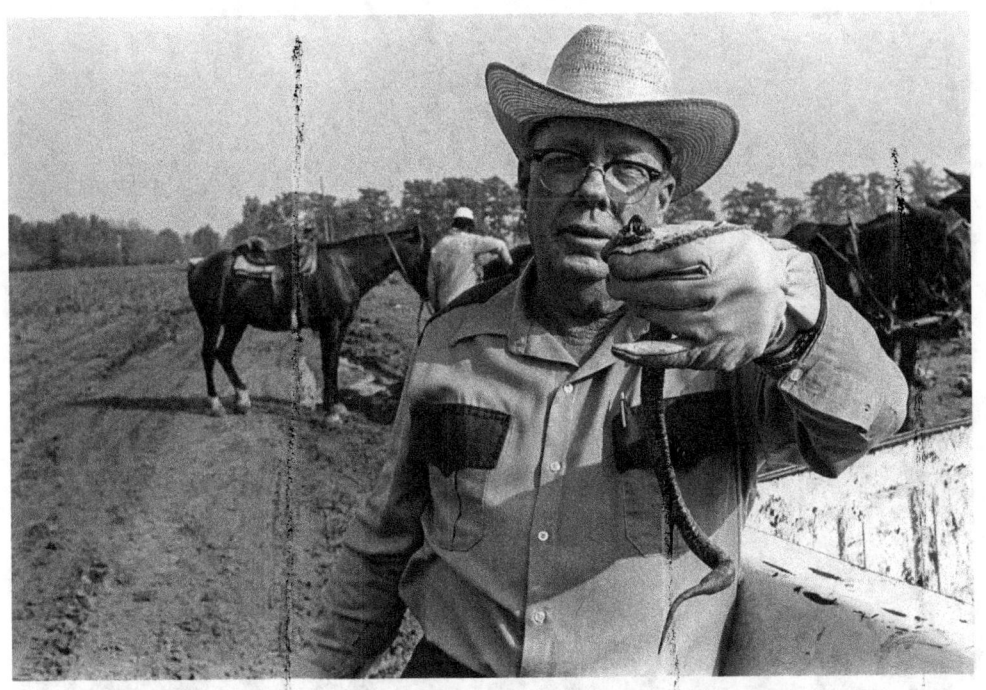

7. Dog sergeant with ground rattler. Cummins prison farm, Varner, Arkansas, 1975.

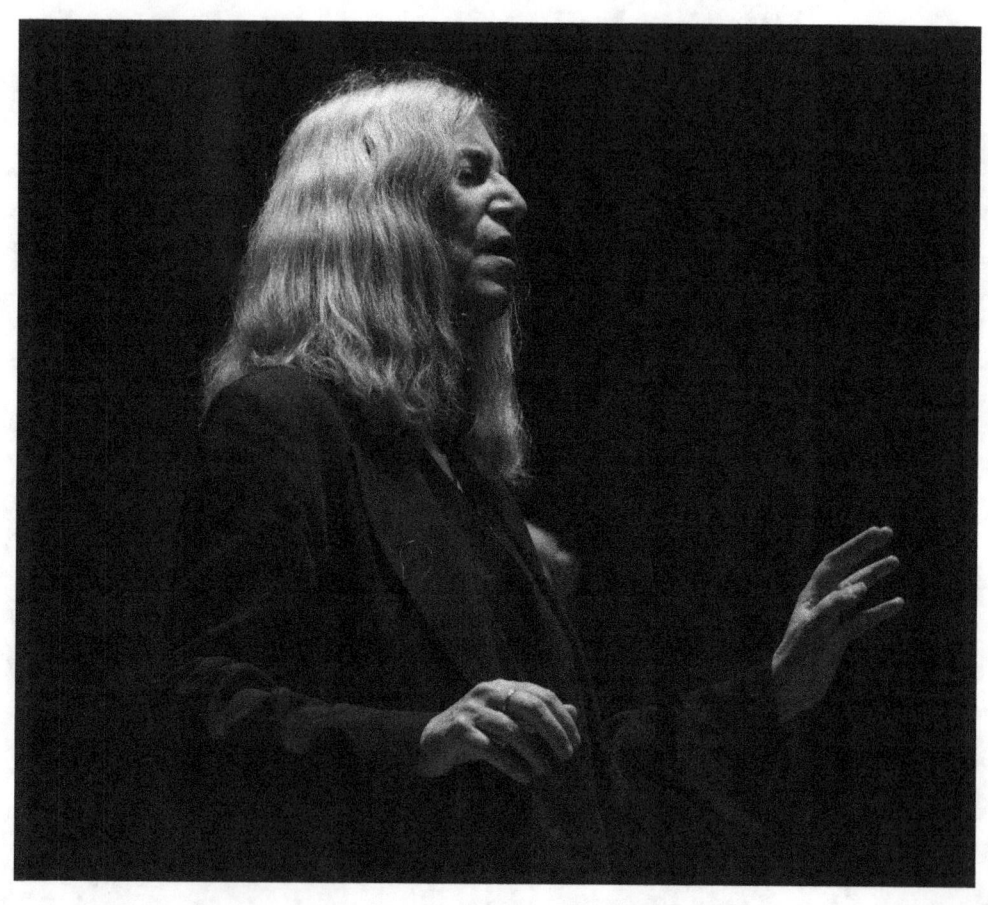

8. Patti Smith (singer and writer) in concert in Just Buffalo's BABEL series. Buffalo, 2015.

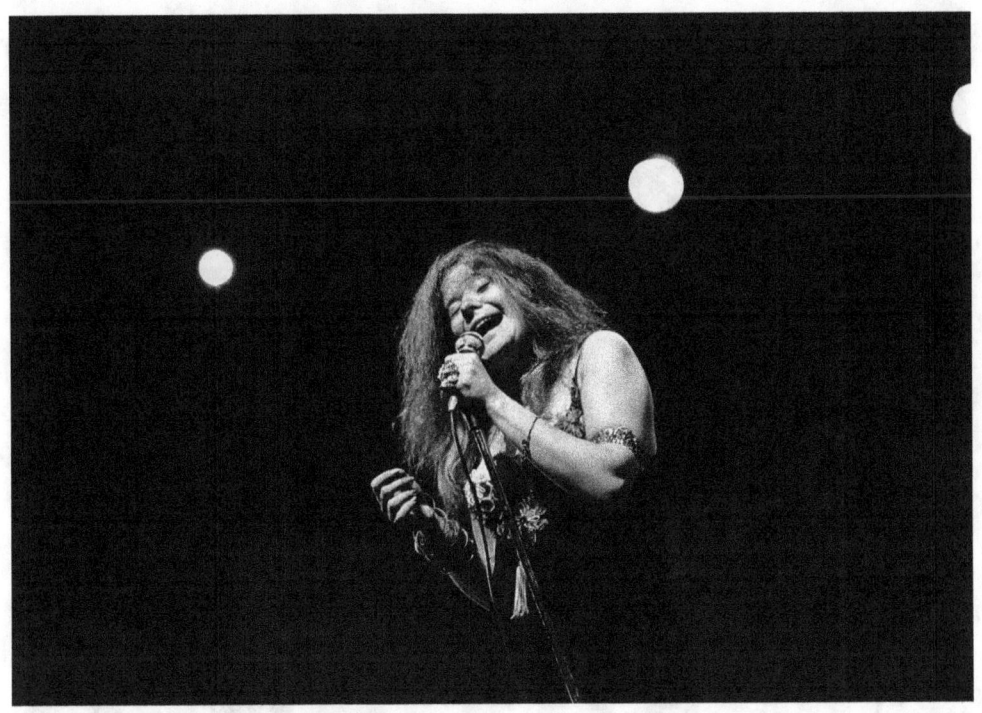

9. Janis Joplin (singer). Newport Folk Festival, Newport, Rhode Island, 1968.

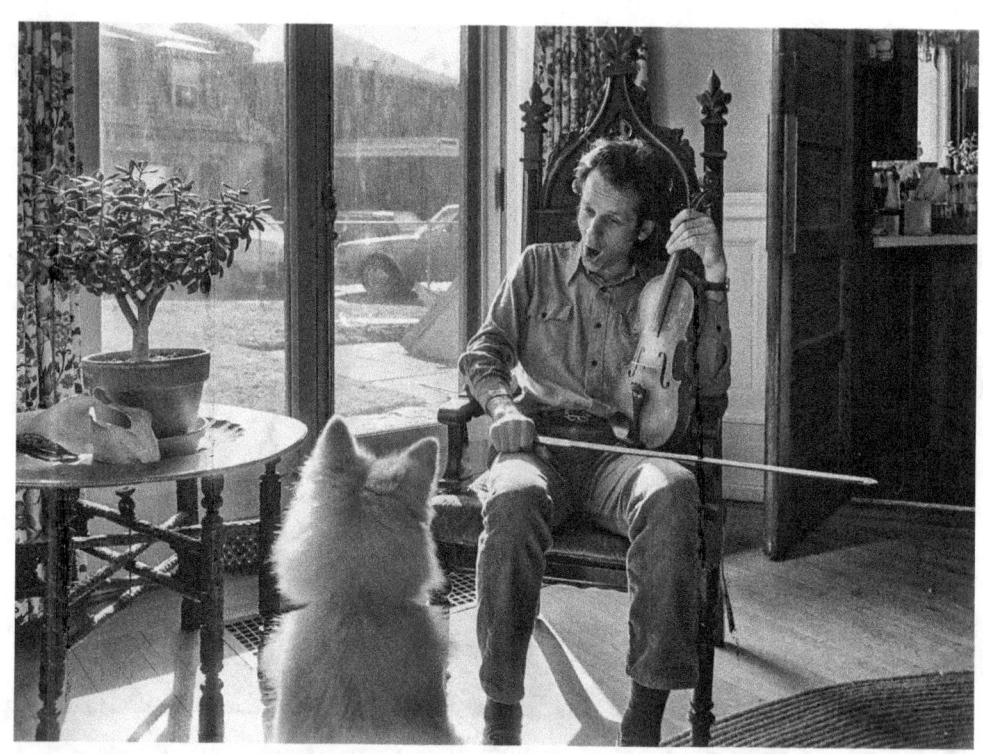

10. Mike Seeger (musician). Buffalo, New York, 1977.

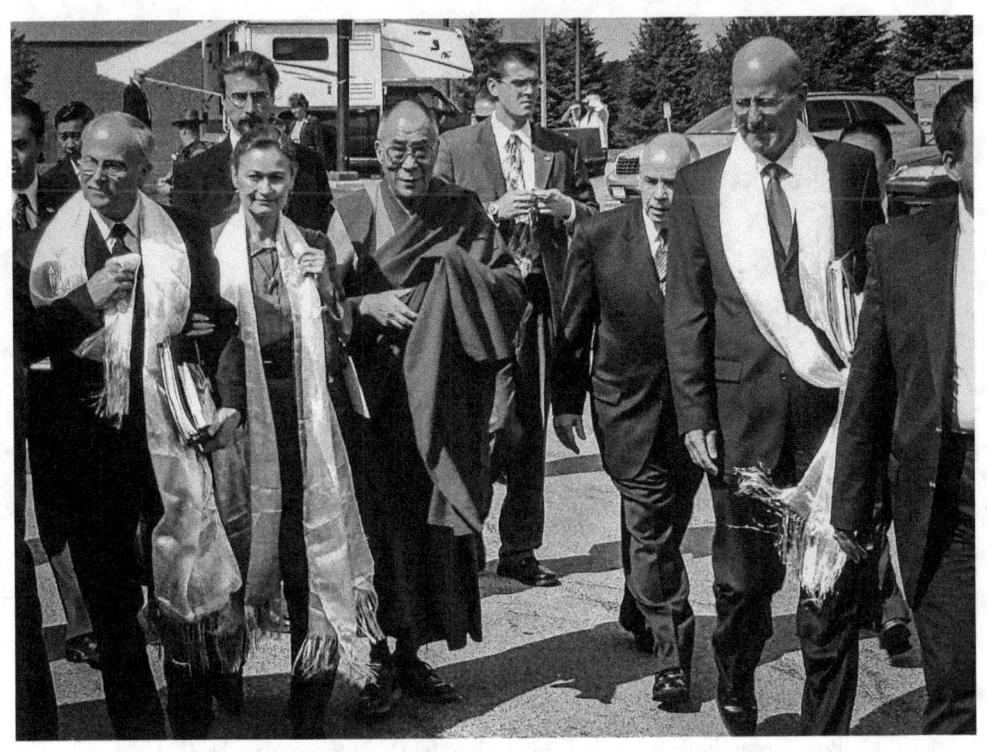

11. Dalai Lama (spiritual leader). Buffalo, New York, 2006.

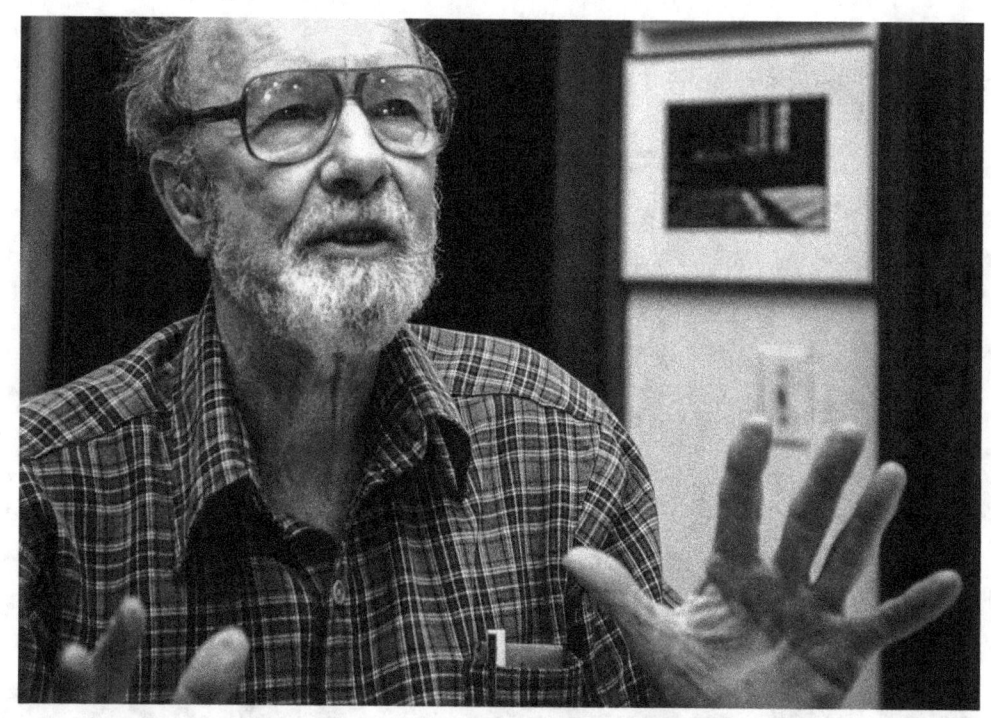

12. Pete Seeger (folksinger and political activist). Buffalo, New York, 1996.

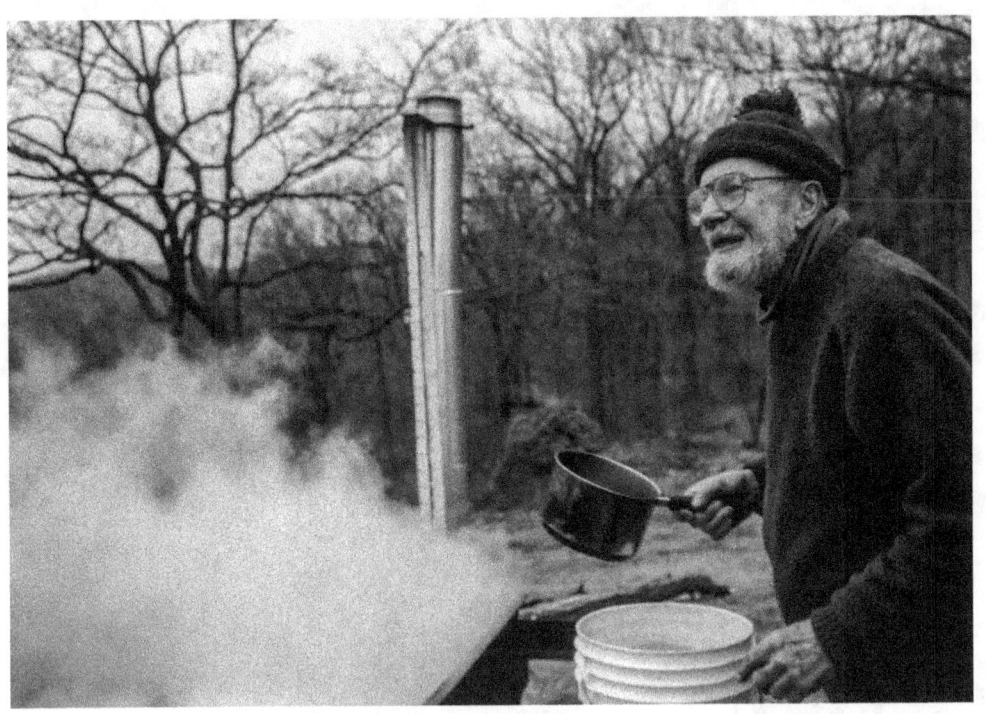

13. Pete Seeger. Beacon, New York, 1977.

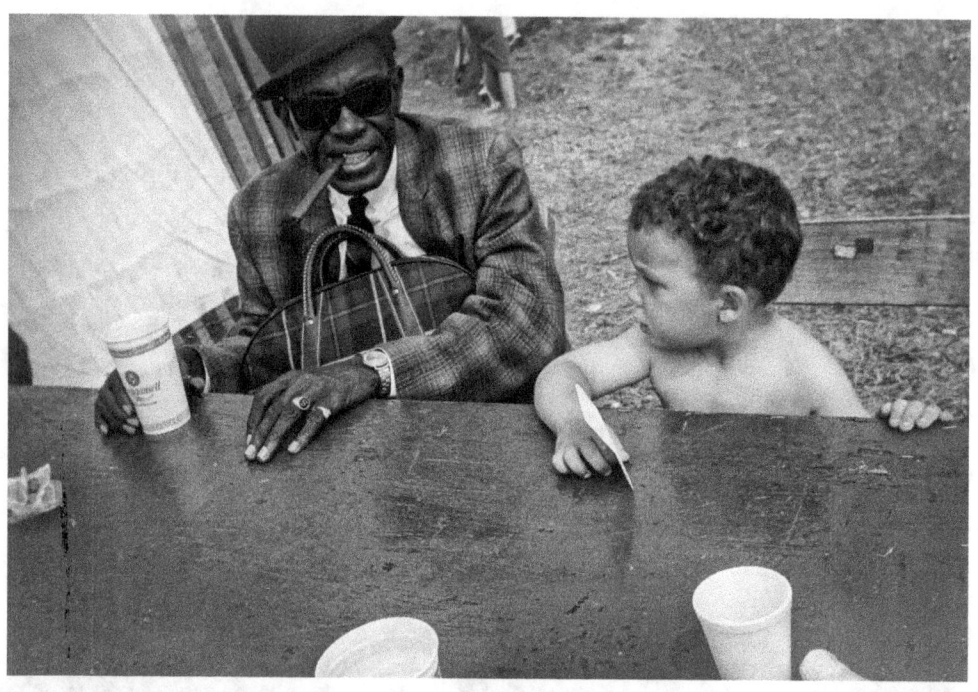

14. Sam "Lightnin'" Hopkins (blues singer) and Michael Lee Jackson, Newport Folk Festival performers' tent. Newport, Rhode Island, 1965.

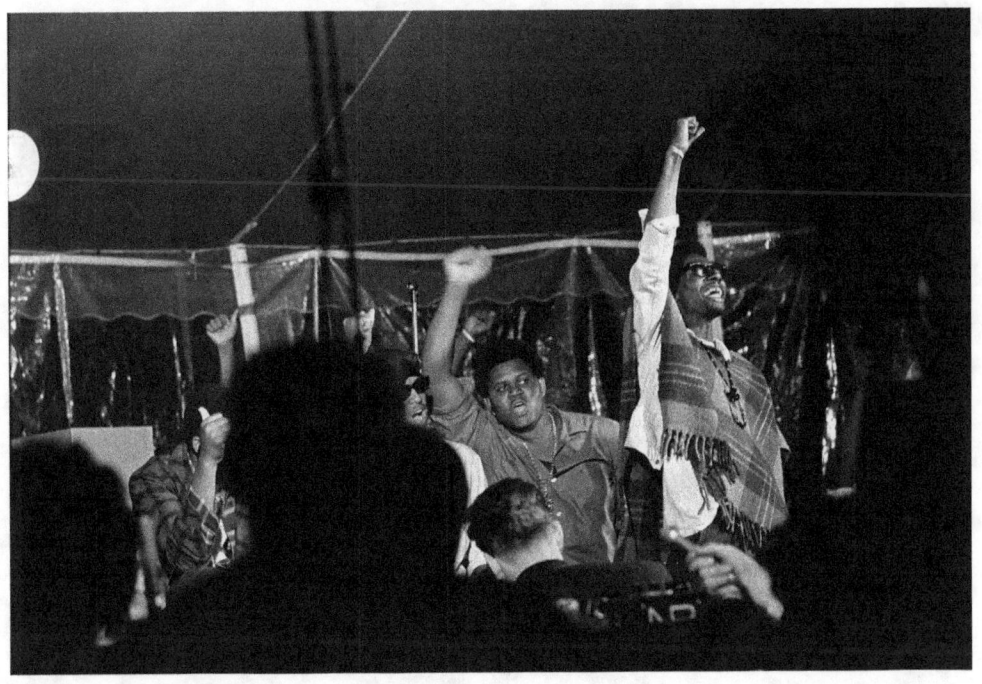

15. Sweet Willie and others. First town meeting. Resurrection City, Washington, DC, 1968.

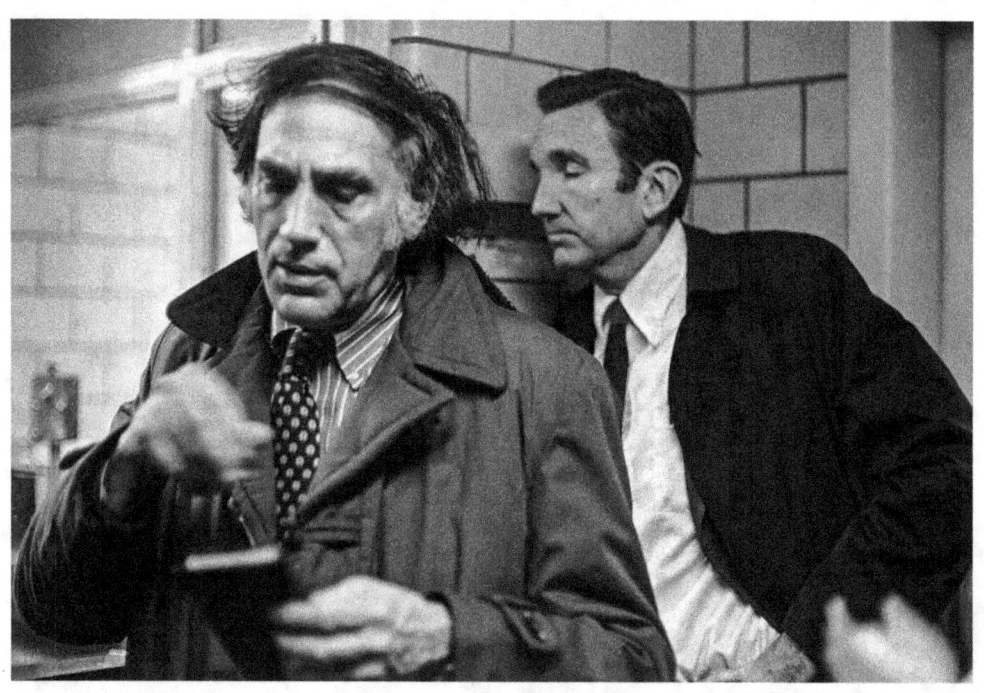

16. William Kunstler and Ramsey Clark (civil rights attorneys). Erie County Holding Center, Buffalo, New York, 1975.

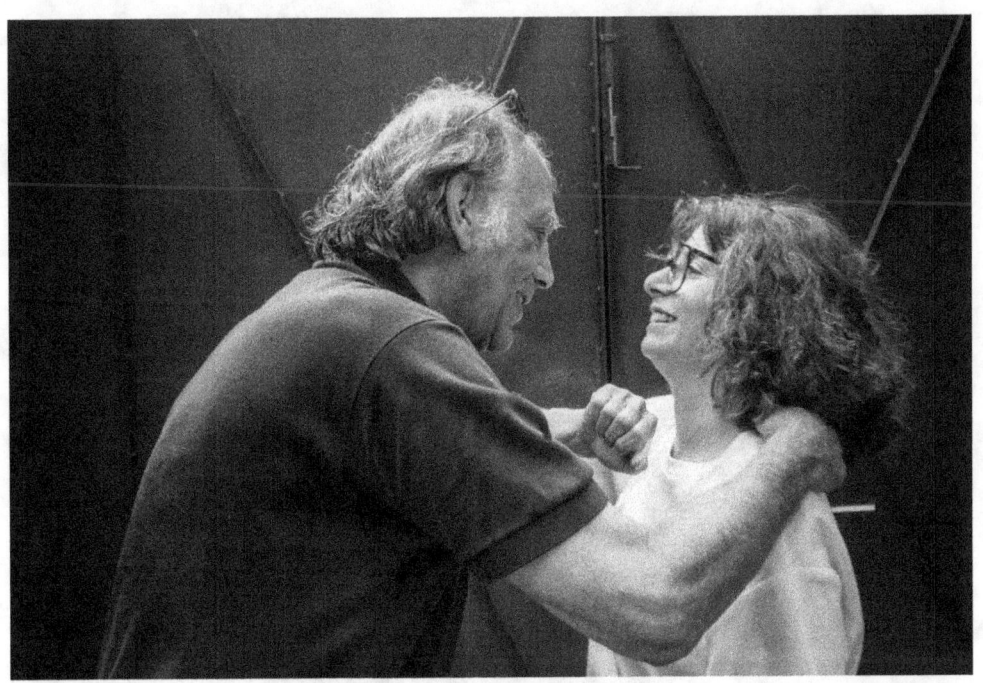

17. William Kunstler and Margaret Kunstler (civil rights attorney). Oaxaca, Mexico, 1990.

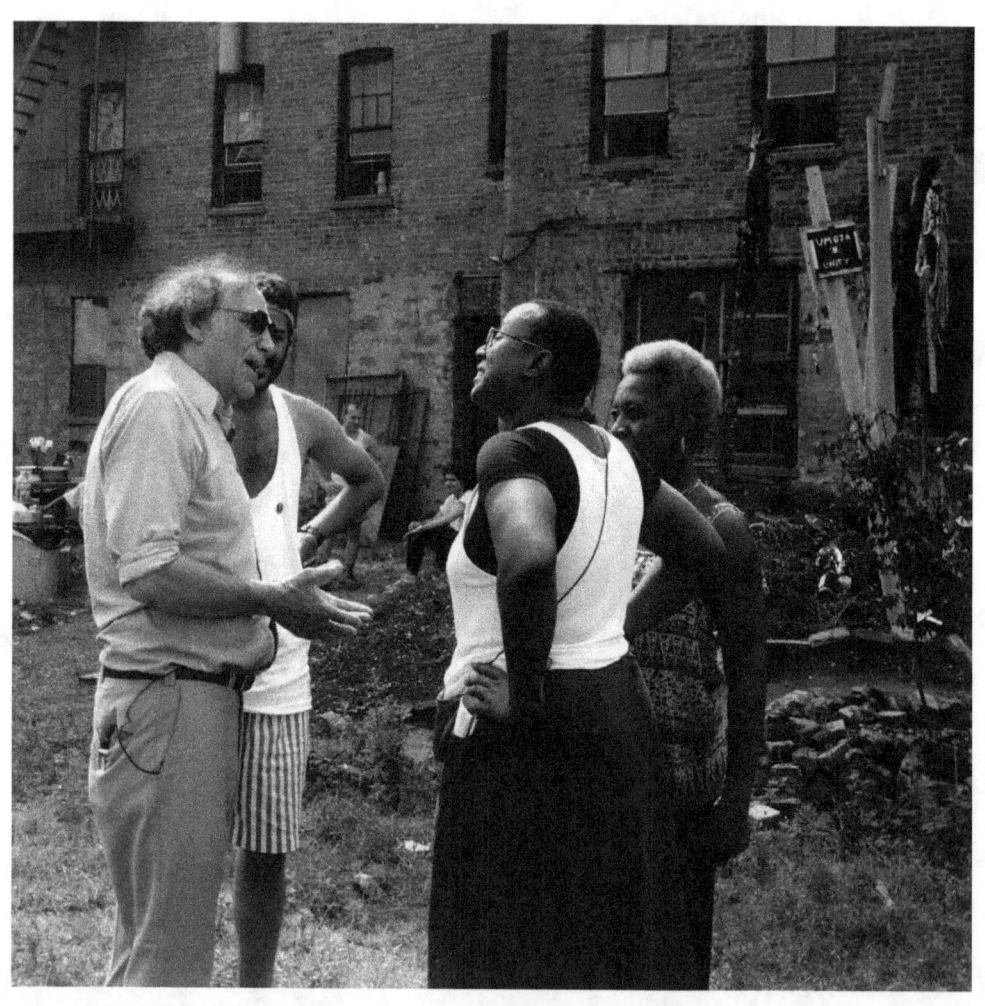

18. William Kunstler and clients. Fort Apache, the Bronx, New York, 1988.

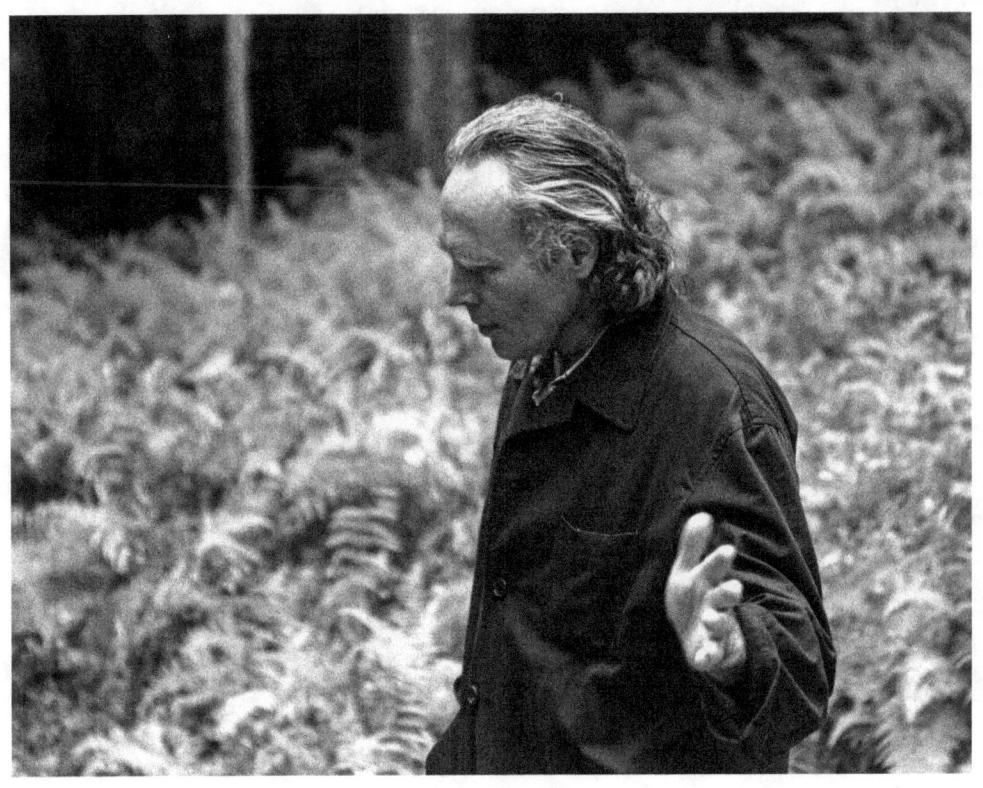

19. Brice Marden (artist). West Shokan, New York, 1995.

Words 1

1. Alexa and Leah Von Essen. Holmdel, New Jersey, 2003.

At that age, you live in a world of story. All you need is the right garment, or part of one. It can even be something you've devised yourself. Nearly twenty years later, I see the same thing in Ali and Leah's younger cousins, Samuel and Michael, only now it is wizards and superheroes: *Harry Potter*, and *Lord of the Rings*. The final image in Michael Ondaatje's *The Collected Works of Billy the Kid: Left-Handed-Poems* (1970) is a photo of Ondaatje himself as a boy, maybe five years old, in his native Sri Lanka, dressed in a full cowboy suit—hat, cap guns, and all. At the same age, in Bed-Stuy, Brooklyn, I had most of the same outfit. Later, our stories get more complicated. They take form and are evoked by the moment, who we're with, an image we're looking at or showing to someone else.

2. Nick Blagona (audio engineer) and Ian Gillan (musician). Dundas, Ontario, 2008.

A kitchen break during an all-day recording session in Nick's studio when Ian and Michael Lee Jackson were laying down tracks for Ian's new CD, *One Eye to Morocco*.

Ian wrote Michael in an email that he'd lifted the title of one of my books—*Get Your Ass in the Water and Swim Like Me*—for one of the verses in a song he'd written for Deep Purple's then-new album, *Infinite*. "I hope Bruce doesn't mind," Ian said.

When Michael told me, I said, "I'm beyond delight."

As a kid, wanting to be a rock star, Michael had played—to a point that nearly drove me mad—the guitar riff on Deep Purple's "Smoke on the Water," which Ian cowrote. All aspiring rockers of Michael's generation did the same. Somehow, Michael and Ian got to be pals, and then they got to be collaborators. And there came a time when Michael performed at Royal Albert Hall with Ian that put my kvetch about "Smoke on the Water" to rest.

Ian knew I loved John Fowles's novels. Fowles was Ian's neighbor in Lyme Regis. For one of my birthdays, he gave me a signed first edition of Fowles's *The Collector*. Ian told me about spending nights in the wooded area across the road from his house, the Undercliff, which you'll know about if you've read Fowles's novel or seen Karel Reisz's film, *The French Lieutenant's Woman*.

Nick had been sound engineer (and sometimes producer) for Cat Stevens, Tom Jones, Chaka Kahn and Rufus, the Police, the Bee Gees, Nazareth, Chicago, Deep Purple, Ian Gillan and Roger Glover, Ian Hunter, Rainbow, April Wine, Kim Mitchell, the Tea Party, Jeff Martin, Crack the Sky, and many others. He died in 2019. There were technical medical reasons why it happened then and in that way, but basically, it was his whole life catching up with him.

A lot of music took place in this easy kitchen moment.

3. Percy Francisco Alvarado Godoy (spy). Rome, Italy, 2005.

Percy had been a spy for Castro among the Florida militias for decades. He broke cover when he learned that the group he'd infiltrated planned to blow up the Tropicana hotel in Havana, killing a lot of people, to disrupt Cuba's tourist industry.

We met in Rome on a forum about US policy in Cuba. I told the person who invited me, "I don't know any more about US policy in Cuba than I read in the *New York Times*." He said, "So what do you think people in Rome know? You have a sense of US politics. Come and put it in that perspective. Business class for both flights."

"How long do you want me to talk?"

"An hour," he said.

"Okay," I said. "I can do that."

I lucked out: not long before the event, then US Secretary of State Condoleezza Rice released a huge report—200 or 300 pages—about US policy in Cuba. It was all red meat for me. I prepared a great one-hour talk.

The Rome forum was Percy, two other people, and me. I was third, after Percy. Neither he nor the woman who spoke before him used a note and neither spoke more than fifteen minutes. I dropped the neatly typed pages that would have filled a mind-numbing hour to the floor and did the same. I think I ended with "*Venceramos!*" So much for data analysis. Percy hugged me and gave me a huge Cohiba cigar.

The next day, he and I did two interviews about US policy in Cuba. The driver who picked me up at my hotel told me he was a Rome policeman. Our first stop was at the office of one of Rome's two Communist Parties, which did not speak to one another. After the interview, waiting for the elevator, he told me he was a communist. He said, "Are there many communist policemen in the US?"

"I don't think so," I said, "and if there are, they're quiet about it."

"Here," said, "you don't have to keep quiet about it." I asked him what his job in the Rome police department was. "Wrestling coach," he said.

After the second interview, Percy gave me another Cohiba. His greatest pain, he told me, was that his parents, who remained in Havana after he went to Florida, died thinking he had betrayed a cause in which they all believed.

"You should come and visit Havana," he said. "It's a beautiful city. I'm a colonel in Cuban intelligence now so I can show you things you wouldn't otherwise get to see."

4. Convict guards returning weapons to armory. Cummins prison farm, Varner, Arkansas, 1971.

I was driving from Buffalo to California to spend a Guggenheim year in Berkeley and San Francisco. I stopped off at Cummins, the first prison in the US to have been declared unconstitutional by a Federal Court (*Holt v. Sarver I* and *II*, 1969 and 1970, respectively).

I had become friends five or six years earlier with Don Hutto, an assistant warden at Ramsey prison farm in Texas. Not long before my California trip, Don had been appointed Arkansas commissioner of Correction. He gave the same freedom to roam around Cummins that I'd had in Texas, when I'd been doing research on Black convict work songs.

The only people I saw carrying guns in Cummins that time were convict guards. There were hardly any civilian employees. Most of them worked in the building. The only people who had uniforms were the convicts working in the fields and the convict guards.

I spent four or five days in the fields with the work crews and in the building. I thought I'd write an article for the *New York Times Magazine* or *Harper's* about daily life in what federal judge J. Smith Henley had declared the worst prison in America. The photos would be aide-mémoire for me and illustrations for the article.

When I got to Berkeley and began working on the notes and photos, I decided I didn't have enough of either; I needed a second visit. I did that on the drive back to Buffalo the following August. By then, the convict guards had been replaced by free world guards and the whole operation seemed like a clone of the Texas prisons. Little wonder: the field major, deputy commissioner, and the Cummins warden were all former Texas Department of Corrections employees. During that visit, I realized that my Cummins story wasn't going to be words with supporting images; it was going to be pictures with supporting words.

I would make six more visits to Cummins over the next three years. On the eighth visit, I realized I was repeating myself—the shots were almost entirely interchangeable with earlier shots. It was time to stop.

I never did the article, but the work resulted in three books and half of a fourth: *Killing Time: Life in the Arkansas Penitentiary* (Cornell University Press, 1977); *Cummins Wide: Photographs from the Arkansas Prison* (Center for Documentary Studies/Center Working Papers, 2008); *Pictures from a Drawer: Prison and the Art of Portraiture* (Temple University Press, 2009); and, *Inside the Wire: Photographs from Texas and Arkansas Prisons* (University of Texas Press, 2013).

I saw Don Hutto one more time. It was in Austin, Texas, at the funeral of George Beto in 1991. George had been director of the Texas Department of Corrections during the first part of my research there (1964–1968). He'd given me free run of the place, which is why Don gave me similar freedom to roam at Cummins. On the church steps after the funeral, he said, "I'm in Tennessee now. I started a new business." The new business was Corrections Corporation of America. It was the start of the infamous private prison industry in America.

5. Lieutenant (with blackjack) and sergeant (with cigarette) in control picket, Maximum Security building. Cummins prison farm, Varner, Arkansas, 1974.

In 1971, Cummins had only a few cells. They were used for punishment or protection. Everyone else was housed in large, crowded spaces they called "tanks." The Max was built in 1973. The solitary cells were as awful as solitary cells everywhere, but the protection cells were spacious. I met some guys I'd photographed in the tanks the previous year. I asked one what got him into Max. "I worked at it," he said.

6. Marine honor guard. Funeral of James Boyer, former president, Road Vultures Motorcycle Club. Lockport, New York, 2010.

In October 1967, shortly after I moved from Cambridge to Buffalo, a member of the Road Vultures Motorcycle Club (RVMC) asked me if I'd write an article about how they were being harassed by Mike Amico, the head of the Buffalo Police Department's narcotics squad.

Amico would turn up at their clubhouse once a month, always accompanied by a camera crew from Channel 7, and would toss the place while the news cameras rolled. They'd never find any drugs or arrest anybody, but Channel 7 ran the footage anyway. Amico always did the raids early enough in the afternoon for the footage to make the 6:00 p.m. broadcast. After most of the raids the Vultures would have to buy a new TV set because the cops tossed their current TV from the clubhouse porch to the sidewalk.

The president of the Club, Tommy Bell, knew I'd recently written about criminal justice affairs for *Atlantic Monthly* and the *New York Times Magazine*. He told me he hoped this would make an interesting article.

One Sunday afternoon, about fifteen members of the Club came to the small suburban house where I was then living. The roar of the bikes as they arrived shook glassware in the kitchen cabinets. They came in, we talked for a few hours, I agreed to write the article, then they mounted up and roared away. A few days later, I visited the clubhouse. They showed me damage from the most recent police visit.

A week after that, I was on the Pentagon porch during the October 21 anti–Vietnam War demonstration. A line of troops with bayonets kept us confined to a small area. I smelled marijuana. I was curious who'd be smoking dope on the Pentagon porch, so I followed the odor. It was Tommy Bell and another Road Vulture. "Who's gonna arrest us for smoking dope *here*?" Tommy said.

Two weeks after that, Tommy was shot to death in an argument over a wristwatch. He was my main contact in the club. I didn't do the article, but I photographed his funeral.

In 2009, the University at Buffalo hosted an exhibition of artwork by underground comix artist Spain Rodriguez (*Trashman, She, Che: A Graphic Biography*). Spain, a Buffalo native, had been a member of Road Vultures. I saw him at Tommy Bell's funeral and then twice again by chance, once in New York when I was visiting Bill Beckman at the office of an alt newspaper, the *East Village Other* (*EVO*) in 1968, then in 1972 at the office of Rip Off Press in San Francisco, when we were both visiting another comix artist, Gilbert Shelton (*Fabulous Furry Freak Brothers, Wonder Wart-Hog*). Both times, at *EVO* in New York and Rip Off in San Francisco, our conversation began with the same ten words: "What are *you* doing here?" and "What are *you* doing here?"

Many current and former Vultures came to that 2009 exhibit. I knew only a few of them. Most of the guys I'd known had by then died or had been killed. It was strange seeing so many old men in the leather colors I'd last seen on young men. The exhibit included a dozen or so of my photos from Tommy Bell's funeral: at the clubhouse, the funeral home, and in the cemetery. The current president of the Club asked if they could get prints for their clubhouse, now located in rural Albion, New York, far away from where a local cop like Mike Amico would make a career bugging them. I sent them a set of prints, which they put on the clubhouse walls. (In return, they invited me to join them on rides and they gave me an RVMC T-shirt. I declined the rides; I still have the shirt.)

A year later, I got a call from one of the Club officers. He told me that James Boyer, who had been president of the Club for years, had died. I was, he said, sort of their Club's president funeral photographer. Any chance I could document Boyer's funeral for them, like I did the last time? "Sure," I said.

7. Dog sergeant with ground rattler. Cummins prison farm, Varner, Arkansas, 1975.

My ten-year-old son, Michael, was with me on my second Cummins visit in 1972. We were driving from San Francisco back to Buffalo. I'd go out photographing in the fields and Michael would find things to do. One day I came back to the place we were staying, and he was sitting on the grass in front of it with a watermelon split cleanly in half. He was happily pulling out and consuming the heart of it.

"Where did you get that?" I asked him.

"Some guys going by saw me. They stopped and one of them got it out of a truck and gave it to me. He opened it up for me."

"Guys in white suits?"

"Yes. In a bunch of carts pulled by a tractor."

That would have been a wagon train of prisoners coming in from the fields. The tractor driver had seen Michael sitting in front of the house where we were staying. He stopped. One of the prisoners got a watermelon from one of the trucks following them, sliced it in half with a machete, and gave it to Michael, after which the wagon train moved on so the prisoners could go back into the building. (Don't tell Family Services.)

One day, Michael and I spent about two hours in the kennel where the dog sergeant told us dog stories. Other than the watermelon heart that was his and his alone, it was Michael's favorite part of the Cummins visit.

I'd see the dog sergeant on some of my subsequent visits. I never learned his name. One day when I was photographing a hoe squad, I saw his pickup coming, a plume of dust following it on the turnrows. He and got out with the snake in his hand. I backed off. "Don't wave that in my face," I said.

"I'm not waving it in your face," he said, "I'm just *showing* it to you."

8. Patti Smith (singer and writer) in concert in Just Buffalo's BABEL series. Buffalo, 2015.

In 2007, a Buffalo arts organization, Just Buffalo, began a visiting writer series called BABEL. They had funding to bring four major writers to town each year. The first year, the series took place in a rehabilitated and repurposed church owned by Ani

DiFranco. The series quickly outgrew that space and moved to Kleinhans Music Hall, home of the Buffalo Philharmonic, where it regularly drew audiences of 1,500 or more.

I began photographing the visiting writers for fun. The camera gave me an excuse to hang out with writers I admired at the preperformance reception and to lurk at the edge of the stage. The first was novelist Michael Ondaatje; the playwright Ariel Dorfman was the second. My intention was to do it just a few times.

I don't know how it came about, but my role in the visits changed. Over the next ten years, I would photograph thirty-five of the forty writers in the series, not only from the edge of the stage and at the receptions, but on the stage during the readings, backstage before they went on, and in their afternoon encounters with local high school students. Many of those photographs appear in *BABEL: The First Ten Years* (Just Buffalo, 2018).

Patti Smith and I had met before her BABEL performance. Twenty years earlier, we'd both been part of the memorial service for our mutual friend, civil rights attorney William Kunstler, at New York's Cathedral of St. John the Divine. She'd sung Kurt Weill's "Lost in the Stars" a capella, and I'd read the text from Whitman's preface to the 1855 edition of *Leaves of Grass* that had, a few months earlier, been carved into the rock outcropping in West Shokan above where Bill's ashes had been buried.

In the middle of the song, Patti forgot the words. The only sound in that vast space was 3,000 people breathing. After what seemed an eternity, she remembered the words and finished the song.

In the Green Room later, she paced back and forth, saying, "I fucked it up. I fucked it up."

"What are you talking about?" I said.

"The song. I forgot the words and fucked it up."

"Nonsense. You were singing about being lost in the stars, you got lost, then you picked it up. Everybody thought it was a bit."

"Really?"

"Sure."

I had no idea what people thought. I recently listened to a tape of the service: that eternity of silence was about twenty seconds. Stage time isn't ordinary time.

When we reminisced about the St. John the Divine event during the reception before her BABEL performance, I pointed at the decoration in her lapel. "The French Order of Arts and Letters," she said. "I'm a *commandeur*."

I pointed to the ribbon in my lapel. "I'm a *chevalier*," I said.

"That means I get to give you orders," she said.

9. Janis Joplin (singer). Newport Folk Festival, Newport, Rhode Island, 1968.

At the performers' party in one of the big Newport mansions after that night's concert, I saw her sitting alone on the staircase, drinking out of a pint bottle of Southern Comfort. Those Newport performer parties were communal—huge tables of food and drink and people making music all over the place. She was the most alone person I ever saw at any of them. There was no way to say that. What I said instead was, "You look bored."

"I'm always bored," she said.

Maybe she was bored in day-to-day life and at after-concert parties. But not onstage. Onstage, she was on fire.

10. Mike Seeger (musician). Buffalo, New York, 1977.

I don't know if Mike ever had any formal musical training, but he was the most accomplished performer in an accomplished musical family. His father, Charles, was an ethnomusicologist; his mother, Ruth, was a composer; his uncle, Alan, was a poet ("I have a rendezvous with death . . ."), his sister and half-brother, Peggy and Pete, were well-known folk singers. Whenever Mike visited we'd hear him practicing or just making himself happy on a wonderful range of instruments: banjo, fiddle, autoharp, dulcimer, guitar, mandolin, jaw harp, pan pipes and more. He was always delighted to have people join in or listen. Sometimes, as here, he'd even play for the dog.

11. Dalai Lama (spiritual leader). Buffalo, New York, 2006.

During his visit to Buffalo, the Dalai Lama talked to a huge audience in the University's stadium. He also did two smaller events: one at the Law School, one in the music building. There was a lunch for him, to which maybe 300 people were invited. While we were inside waiting for him to arrive, I got a cell phone message from my son in LA, but the building blocked the signal, so I went outside to take the call. When I tried to go back in, the Secret Service guys bodyguarding the Dalai Lama (he's a head of state) told me I'd have to stay at the entranceway until he was in the room, then I could reenter. That injunction didn't make much sense, but you don't win arguments with the Secret Service, so I stood with one of the rows of people bracketing the path to the entranceway.

The official party approached: the Dalai Lama, university officials, more Secret Service guys. Suddenly, he broke out of the formal line and came up to me. "Moishe Dayan, my old friend," he said. We bowed to one another; we hugged. He rejoined the procession.

I was, at the time, suffering from a transient episode of double vision, so, that day, I was wearing an eye patch. The Israeli general Moishe Dayan (1915–1981) who, late in his life became an advocate for a sane peace with the Palestinians, had lost an eye early on, during his Irgun days, and was always photographed wear a large black eye patch. The Dalai Lama was making a joke that only I heard. We had never seen one another before that moment.

The procession moved on. John Simpson, the University president, who had watched our entire encounter but heard none of anything either of us said, said to me as he passed by, "You just know everybody."

12. Pete Seeger (folksinger and political activist). Buffalo, New York, 1996.

In our kitchen. He was staying with us while he was in town for a concert. Earlier, we'd been at the university campus where I worked. As we walked from one building to another, he said, "This is a pretty bleak place." I acknowledged that it was. "It's got a lot of empty walls." He pointed to one large windowless wall on the side of the music building. "A wall like that. You could have a competition among high school kids to design a mural for that wall. The best one gets painted on the wall. But you do it with paint that won't last more than a year, to the next year you can have another competition." I don't think I ever saw Pete when he didn't come up with at least one new project worth thinking about or even doing.

13. Pete Seeger. Beacon, New York, 1977.

Pete was boiling down maple syrup he had tapped earlier that day. He and his wife, Toshi, had built their house themselves years earlier. He looked across the Hudson and pointed to some housing developments. "It didn't used to be like that here," he said. "In the night, it was dark as far as you could see."

The first time I'd visited them in Beacon had been in 1966, when we were doing the final edit of a film Pete, Toshi, their son Dan, and I had shot in Ellis prison a few months earlier, *Afro-American Worksongs in a Texas Prison*. I noticed an old Japanese man on his knees in a flower bed.

I mentioned him to Pete. Japanese gardeners are rare in this part of the country. "That's Takashi Ohti, Toshi's father," he said. "He's living with us."

Takashi had been born in Japan, Pete said. He'd met Toshi's mother, an American citizen, in Berlin, where Toshi was born in 1922. They all came to the United States, where Takashi became a US citizen. During the war, he was smuggled into Japan where he served as a spy for the Americans. When the war ended, he identified himself to the occupation forces and asked them to get him back to his family in the US.

When they checked his story, Pete said, they discovered that he had, in his youth, belonged to a communist or socialist organization. Because of that, the US wouldn't let him back in.

It took years, but he was eventually allowed to come home. "It took more time for him to get home," Pete said, "than he spent in Japan working as an American spy. If he'd ever been caught, he'd have been tortured and executed. All those years he was fighting to get home, he was a man without a country. The Japanese had no use for him because he had worked for the Americans. The Americans had no use for him because of his political activity as a kid. It's a terrible story."

14. Sam "Lightnin'" Hopkins (blues singer) and Michael Lee Jackson, Newport Folk Festival performers' tent. Newport, Rhode Island, 1965.

Some of my favorite moments in the years I was involved with the Newport Folk Festivals (1964–1968) occurred in the performers' tent and lunch area, and during the performers' dinners/parties after the evening concerts. There would be music and talk all over the place. I remember one night in one of the large Newport mansions we rented when the Clancy Brothers were singing Irish songs in one room, while in the adjacent room Junior Wells and Buddy Guy sang the blues: Buddy Guy played his harmonica and sang from a chair; Junior Wells strutted back and forth with his guitar atop on a highly polished dining room table. Earlier that day, in the performers' tent, Joan Baez was in intense conversation with Maybelle Carter, while outside, civil rights activist Fannie Lou Hamer sat at a picnic table in an equally intense conversation with Skip James, Mississippi John Hurt, and several other people. Another time, that same weekend, my three-year-old son Michael (now an intellectual property lawyer and accomplished rock musician) and bluesman Lightnin' Hopkins started hanging out. I don't know what they were talking about, but I have photos of them doing it in three different places that weekend.

During the performers' lunch one Saturday, a few people started singing "Diamond Joe," a beautiful song performed by a convict named Charlie Butler and recorded by John A. Lomax in 1937. The song appeared on one of the phonograph albums published by the Archive of American Folk Song, *Afro-American Blues and Game Songs* (AAFS-4). Those albums and Harry Smith's six Folkways LPs, *Anthology of American Folk Music*, provided the core repertoire for many of the urban folksingers of the 1950s and 1960s.

After a few minutes, the group singing "Diamond Joe" grew. Now there were guitars and banjos. The promotions lady from Hohner showed up and gave harmonicas to anyone who looked to her like a real musician. Someone from the Kazoo company gave kazoos to people who couldn't play one of the other instruments but could hum.

The melody for the chorus and verses differs, but the song consists mostly of the chorus, so even people who'd never heard it before were able to join in. We sang "Diamond Joe" again and again, with more and more voices and instruments taking part.

Then, just as the group came together, it began to dissolve: people went back to conversations that had been in process when the music started or hit the food tables again or got ready for one of the afternoon workshops.

There is no recording of it and no photographs: I have no idea how long we sang "Diamond Joe" or how large the group became. All that remains is what I just told you.

15. Sweet Willie and others. First town meeting. Resurrection City, Washington, DC, 1968.

The Poor People's Campaign was Martin Luther King's last big project. He was murdered before it happened, but his colleagues at the Southern Christian Leadership Conference (SCLC) carried it on. The plan was for poor and working people from all over the country to come to Washington to lobby Congress for a fair piece of the American Dream.

The Newport Folk Foundation was one of the many organizations involved. Ralph Rinzler, Alan Lomax, and I worked with SCLC and Smithsonian Institution staff setting up a music program at Resurrection City, the A-frame complex set up near the Reflecting Pool. There were daily events for kids, music at meetings, and concerts (my favorite of which was a Muddy Waters concert on a stage in the Reflecting Pool, with the steps leading up to the road and the steps in front of the Lincoln Memorial as the seats).

This photo is from one of our first days there. The A-frames were still being built and the buses from various parts of the country hadn't arrived yet. But the big tent was filled anyway. There were only a few white faces, most of them at the press table in front of the speakers' platform. There was speechifying, music, more speechifying. Alan Lomax and I stood at the back, listening to one incredible speaker after another.

Sweet Willie had only one arm; he'd lost the other in Vietnam. His words were electric.

The speaker after him said, "The beautiful thing about history is, it doesn't liberate you, but it does locate you."

"Have you been to the top of the mountain?" someone yelled.

"Yeah."

"What did you see?"

"I seen the world playin' with itself."

16. William Kunstler and Ramsey Clark (civil rights attorneys). Erie County Holding Center, Buffalo, New York, 1975.

In spring 1975, I was teaching a University at Buffalo Law School seminar on prison law with Constitutional scholar Herman Schwartz. Herman—who had been one of the prisoner-invited observers in the 1971 Attica Uprising—told me he was assisting civil rights attorneys William Kunstler and Ramsey Clark in their preparations for one of the key prisoner felony trials: John Hill and Charles Joseph Pernasalice, charged in the death of guard William Quinn in the first few minutes of the uprising. Bill was then one of the best-known civil rights lawyers in the country; Ramsey had been US attorney general. I told Herman I was envious.

"Would you like to meet them?" he asked.

"Absolutely."

Herman said they were staying at the Statler Hotel downtown and were no doubt bored with hotel food. "Invite them to dinner," he said, "they'll be delighted."

A few nights later, Bill and his associate, Margaret Ratner (they would later marry), Ramsey, and Herman came over for dinner. Bill and Ramsey were both great storytellers and extremely funny, but in very different ways: Bill performed stories; Ramsey was dry, and subtle. As they were leaving, Diane said, "That was wonderful. We have to do it again."

Ramsey said, "How about tomorrow?"

We reassembled a few days later (without Herman). It was even better.

Something else happened: Bill, Margaret, Diane, and I fell into immediate friendship. We would, in the years that followed, stay at each other's houses in New York, Buffalo, and West Shokan, and vacation together in Bermuda and Mexico. The relationship with Bill continued until his death in 1995; Margaret is still Diane's closest friend.

Not long after those two dinners, Charley Joe and Johnny went to trial. The day the jury began deliberations, Bill and Margaret were having dinner at our house. Bill got a telephone call: the jury had reached a verdict. We rushed downtown.

Charley Joe and Johnny were both convicted. They were taken from the courtroom immediately. Bill, Ramsey, and Herman were told they could talk to them across the street in the Holding Center in thirty minutes. This photo was while we were waiting for them to be brought down.

I said to Herman that it must be terrible to put so much work and care into a trial, only to lose, to go home with nothing. "Bill got something out of it." His voice was unusually tight, and his face seemed to be constraining anger.

"What?" I asked.

"A friend," Herman said.

17. William Kunstler and Margaret Kunstler (civil rights attorney). Oaxaca, Mexico, 1990.

Bill and Margaret were in Oaxaca with their daughters, Sarah and Emily, who were spending a month there learning Spanish. We joined them for part of it. Mostly, we hung out, which is what we always did, but we also visited Coyotepec, Mitla, Teotitlán, and Monte Albán. In Coyotepec I bought a black pottery flute that plays a scale unique to itself. When we were going single file through a dark tunnel in one of the smaller structures at Monte Albán, someone ahead of us heard Bill's voice, turned, and said, "You're William Kunstler!"

"Of course I am," Bill said.

A few years later, the four of us went to Bermuda. In the hotel elevator one night, someone recognized Bill and mentioned an event at which he'd seen him. Bill immediately told a wonderfully detailed story about that event. He finished just as the elevator doors opened. "Isn't that right?" he said to Margaret.

"No," she said. She was every bit as taciturn as he was voluble, and equally eloquent.

Every night, after dinner, we sat on our joint patio and played Rummy Cube, which Diane, Margaret, and I always conspired to let Bill win.

One afternoon we were walking from our hotel to a nearby beach to go snorkeling. Bill forgot which way the traffic was coming from (British rules in Bermuda) and almost got hit by a moped. He stood in the middle of the road and looked at it as it rounded a curve.

"Oh, to die in Bermuda by moped," he said in his great baritone. "How inappropriate!"

18. William Kunstler and clients. Fort Apache, the Bronx, New York, 1988.

Bill's staff was usually on guard to keep strangers from approaching him. It wasn't a security issue. It was rather that if someone had a problem that interested Bill, he'd take the case, whether or not there was any money. Most of the time, there wasn't.

In 1988, Bill was defending Larry Davis, charged with shooting six New York Police Department officers two years earlier. (Davis claimed self-defense. Bill got him off everything but illegal gun possession, for which he got a sentence of five to fifteen years. Davis was also convicted in 1991 for the murder of another drug dealer; he got twenty-five-to-life for that. He was stabbed to death in Shawangunk Correctional Facility in 2008.)

A group of people got to Bill on the steps of the Bronx County Courthouse. They told him that the owner of a derelict apartment house had promised them that if they rehabilitated the building, he would give it to them and walk away with a tax deduction. They did rehabilitate it. When they were done, he sold the building. The new owner said he wasn't bound by the previous owner's promise. He got a Bronx judge to issue an immediate eviction order: any of their possessions in the building would be tossed onto the street by bailiffs.

That kind of case was irresistible to Bill. He talked to another New York judge, Bruce Wright in Brooklyn, to issue an order countermanding the order of the Bronx judge. (Wright was often referred to as "Turn 'em loose Bruce" by Brooklyn cops and prosecutors. He was not a fan of cash bail. He had presided at Bill and Margaret's marriage.)

Wright told Bill that an order from him was meaningless: he couldn't override an order by a judge at the same level in the Bronx.

Bill said it didn't matter. He'd show Wright's order to the bailiffs, who wouldn't know the law and who wouldn't want to get into trouble, so they'd go away. It was a Friday. "By the time they get it sorted out," Bill said, "I'll have time to get a legitimate order blocking the eviction."

Which was exactly what happened. Not only were the evictions blocked, but the residents got ownership of the house. This photo was at a party celebrating the victory next to their vegetable garden in an adjacent empty lot.

19. Brice Marden (artist). West Shokan, New York, 1995.

Bill Kunstler died on September 4, 1995. His memorial service, at St. John the Divine on November 19, was a quilt work of his life: brief statements by family, friends, and clients, and a dazzling range of musical performances: Danny Glover, Patti Smith, Ritchie Havens, the Harlem Boys Choir, Lakota drummers and dancers, Jimmie Breslin, Amiri Baraka, Allen Ginsberg, David Dellinger, Angela Davis, Ossie Davis, Ruby Dee,

Diane Christian, Michael Ratner, Margaret Kunstler, and more. The cathedral was packed. An improvised sound system carried the audio part to an overflow audience in the street. One protestor from the Jewish Defense League walked back and forth, shouting, "William Kunstler is where he belongs!"

The musical performances took place on the altar; the statements were read from pulpits on either side of it. There was a visual problem: on the wall behind the altar and two pulpits was a huge cross. During the entire ceremony, the audience there to honor an atheist Jew would be looking at the speakers and performers against a cross bigger than any of them.

Bill's friend Brice Marden solved the problem. Behind the altar and adjacent to the two pulpits, he built a huge frame containing a portrait of Bill. The afternoon he set it up coincided with St. Francis's feast day: as Brice's crew worked with hammers and saws, New Yorkers came and went with their animals needing blessings: dogs, cats, goats, snakes, fish, pigs, turtles. Memorials are one-day things, but the work of the church has its ineluctable calendar.

A few months earlier, Bill's family and a small group of friends had gathered to put Bill's ashes at the foot of a stone outcropping about a hundred yards up a dirt road from Bill and Margaret's cabin in West Shokan (near Woodstock). All afternoon, as we hung out and told stories, we heard the *chip-chip-chip* of the hammer and chisel of the stonemason from St. John the Divine, as he carved into the rock these lines from Whitman's Preface to the 1855 edition of *Leaves of Grass*:

> This is what you shall do: Love the earth and sun and the animals, despise riches, give alms to every one that asks, stand up for the stupid and crazy, devote your income and labor to others, hate tyrants, argue not concerning God, have patience and indulgence toward the people, take off your hat to nothing known or unknown.

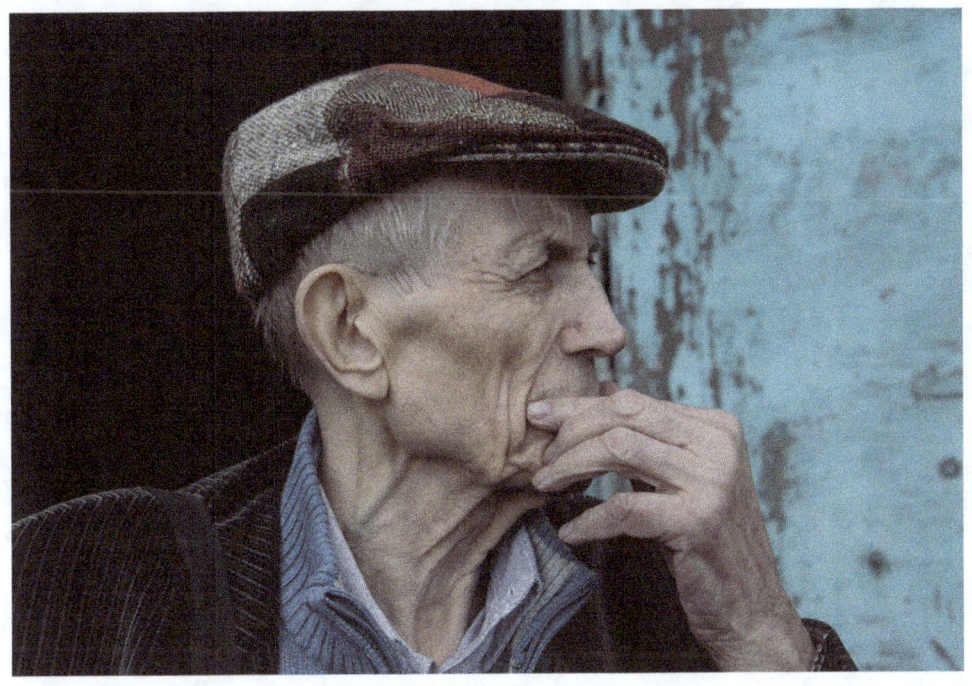

20. Yevgeny Yevtushenko (poet). Perot Grain Elevator. Buffalo, New York, 2012.

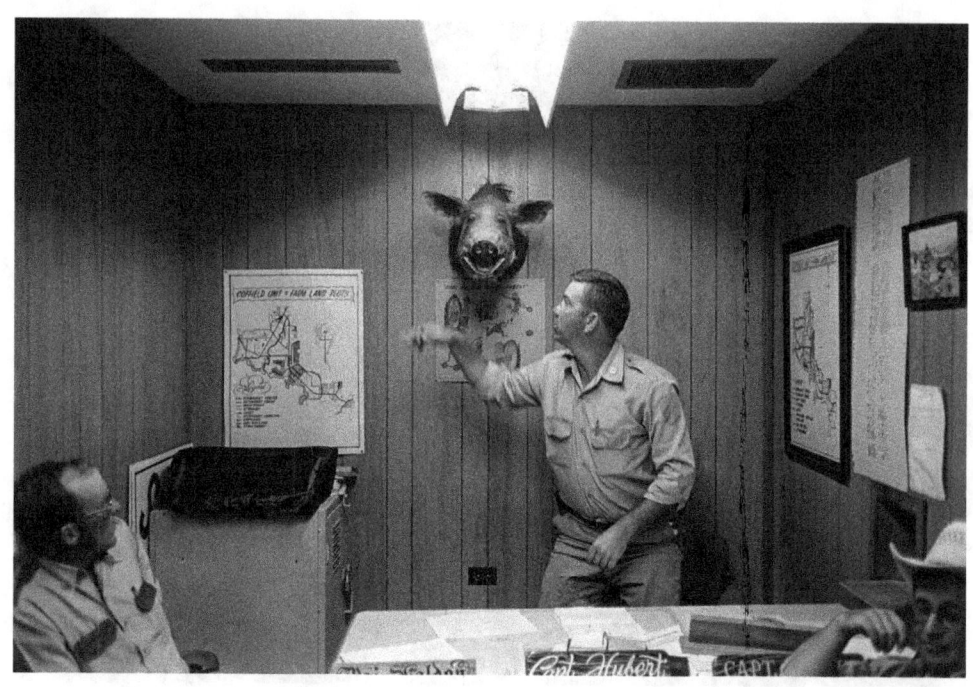

21. Captain Hubert. Coffield unit. Texas Department of Corrections, Huntsville, Texas, 1978.

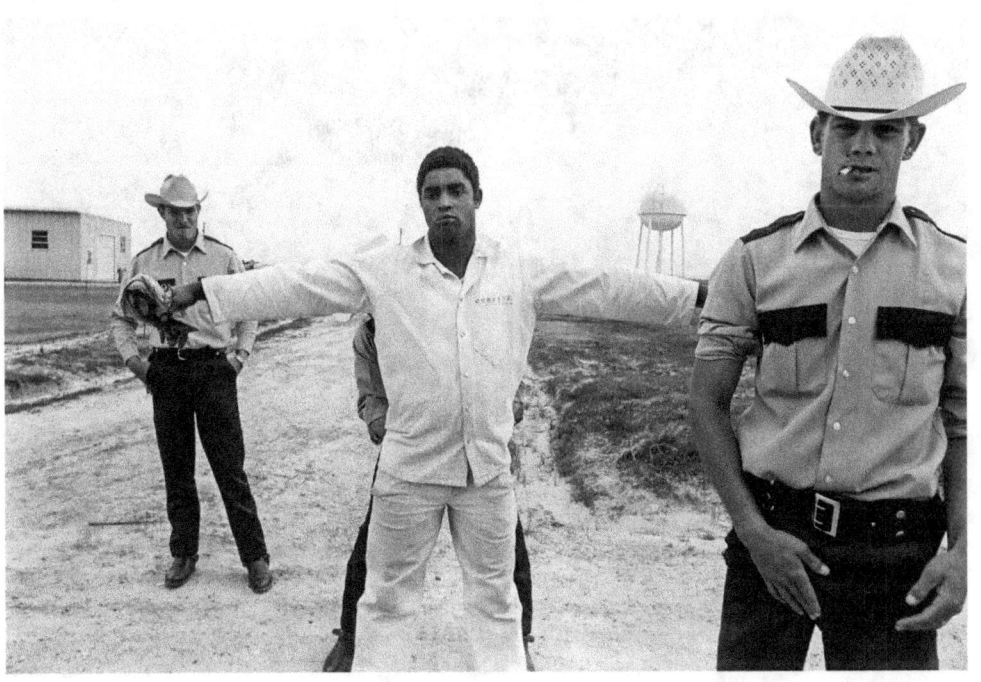

22. Shakedown. Cummins prison farm, Varner, Arkansas, 1973.

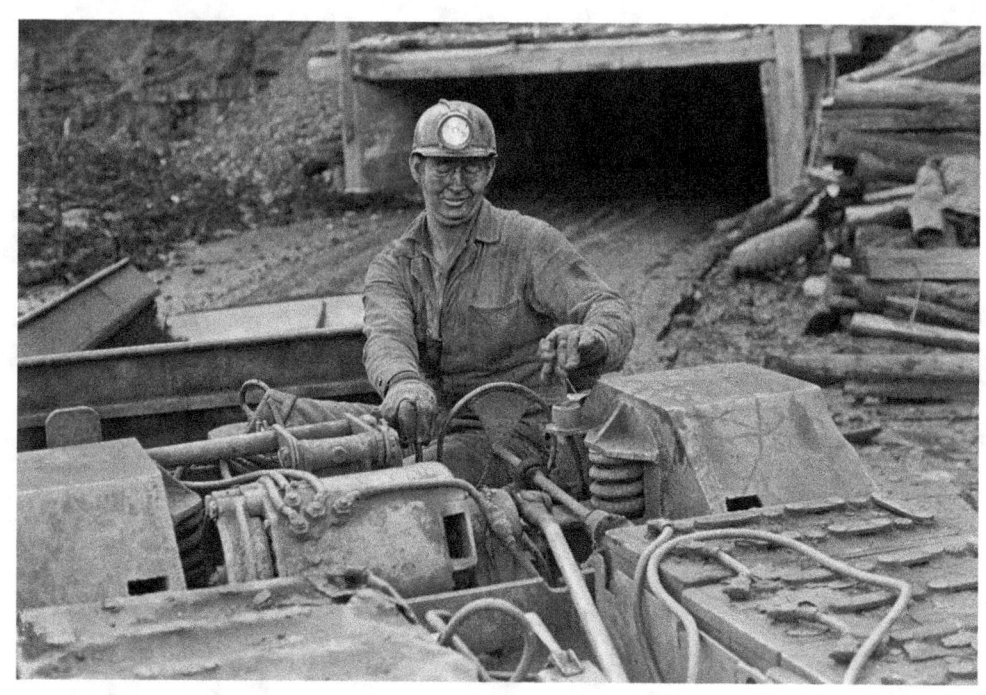

23. Truck Miner. Pikeville, Kentucky, 1969.

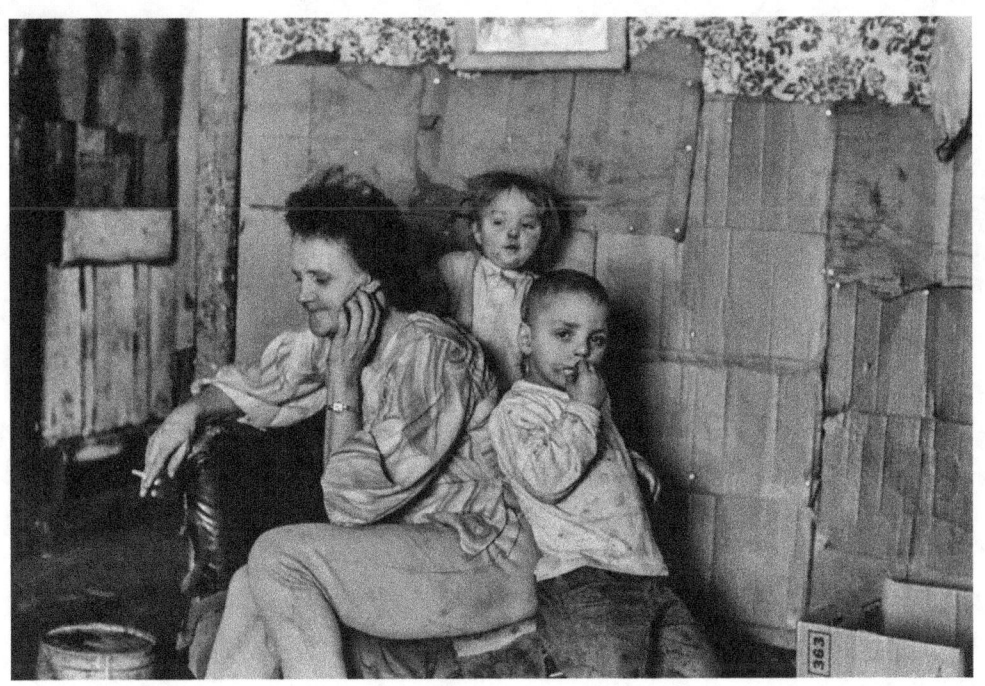

24. Family in Poorbottom, Marrowbone Creek. Pikeville, Kentucky, 1969.

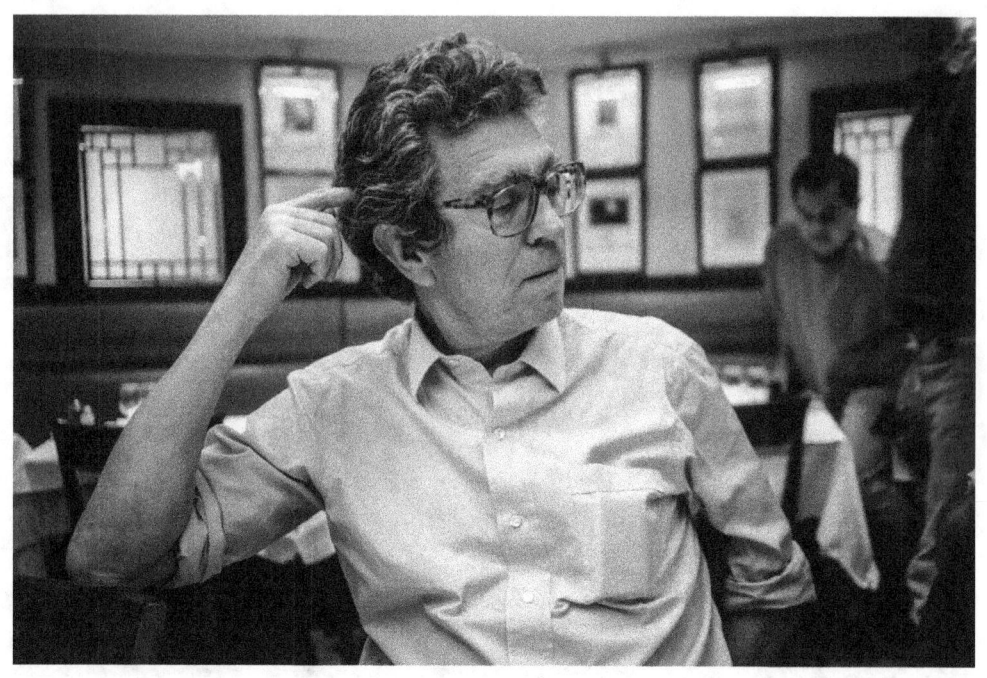

25. Pierre Joxe (politician and judge). Paris, France, 1996.

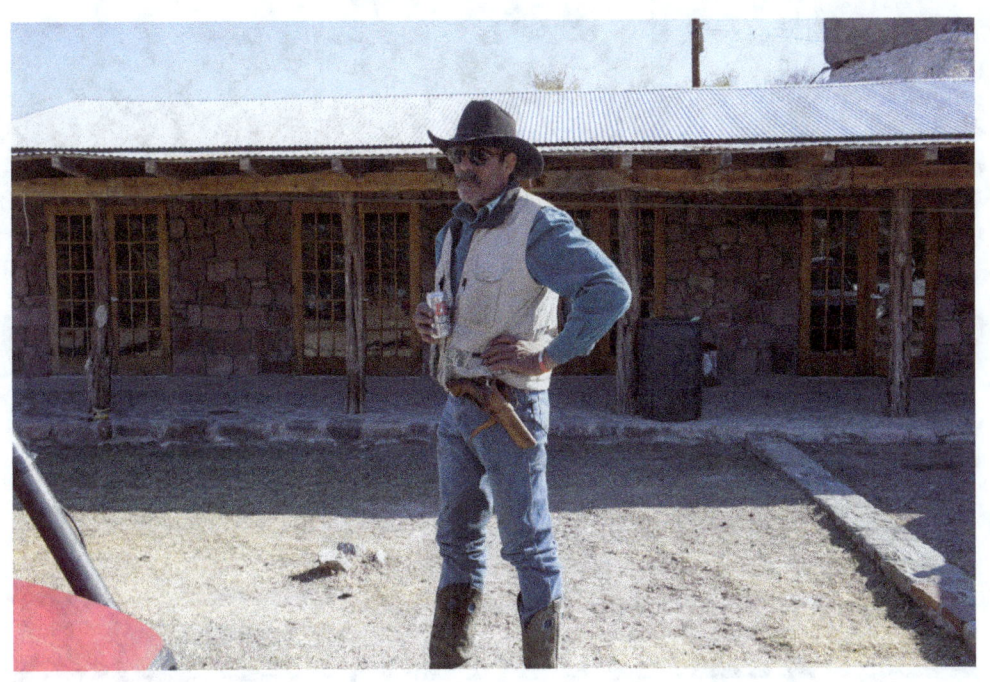

26. Ranch hand, Circle Dug Ranch. Candelaria, Texas, 2012.

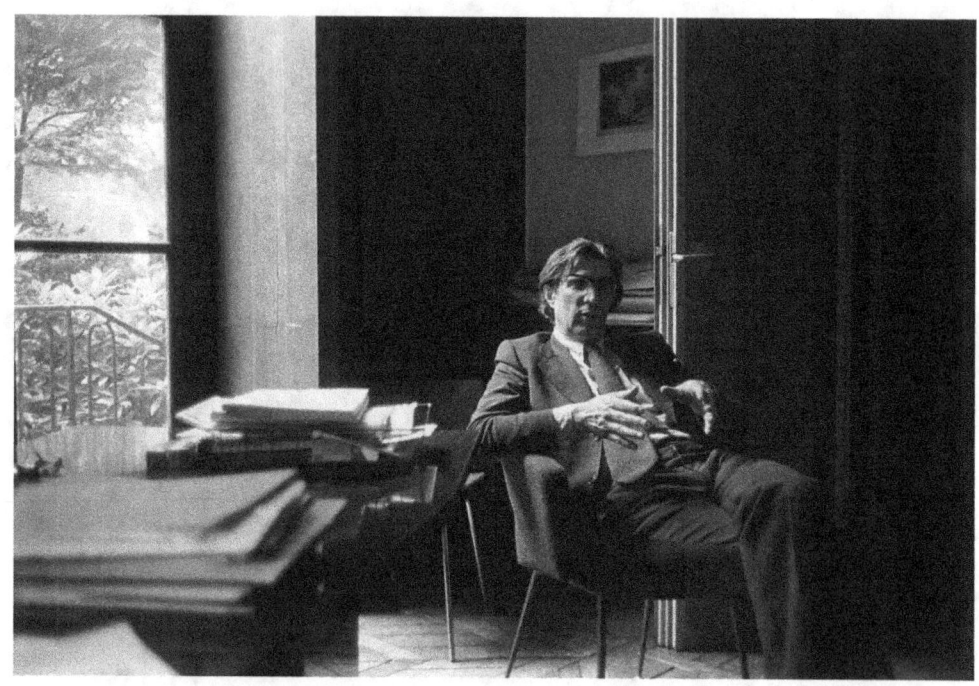

27. Jean Malaurie (geomorphologist, anthropologist, and publisher) in his study at Écoles des hautes études en sciences sociales. Paris, 1975.

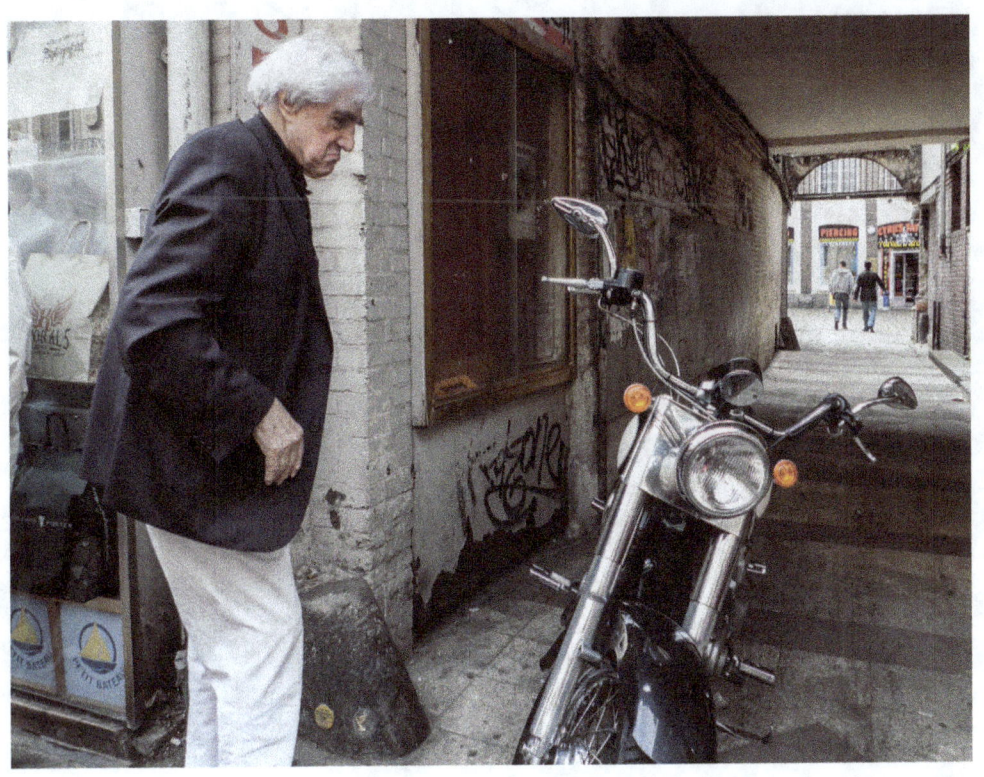

28. Jean Malaurie. Dieppe, France, 2010.

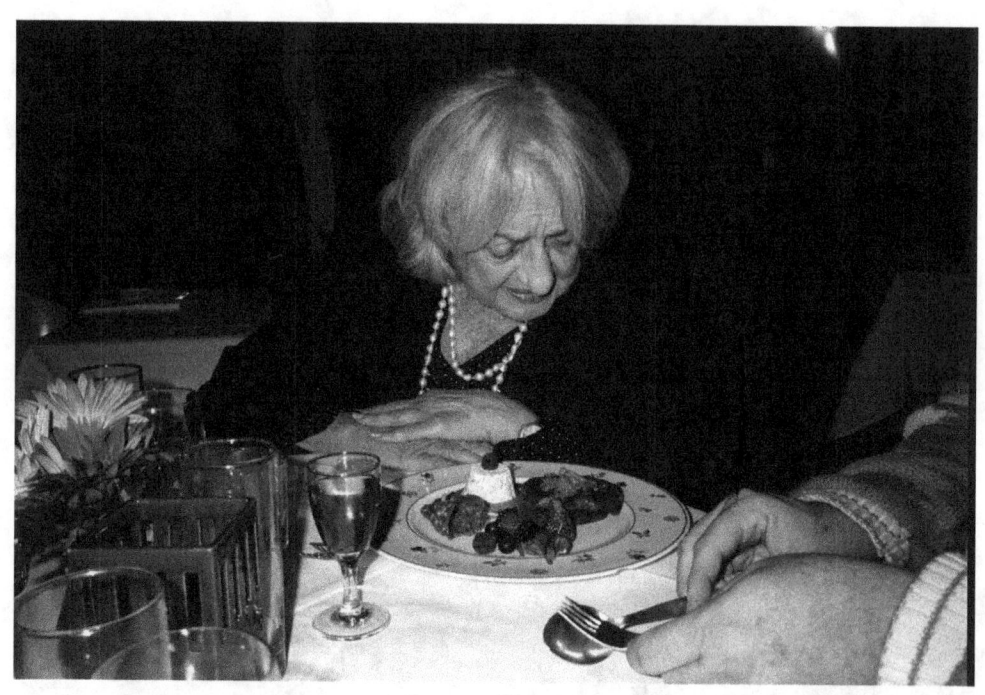

29. Betty Friedan. Santa Monica, California, 1995.

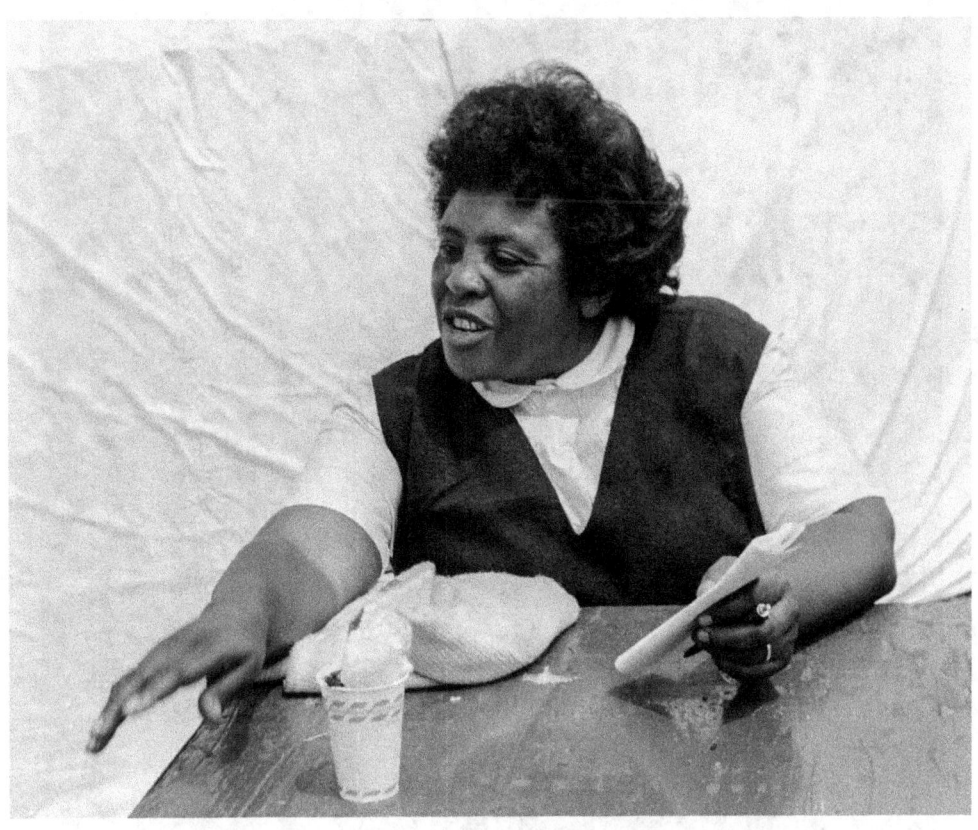

30. Fannie Lou Hamer. Newport Folk Festival performers' tent. Newport, Rhode Island, 1965.

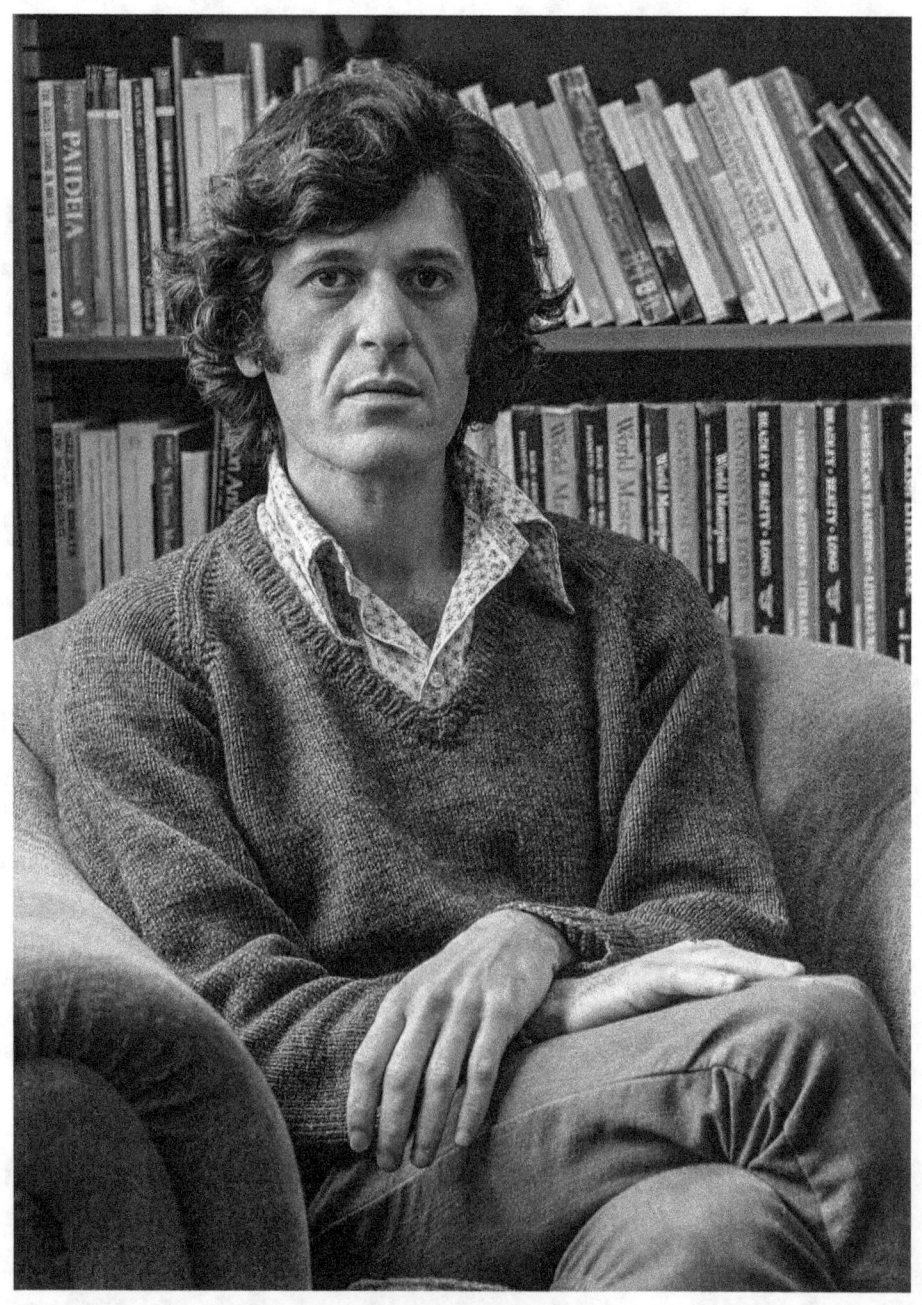

31. Leonard Michaels (writer). Berkeley, California, 1971.

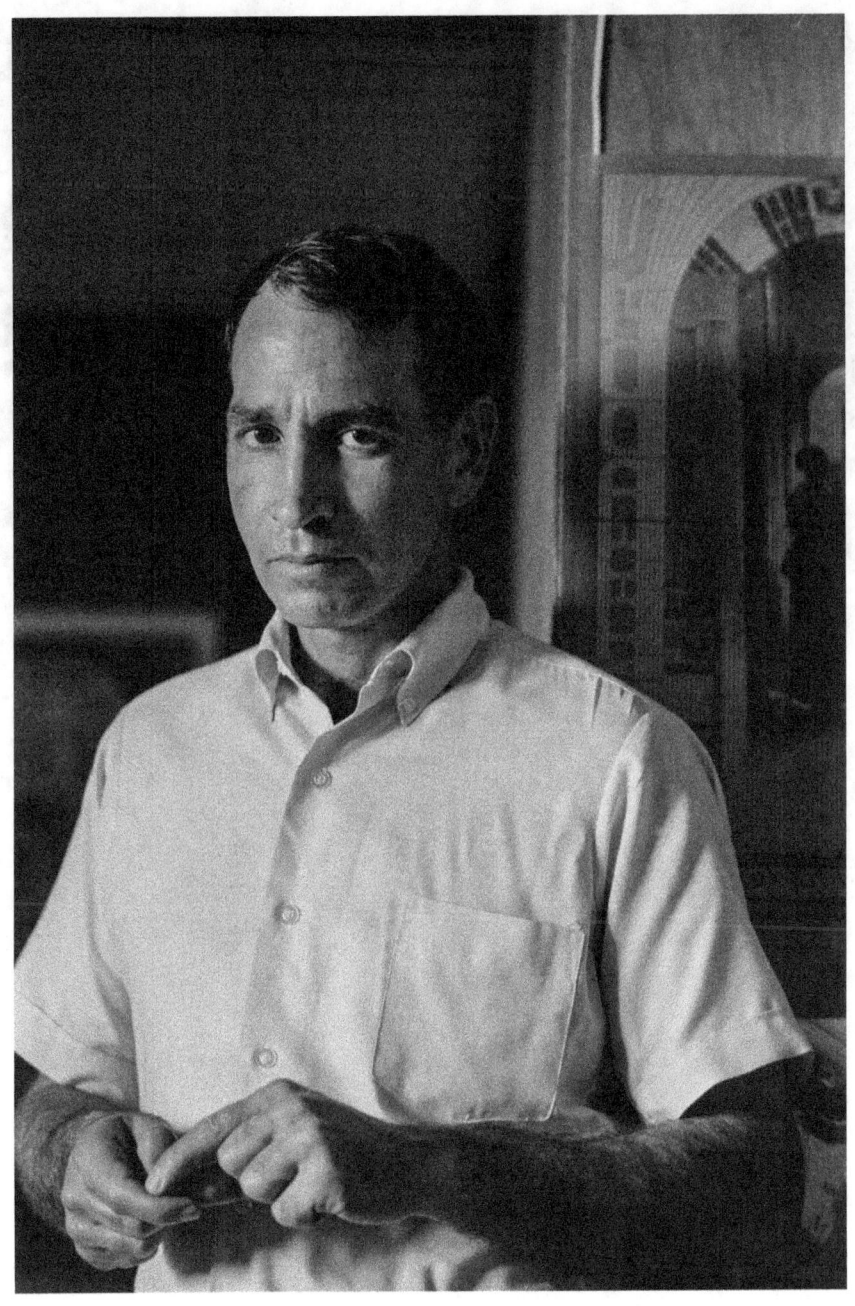

32. Billy Lee Brammer (writer). San Antonio, Texas, 1967.

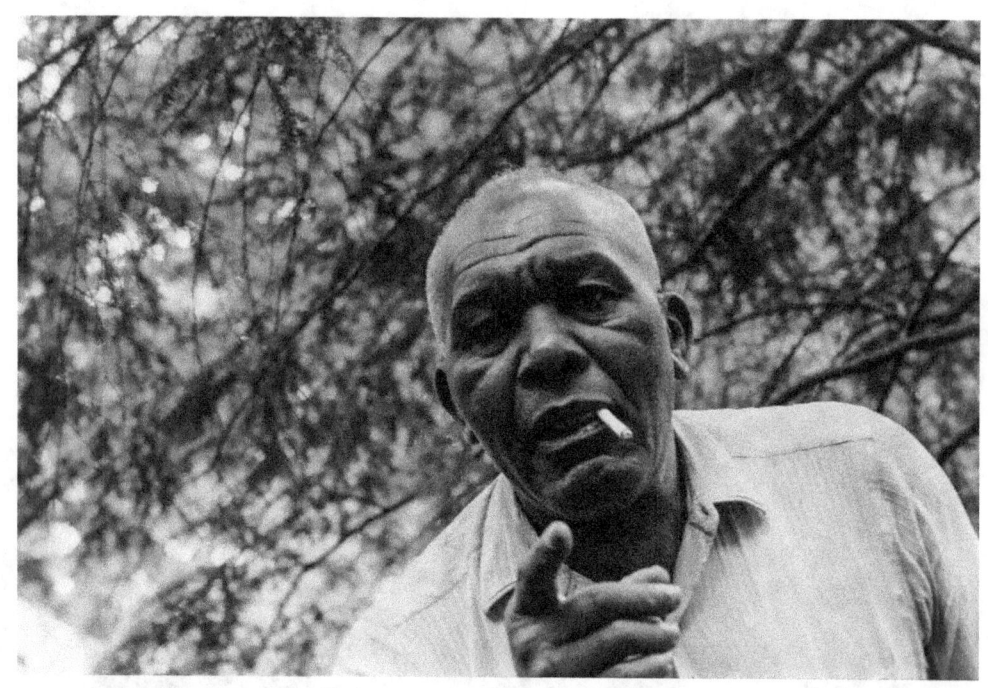

33. John Davis (singer). Washington, DC, 1968.

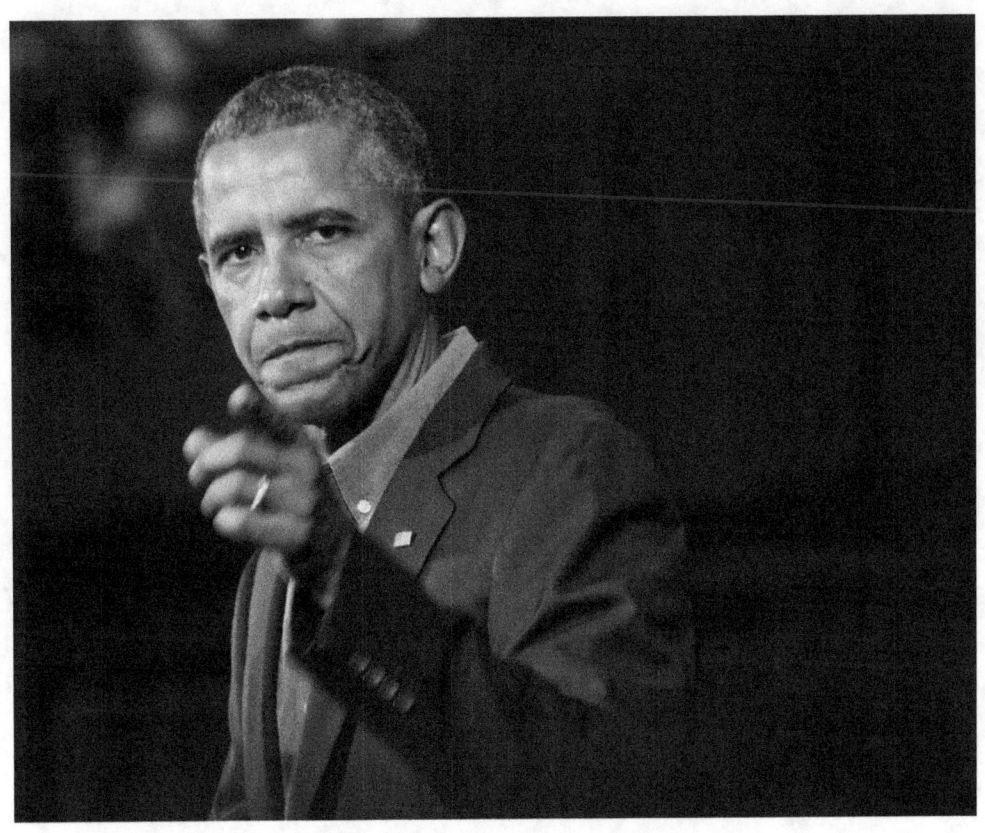

34. Barack Obama (US president). Buffalo, New York, 2013.

Words 2

20. Yevgeny Yevtushenko (poet). Perot Grain Elevator. Buffalo, New York, 2012.

Yevgeny Yevtushenko was in Buffalo to read his famous poem, "Babi Yar," as part of the Buffalo Philharmonic's performance of Shostakovich's Symphony No. 13. He wanted to meet with students. My English Department colleague, Tanya Shilina-Conte, who is from St. Petersburg, did much of the arranging. He did a Q&A with a large group of students and a poetry reading. I photographed him at everything. (That became a small book with text by Tanya and photos by me, *Yevtushenko in Buffalo* [Center Working Papers, 2020].)

He said he wanted to visit the Albright-Knox Art Gallery and the grain elevators on the city's waterfront. At the Gallery, Douglas Dreishpoon, then senior curator, noticed that Yevgeny was having difficulty walking, so he found a wheelchair, then spent two hours wheeling him around the Gallery, talking about the art, bent over almost the entire time.

The next day we took him to the grain elevators. He was particularly taken with a large space in Perot Grain Elevator that caused sound to have a brief hang time. I demonstrated it by clapping my hands. He was delighted and immediately began reciting poetry in Russian. Two students who were filming in another part of Perot heard the sounds and joined our group: Tanya, Diane, Rick Smith (who owns that group of elevators), and "Swanee Jim" Watson (the resident guru of the place). Every time Yevgeny stopped, we begged for more. Tanya was the only one of the group who understood a word he said. It didn't matter: his voice was like music.

We went outside to the dock, where I took this photo, then we walked back through a field between Perot and another elevator. He saw a covered walkway maybe twenty feet above the ground connecting the two elevators. He said he wanted to come back to give a poetry reading from the walkway. "That would be wonderful," I said. "A lot of people could fit in this field."

"Not the field," he said. "The river. It will be for people in boats."

It didn't work out. The next year, his right leg was amputated. Not long after that, he was diagnosed with kidney cancer. He died in 2017.

21. Captain Hubert. Coffield unit. Texas Department of Corrections, Huntsville, Texas, 1978.

It's rare to see a guy get up and punch a stuffed hog in the snout.

Earlier that year, George Beto, who had been director of the Texas Department of Corrections when I began my research on Black convict work songs in 1964, and who was now acting director of the Criminal Justice Institute at Sam Houston State University, invited me to give the Institute's annual Distinguished Lecture.

Billy MacMillan, whom I'd met on Ramsey prison farm in 1964, when he was a field major, then a few years later when he was deputy warden at Ellis prison farm, came up afterward to say hello at the reception. He invited me to a barbecue the next day at Goree, the women's prison. Many prison officials I'd encountered in TDC a decade earlier were there. Stories were told.

Billy told me about a prisoners' civil rights case, then in the preliminary stages. He said, "Would you be willing to testify in it?" I said I didn't have anything to contribute: I hadn't been in a Texas prison for a decade. He said I could talk about how my experience of Texas prisons differed from other prisons I'd visited (Indiana, Missouri, Massachusetts) and how things had changed since I'd visited there more than a decade earlier. I said I didn't know how things had changed. "You could visit," Billy said.

"I won't lie for you," I said.

"I'm not asking for that," Billy said. "I'm just asking for you to say what you saw."

I couldn't say no to that. George Beto had given me free range fourteen years earlier, and the prison system had stuck to George's license even when I criticized the system in articles. I said I'd do it, but I had to revisit all the Texas prisons I'd worked at a decade earlier, and the few I missed. He said that could be arranged.

Billy then said, "You're going to get some heat from your pals if you do this."

"Why?"

"Because you're testifying for the enemy."

"I'm not going to say anything but what I know about the place."

"That ain't gonna matter."

Over the next several months, I visited all but one of Texas's fourteen prisons. I also made my first visit to Death Row on Ellis prison farm.

Billy was right: I did get some flak for it. One Austin minister took me on as a cause: after I testified: any time I had anything about prison in *The Nation* or *Texas*

Monthly, he fired off a letter about my questionable associations. Most of my friends said nothing. The screeds from the Austin minister were more than offset by Bill Kunstler, who said he thought my testifying was perfectly reasonable.

The night before my testimony in federal court in Houston in *Ruiz v. Estelle*, Diane and I had dinner with the lead counsel for the plaintiffs in that case, William Bennett Turner. He said, "I don't understand why you're not testifying for us."

I said, "I'd be saying the same thing. You didn't ask me. They did."

Only later, reading the testimony in that case, did I learn how much I hadn't seen during my visits to TDC in earlier years. I'd known the "building tenders," the convicts who maintained the cellblocks, had power, but I'd never known how much, and how much brutality went on when I was not freely roaming about. I'd seen what there was there for me to see, but that wasn't the real story.

During one of those 1978 visits, I spent some time at Coffield unit, which housed the prison system's abattoir. The Texas prisons, in those years, grew most of their own food. The prisoners' clothes were made from cotton the prisoners chopped, picked, spun, wove, and sewed. Their boots and belts were made from the hides of cattle they maintained and slaughtered.

This day, I was sitting in Captain Hubert's office, listening to him talk with a building officer and a field officer. For a reason I never knew, Captain Hubert suddenly stood up, punched the stuffed boar's head in the snout, then sat down and finished his sentence.

22. Shakedown. Cummins prison farm, Varner, Arkansas, 1973.

This is, for me, one of the archetypal photographs of life in a southern plantation prison, or in any prison. If you're a prisoner, your body is not your own. Here, one white guard with his hands in his pockets, the Black prisoner in crucifixion position being patted down by a guard almost hidden by his body, the third guard fondling his crotch as a cigarette dangles from his mouth. Who gets to wear a hat, who gets to smoke, who gets to touch whose body?

23. Truck Miner. Pikeville, Kentucky, 1969.

I was on assignment from *Harper's* to do a piece on how the Poverty Program had been taken over by politicians and mine owners in eastern Kentucky.

Around town, mountaintops were being shaved off by D9 bulldozers so coal could be scooped out of open seams by huge shovels. Toxic exudate ran downhill and poisoned the streams.

Old deep mines—the ones that tunneled in—sold or leased what was left to smaller operators who ran what were called "truck mines." They dug out what was left in the underground seams. One of them let me visit one of his operations.

We went about a mile in on the cart that miner is driving. The tunnel was thirty-eight inches high. All day long the miners worked on their bellies or on their knees. I wore a helmet just like his. It cast a perfect beam of white light wherever I turned my head. I have never seen a narrow beam of light so sharp, nor had I ever been in a place so perfectly dark.

Then I realized why the beams were so bright and sharp: you only see light when it hits something. Those helmet lamps were illuminating millions of bits of particulate matter in the air—air those men breathed all day, every day.

Later that week, I'd sit on porches and talk with men who were old past their years, suffering from black lung or silicosis. There would be bottles of pills nearby, and oxygen tanks. Again and again I heard, "You don't never get well from this."

24. Family in Poorbottom, Marrowbone Creek. Pikeville, Kentucky, 1969.

After I spent a few days talking with the disabled Pikeville miners, many of whom had been abandoned by United Mine Workers, Edith Easterling, a Vista worker, said, "There's somebody I want you to meet."

She drove along Marrowbone Creek until we got to a log house. Edith said, "Let's go inside. Bring your camera." I looked at the littered yard and ratty house, and I left the camera in the pickup. Inside, we talked with the mother, Venita Coleman. Edith told me to go get my camera and takes some photos.

I said, "No. It's okay."

The poverty was so awful, I didn't want to intrude with a camera. I've no gift for photographing people in pain or in dire straits. Edith again urged me to get my camera. I again demurred.

Venita said, "That's okay, sonny. You go get your camera. Show them folks who live up where you do how us folks down here live." So, I did.

25. Pierre Joxe (politician and judge). Paris, France, 1996.

When this photo was taken, Pierre was first president of the Court of Audit, one of France's two supreme courts. He'd previously been, among other things, minister of Defense, minister of Interior, minister of Industry, president of the Socialist Party Group in the National Assembly, and president of the Regional Council of Burgundy.

When our film *Death Row* was broadcast on Antenne II in 1981, he had a dinner for us at his family house on Île de la Cité. The dining room was on the third floor. While we were talking, I saw someone go by outside a window. The person appeared briefly again, was gone, then swept past the window again.

I looked out the window and saw it was an acrobat group, working from a rig on Pont Neuf, two or three doors down.

"A little something we put on for our American friends," Pierre said.

"It's a celebration for the 300th anniversary of the bridge," his wife said.

The wine was superb. There was no label on the bottles. I asked Pierre what it was.

"From our family vineyard."

I waved my hand around the magnificent house and said, "Pierre: you're a Socialist. How can you have this house and estates in Burgundy and be a Socialist."

He shrugged. "Bruce: I am a *French* Socialist."

At that time, he was minister of Defense. "What happens to you if the Socialists lose power."

"There will always be a place for me in the French government. You should perhaps think of me as the Duke of Burgundy."

A year later his friend Henri Korn said Pierre was in New York. He had come in on the Concorde to give a speech at the United Nations. It was Thanksgiving weekend. Henri said Pierre had never had an American Thanksgiving dinner. Might he bring him by? We said sure. The next day, they joined us for our usual family Thanksgiving mob event. Pierre loved it. He was particularly delighted, he said, that no one in the French delegation in New York had a clue where he was. He hadn't told them he was going to Buffalo.

The Erie County Savings Bank had recently issued three very heavy ceremonial brass belt buckles celebrating the city's 150th anniversary. All three had the dates—1832–1982—and the city's name. One had an outline of downtown; one had a charging buffalo; one had the Erie Canal. Diane and I were about to go on a United States Information Agency lecture tour in Europe, so the bank gave us a dozen of each of them to give to interesting people we met on our trip.

We showed them to Pierre. He said he liked them. I said, "Take one." He did.

As they were leaving, Henri said, "Pierre was only being polite. Those are so *tacky*."

When we were next in France, about a year later, Henri said, "Pierre wears that Buffalo belt buckle all the time! I don't understand it."

The last time I saw Pierre, he said I should come to the Court with him one day. "You'd find it interesting." I said that the only clothes I had with me were the jeans I was wearing, a few casual shirts, and a street jacket. I was wearing boots or running shoes.

"No problem, Pierre said. "I'll give you one of the Supreme Court judge's robes."

"My French is lousy and—" I pointed at the boots or running shoes. "Won't someone say something?"

"If you're with me, no one will say a word."

26. Ranch hand, Circle Dug Ranch. Candelaria, Texas, 2012.

In 2013, the Burchfield Penney Art Gallery in Buffalo did a large retrospective of my photographic work—about 350 prints, some of them twelve feet on the long side. There was one photo I'd taken on a 1977 trip with my French friend and publisher, Jean Malaurie, on the Nome-Council Road in the Norton Peninsula in Alaska: small-gauge railroad engines and cars mired in the tundra. Locals called it "the Train to Nowhere." But the print wouldn't go big. It looked fine on a thirteen-inch-by-nineteen-inch sheet; bigger than that it turned to mush. (We didn't have the fractal pixel interpolating technology we have now.) It was my own fault: I'd been in a hurry to get to Council, and I didn't take enough time when I stopped to photograph the train.

I really wanted that mired train image in the exhibit, so I decided to go back to Alaska to get it. But I found out that the tundra I'd photographed in 1997 was gone. Global warming had altered everything. "The Train to Nowhere" had shifted: part of the permafrost level supporting it had melted, and all the vegetation around it had changed.

My son, Michael, mentioned this to a Texas friend of his, Mike Wilson. Mike said, "If your dad wants to photograph desolate, he's welcome to my ranch on the Rio Grande. It's got a lot of desolate." Mike and a few friends had bought the ranch at a government auction for a song: it had been seized because the previous owner had been using the landing strip to import drugs from Mexico. It borders on the Rio Grande to the south and the foothills of the Sierra Vieja (the southern tip of the Rockies) to the north. The ranch is about 150 miles east of El Paso; it is about the size of Manhattan, with pretty much the same shape.

So, instead of going north, I went south. I did a little book about what I saw there (*Candelaria West* [Center Working Papers 2012]). One of the photos I took on that trip—an abandoned, roofless stone house in the desert between El Paso, Guadalupe Mountains, just north of Cornudas on US 62 (which runs from the Mexican border at El Paso to the Canadian border at Niagara Falls, and passes only a few miles from my house in Buffalo)—was one of the twelve-foot photos in the Burchfield Penney exhibit. It took the place that the train to nowhere would have occupied.

I would make four more trips to the northern Chihuahuan Desert, two of them to the Big Bend area, another a meandering trip from Albuquerque to El Paso, and the last to El Paso itself, with Michael. I'm still working on that project.

27. Jean Malaurie (geomorphologist, anthropologist, and publisher) in his study at Écoles des hautes études en sciences sociales. Paris, 1975.

Jean had just published my book, *In the Life: Versions of the Criminal Experience* (Holt, 1972) in his *Terre Humaine* series (*Leurs prisons*). We would remain colleagues and friends ever after.

28. Jean Malaurie. Dieppe, France, 2010.

Every time Diane and I were with Malaurie in Paris, he would tell us stories about the history of just about everything we saw: *That's where X met his mistress . . . that's where the Germans had one of their torture places . . . during the Revolution, that building was . . .* If I hadn't known that he was a geomorphologist, anthropologist, Arctic explorer, and publisher, I would have thought him the Ultimate Paris Guide. Then, in 2009, he moved to Dieppe in Normandy. He'd had family in Normandy and had spent some time there as a child, but that didn't explain the move. He invited us to visit him and his wife, Monique, there for a few days. He said he would explain everything. He never did, but he explained everything else: it was just like Paris: we walked around, he told stories and explained history of everything we saw. We walked through a church, where he and Diane talked about the holy artifacts and the stained glass; we walked on a beach where hundreds of Canadian soldiers died on D-Day; we had oysters. One day, we explored a market and then came upon this motorcycle. He got really pissed off at this motorcycle. He didn't say why. For a moment, I thought he was going to kick it over, but he just scowled at it, then we walked on, talking.

29. Betty Friedan. Santa Monica, California, 1995.

She is still best known for her 1963 book, *The Feminine Mystique*, which was a key document in that decade's feminist movement. She was the first president of the National Organization of Women.

I was in Los Angeles working for Dustin Hoffman on a film project (which, like most film projects, went nowhere). My old friend Warren Bennis, who was then living in a condo in Santa Monica just north of Venice, said, "Come to dinner. I've got an old friend I want you to meet: Betty Friedan. You'll like one another."

Warren told me that his then-wife had a long-standing jones against Betty and wouldn't come with us. Two other friends of Warren's would: Ron Gottesman, who taught at University of Southern California (USC), and Ron's wife, who worked in a trendy Melrose Avenue bookstore where interior decorators sometimes bought books by the running foot and binding color to go with the movie or rock star client's decor.

The conversation was lively. At one point, Betty stopped talking and looked at her plate as if she were about to attack it. That's when I took this photo.

Later, when I drove her back to her hotel, which was on the way to mine, she said her daughter lived near Buffalo and we must get together next time she was in the area. Like most plans of that sort, it never happened. But there was a curious collateral connection. She figures in *Town Bloody Hall* (1979), Chris Hegedus and D. A. Pennybaker's film about a contentious encounter in 1971 between Norman Mailer and a group of feminists. She's not one of the onstage characters, but she's in the audience, and her work informs much of what they say. That film would be adapted into a play by New York's premier experimental theater company, the Wooster Group, in 2017. The play—*The Town Hall Affair*—was directed by Elizabeth LeCompte and had, as a key member of the cast, Kate Valk. The next year, Kate would direct, and Liz would design, a Wooster Group play based on my early prison work, *The B-Side: "Negro Folklore from Texas State Prisons": A Record Album Interpretation*.

30. Fannie Lou Hamer. Newport Folk Festival performers' tent. Newport, Rhode Island, 1965.

The Newport Folk Festivals, in the years I was involved with them (1964 as a reporter; 1965–1968 as a board member; after that as a trustee of the Foundation) were always political. Pete Seeger was a driving force in Newport. He, Theodore Bikel, and Oscar Brand had joined with jazz promoter and musician George Wein to create the Festival. Joyce Wein, George's wife, was a college roommate and lifelong friend of Coretta Scott King. Each year, the festival presented an astonishing range of musical voices and styles, and each year, there were major political components in the concerts and workshops, which is why Fannie Lou Hamer, one of the great heroes of the civil rights movement was there.

31. Leonard Michaels (writer). Berkeley, California, 1971.

Lenny had the office next to mine at Berkeley the first half of my 1971–1972 Guggenheim year in California. I got the office because Stanley Fish, who had taught at University at Buffalo English Department summer school just before I was about to head west, offered to get me a Berkeley English Department office. I accepted happily.

I got there and got my family settled in our rented house in Kensington Heights. My first marriage was breaking up and the plan was for everyone to get comfortable in Kensington Heights, then I'd move out. It was a nice idea, but in practice, it was, like most such things, a drawn-out mess.

The Berkeley office, it turned out, had been the office of a Johns Hopkins friend of Diane's who, a short time before, had been denied tenure by Berkeley. Before I moved into the flat of my Texas friends, Hugh and Claudette Lowe, in the Mission District of San Francisco, and while I was still getting things sorted out in Kensington Heights, it was my daily hideout.

Almost every day of my first two weeks there, Stanley would come by my office and say, "Let's go outside." We would go to Sproul Plaza and get on-the-spot squeezed orange juice, which I loved. The oranges were right off the trees. Then we'd sit by the fountain, drink our OJs, and Stanley would say, "Look at the tits on that one," or, "Wow, did you see her," or, "Over there, look over there, the one in the pink sweater."

That got old pretty fast. That's when I started hanging out with Lenny.

We'd sit in his office or mine and talk. We talked about books, the ones we were writing and the ones we liked. I remember particularly our conversations about Kafka, the subject of Lenny's Ph.D. thesis. There was something about his sensibility that made Kafka seem perfectly appropriate.

And we talked about divorce. I was about to get one. He said comforting things. I said, "I know that you've been through this, too."

"Not quite the same. She killed herself. We were about to reconcile, too. I didn't want to reconcile but she did, and I agreed to it. She came out of the bedroom and told me she'd taken forty-seven sleeping pills and some bourbon. She went into the bathroom and went into a coma. She lived for three days. The doctors were very interested and very proud. They thought they had a real achievement and that she would live. The cops were really nice, though. They said to me, 'No, man. She's gonna die. Get ready for it. She won't make it.' They were right. I never understood why she did it."

"You're tied to her for good now," I said.

"Yeah," Lenny said. "That's why she did it."

Lenny had one of my favorite book titles, one I often quote when people talk to me about work or family problems that are beyond their capacity to fix: *I Would*

Have Saved Them If I Could (1975). Some of the stories in it remind me of our conversations about marriage.

One night that fall, leaving our house in Kensington Heights, Lenny leaned out the car window and yelled, "Watch me as I back out. I don't want to hit that wall across the road."

There was nothing across the road except a steep drop-off into Wildcat Canyon. I said, "Lenny, there isn't any wall across the road."

"Bruce," he said, "that doesn't mean I won't hit it." I dutifully guided him as he backed out.

32. Billy Lee Brammer (writer). San Antonio, Texas, 1967.

Whenever I was doing research at the prisons around Huntsville, Texas, in the mid-1960s, I'd take a break and visit Billy Lee and his wife, Dorothy Browne, in Austin. Almost every illegal chemical I ever had, I had for the first—and sometimes the only—time was at Billy Lee's apartment or houses.

Their place was always swarming with writers, painters, comix book geniuses, and others. I met underground comix artist Gilbert Shelton (*Fabulous Furry Freak Brothers)* there. When I met novelist Larry McMurtry in Houston two years later, I mentioned Billy Lee's great political novel, *The Gay Place* (1961). Larry said he had been friends with Billy Lee for years. We told each other Billy Lee stories for hours, long after our host passed out on the couch. Billy Lee was the reason I got to write for *Rolling Stone* and *Texas Monthly.* When Willy Morris and I met to talk about me writing for *Harper's,* we spent half the conversation telling Brammer stories. When Diane and I connected with writer and former *Texas Observer* editor Molly Ivins in Sun Valley, we told Brammer stories.

After this visit in San Antonio (his friend Hugh Lowe had gotten him a job on the HemisFair project), I didn't see him again until I moved from Kensington Heights to San Francisco in January 1972. His Texas friends, Hugh and Claudette Lowe, were back in San Francisco by then. As I noted earlier, they lent me their apartment in the Mission for a few weeks while I looked for a place after my marriage to Susan broke up. Before they left town on a Texas trip, they told me that Billy Lee was living in the Haight. Claudette told me how to find him.

Billy Lee opened the door and we stared at one another. The corridor wasn't very well lighted. Neither of us looked the same as the last time we'd met: I'd quit cigarettes and had put on more than twenty pounds; he'd developed cataracts and was wearing Coke-bottle glasses. After we decided that it really was us, we talked a while, then he showed me about fifty pages of the novel he said he was working on. The working title was, he said, "The Spy Who Came into His Hand."

They were exactly the same pages he'd shown me in Austin in 1966, and that was just what he'd said when he'd handed them to me then.

We went to a poetry reading by Robert Creeley and Andrei Codrescu at the Castro Theater, not far from where I was living on Russian Hill. On the way out of his apartment, Billy Lee scooped a spoonful of white powder from a jar and swallowed it. "Speed?" I asked.

"Mescaline," he said.

Judy Sullivan, a Buffalo friend who had known Billy Lee in Austin, called in 1978 to let me know that Billy Lee had died of a meth overdose, a few months before what would have been his forty-ninth birthday.

33. John Davis (singer). Washington, DC, 1968.

He was there with Bessie Jones as part of a group from the Georgia Sea Islands, working on the music program at Resurrection City.

"They took me to the Capitol yesterday," John said. "A lot of lies been told in that place." He said he particularly disliked the Rotunda: "I want a house with four corners so I can get my mind straight. In there, I would just go around and around all day long and just get dizzy."

34. Barack Obama (US president). Buffalo, New York, 2013.

He wasn't looking at me like that and neither was he pointing at me. I just happened to be where he was looking and pointing. The only other politician I saw work a room so well was Bill Clinton. Both could turn a performance in a huge arena into an intimate conversation.

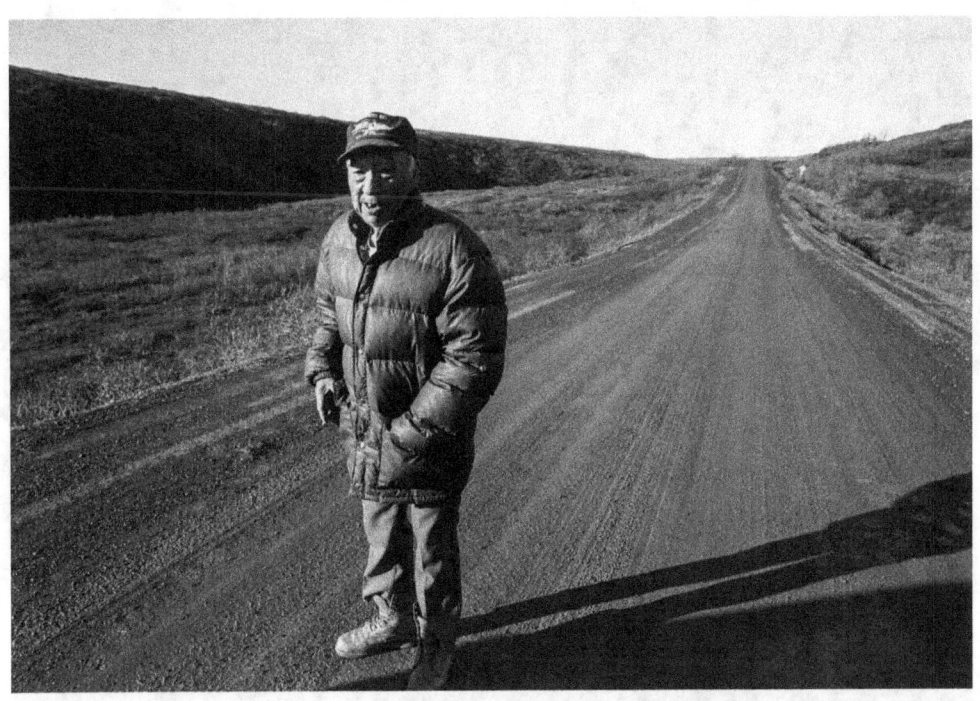

35. Hitchhiker. Nome-Teller Road, Alaska, 1997.

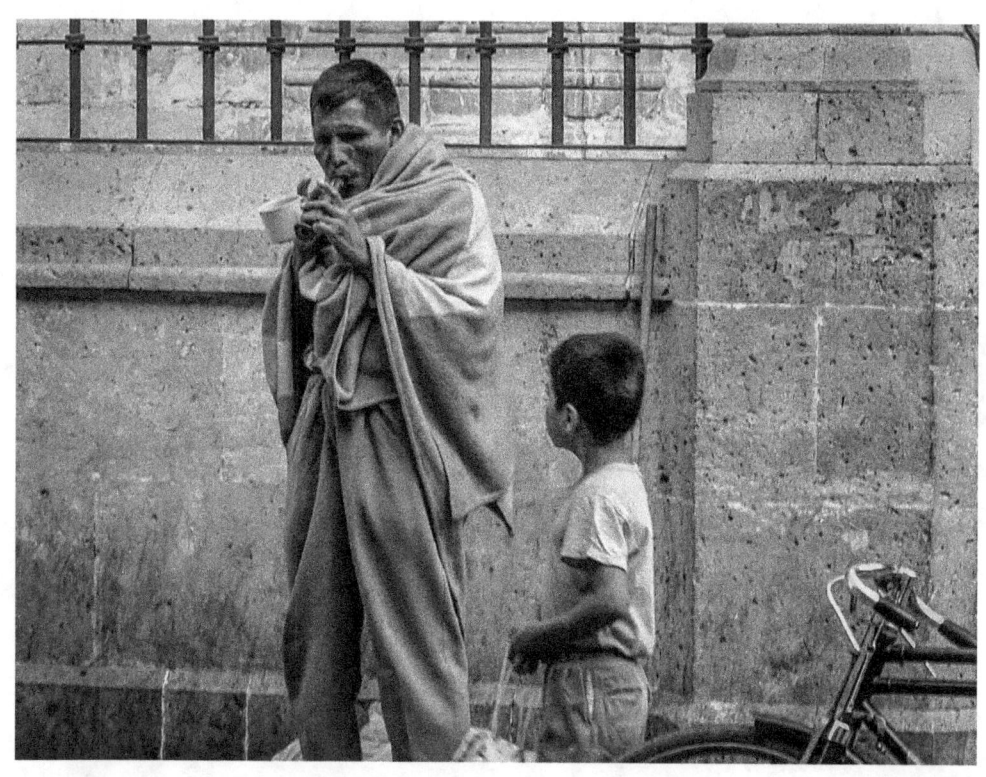

36. Flute player. Oaxaca, Mexico, 1970.

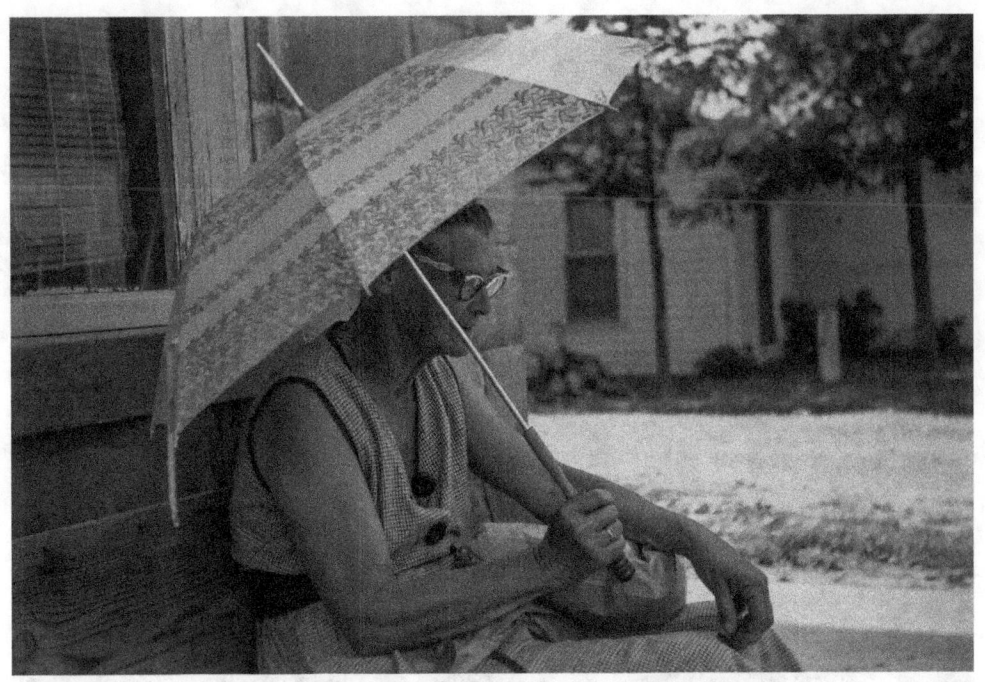

37. Mrs. Esrie Vickers. Big Flat, Arkansas, 1964.

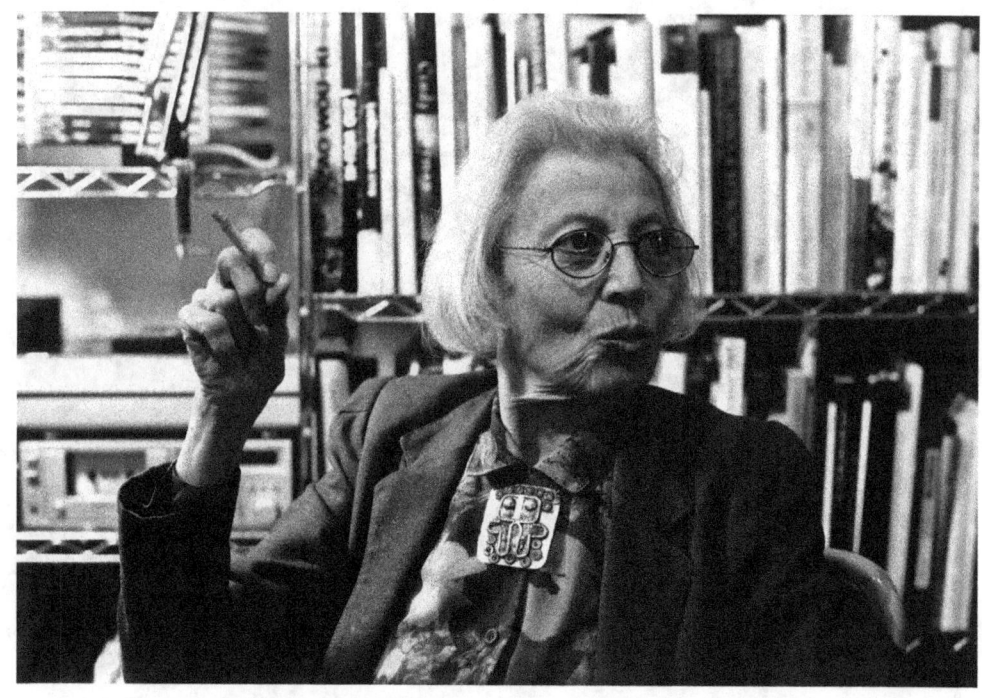

38. Magda Cordell McHale (artist). Buffalo, New York, 1997.

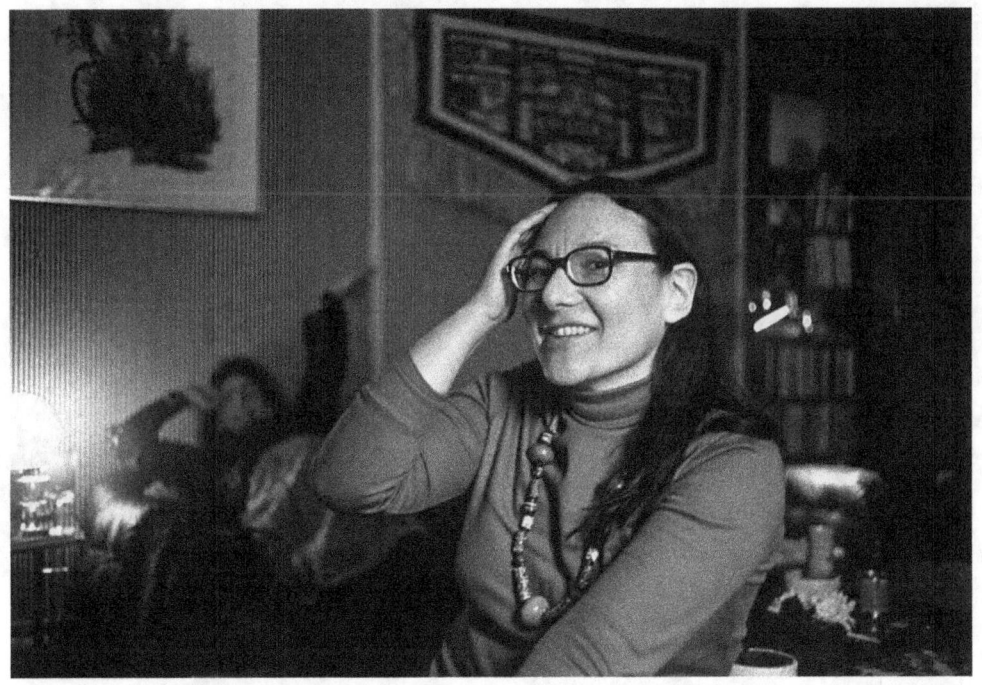

39. Diane Christian (professor, filmmaker, and author) and Elsa Dorfman (photographer). Buffalo, New York, 1974.

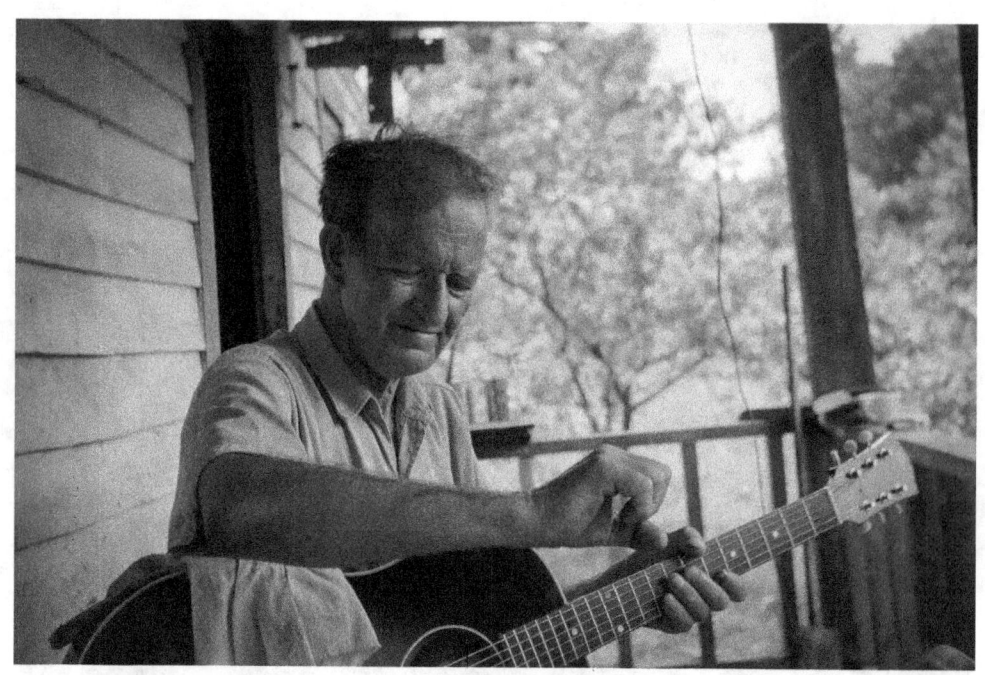

40. John Gallagher. Saltville, Virginia, 1965.

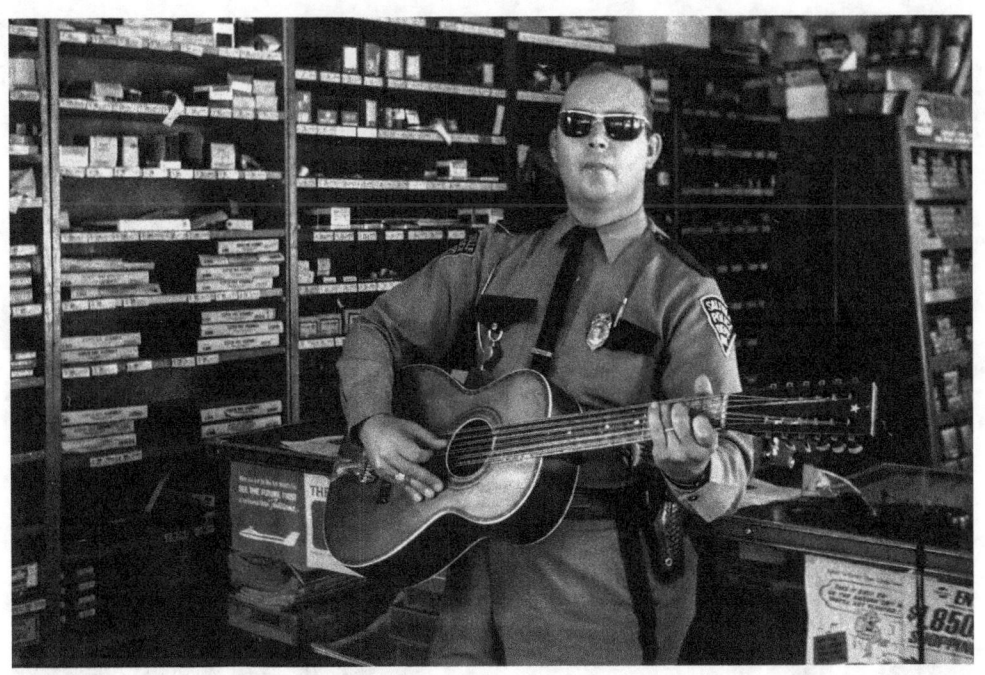

41. Melvin "Sam" Holmes (police officer). Saltville, Virginia, 1965.

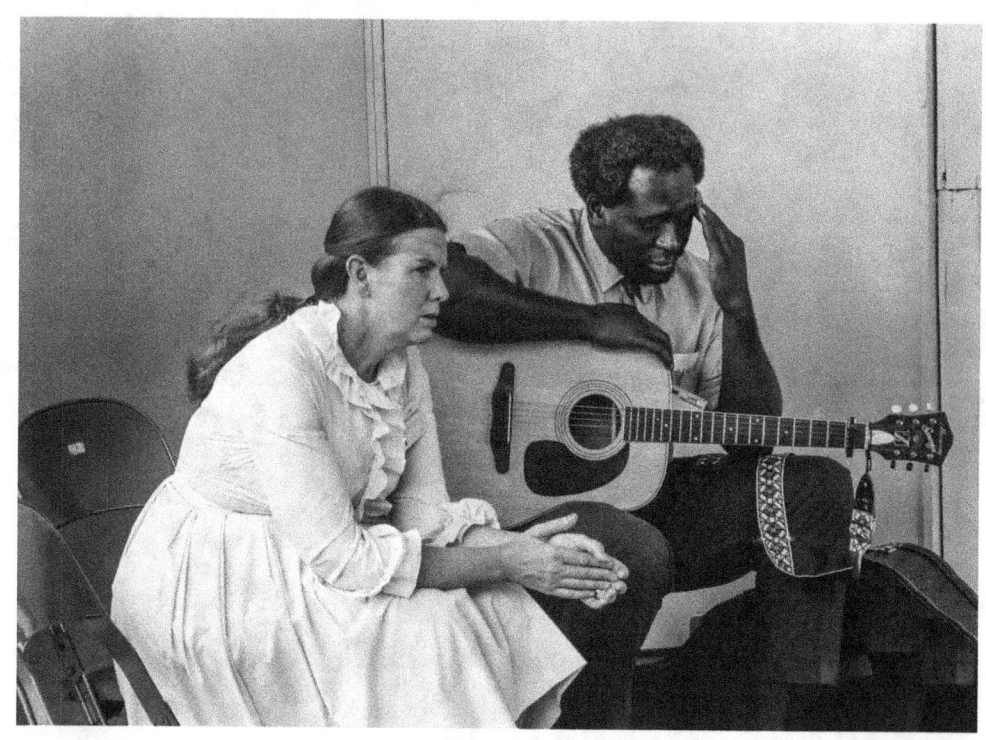

42. Jean Ritchie and Rev. Frederick Douglas Kirkpatrick (musicians). Newport Folk Festival, Sunday morning gospel concert. Newport, Rhode Island, 1968.

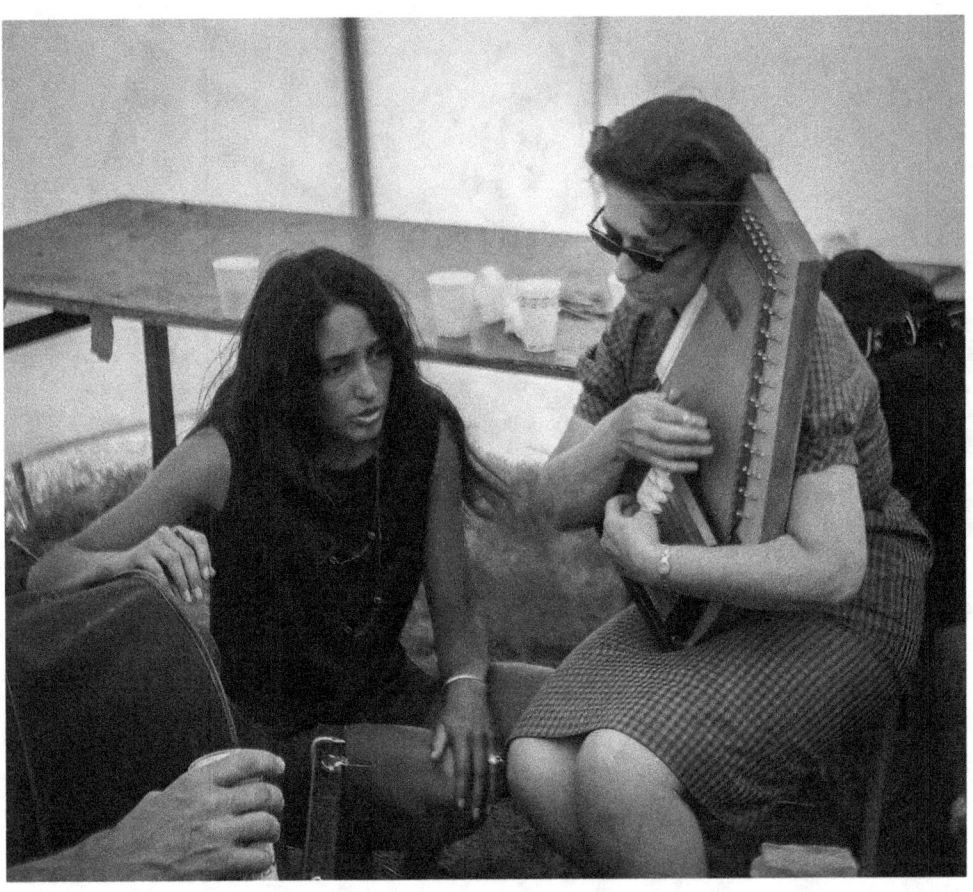

43. Joan Baez and Mother Maybelle Carter (musicians). Performers' tent, Newport Folk Festival. Newport, Rhode Island, 1965.

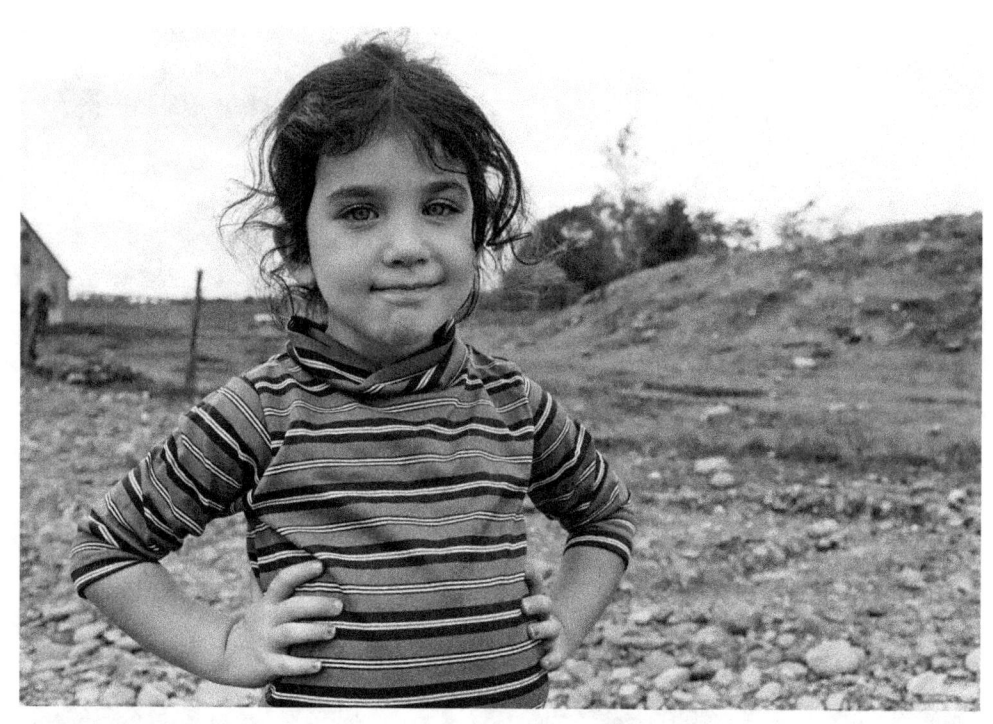

44. Rachel Jackson. Eden, New York, 1973.

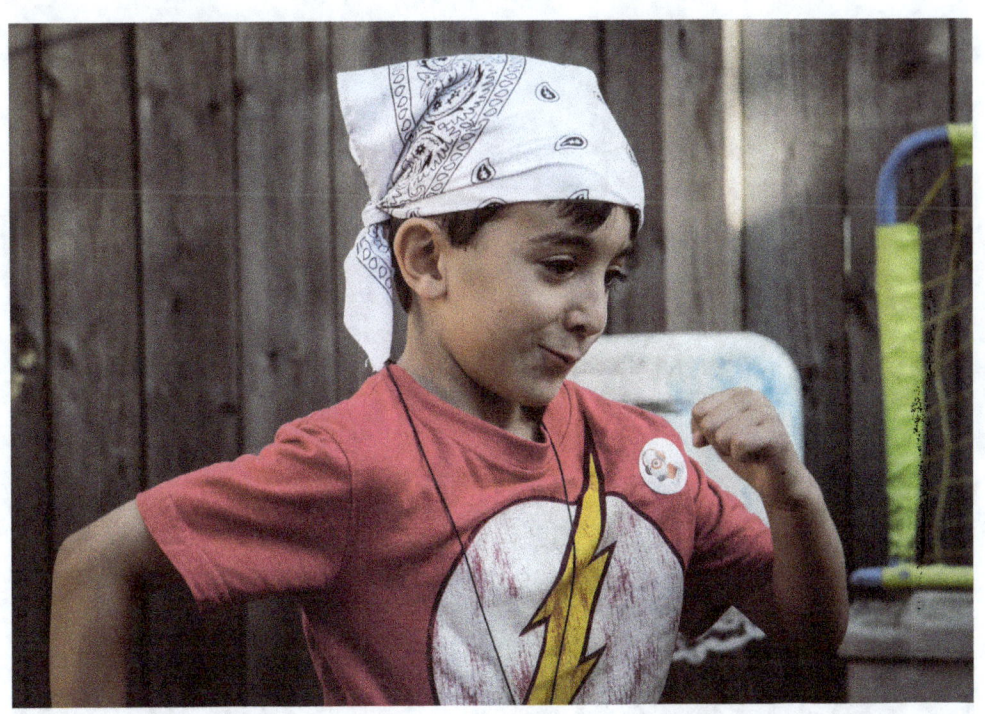

45. Rachel's son, Samuel Caico. Buffalo, New York, 2017.

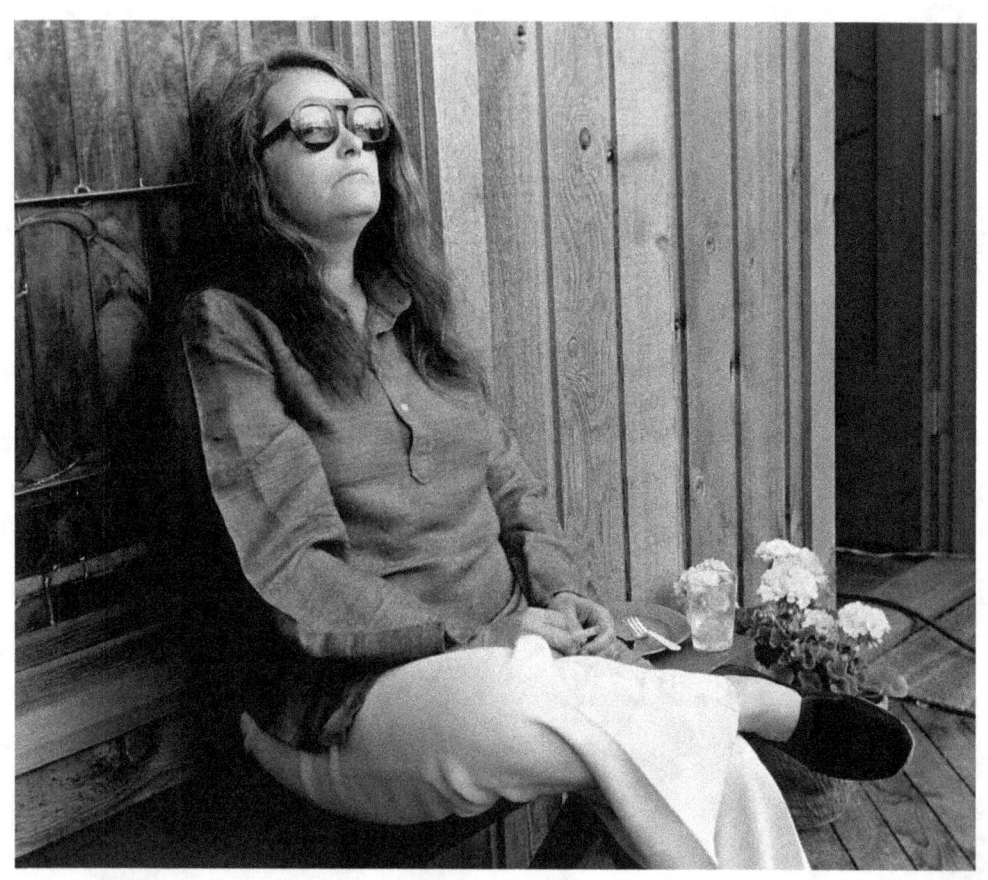

46. Kate Millett (writer). Hailey, Idaho, 1977.

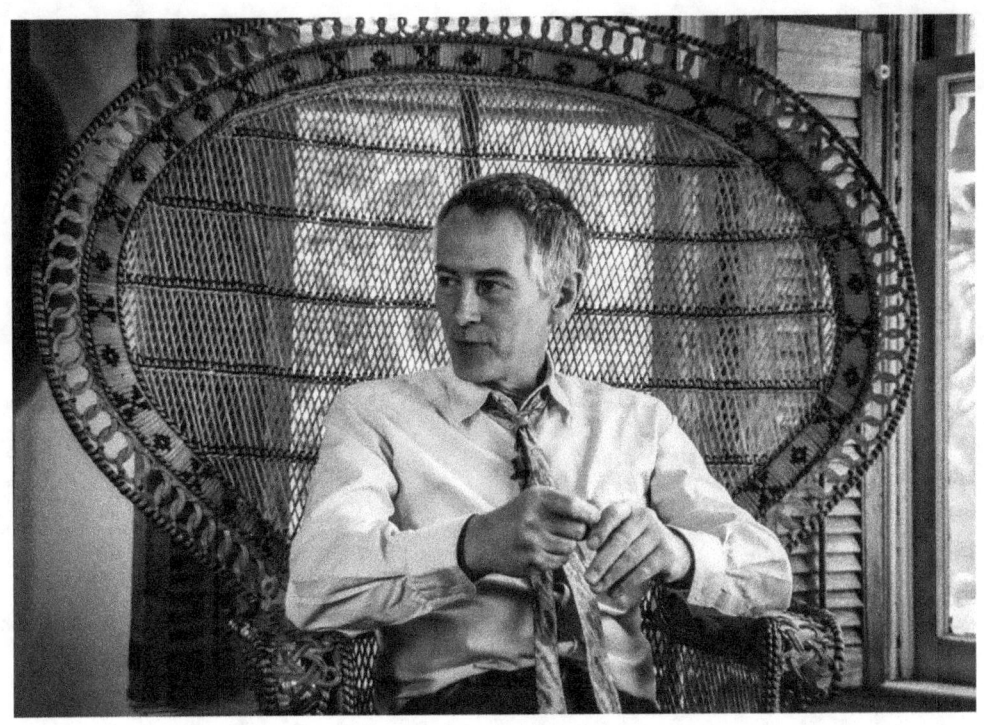

47. Michael McClure (writer). San Francisco, California, 1982.

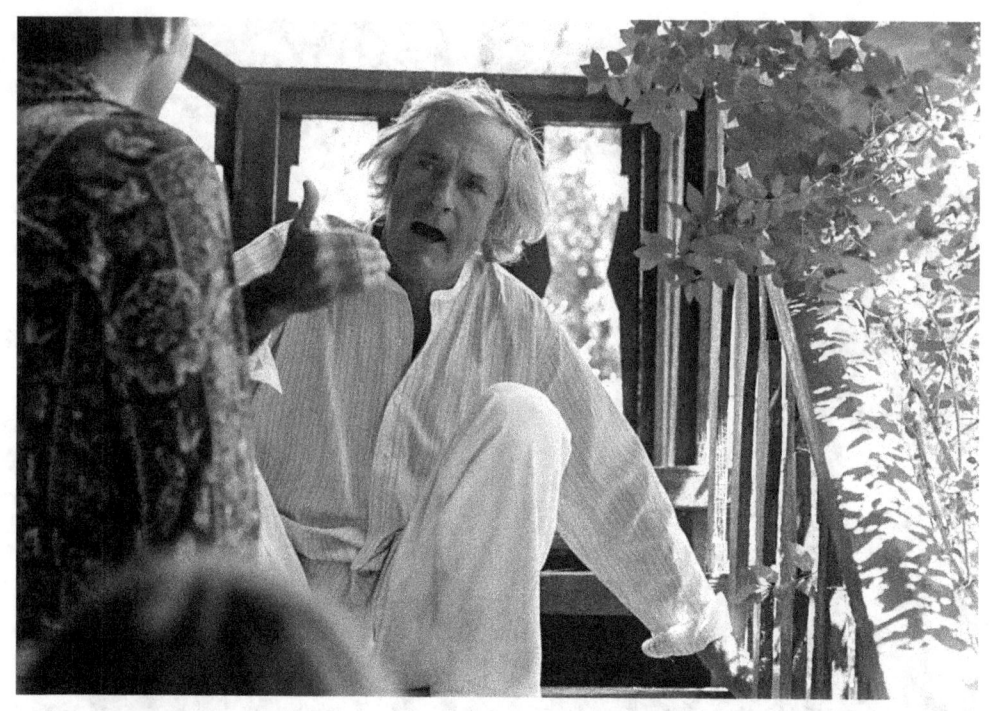

48. Timothy Leary (LSD evangelist). Sun Valley, Idaho, 1977.

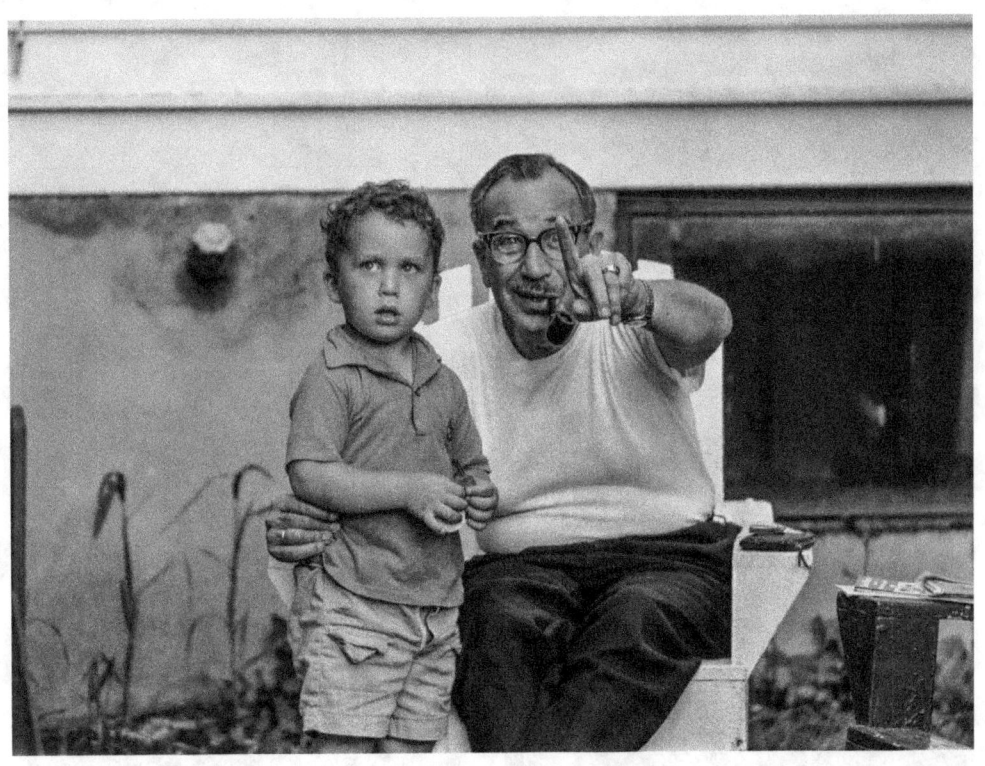

49. Michael Lee Jackson and Irving Jackson. Fords, New Jersey, 1965.

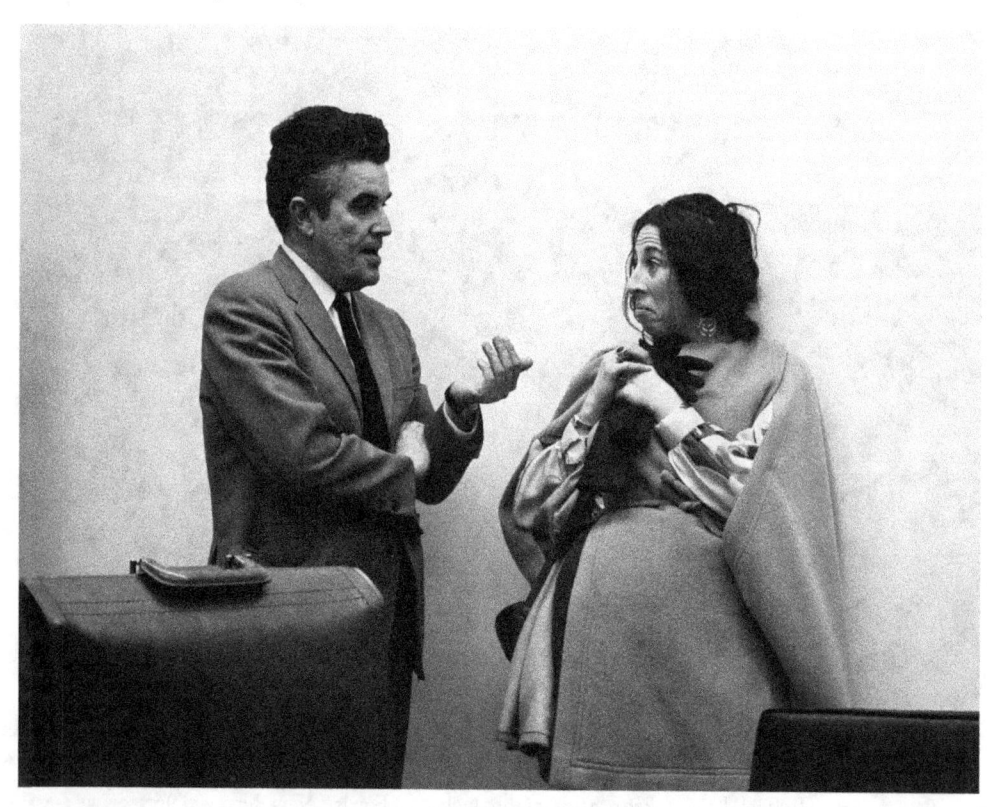

50. René Girard (philosopher) and Diane Christian. Buffalo, New York, 1971.

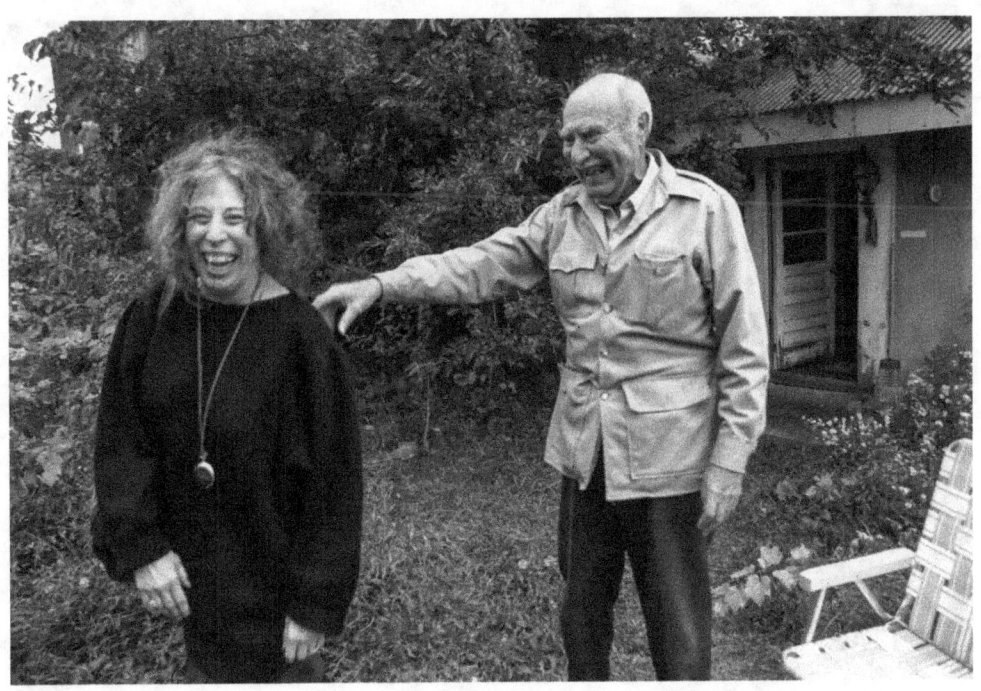

51. Diane Christian and James Card (film preservationist). Canandaigua, New York, 1995.

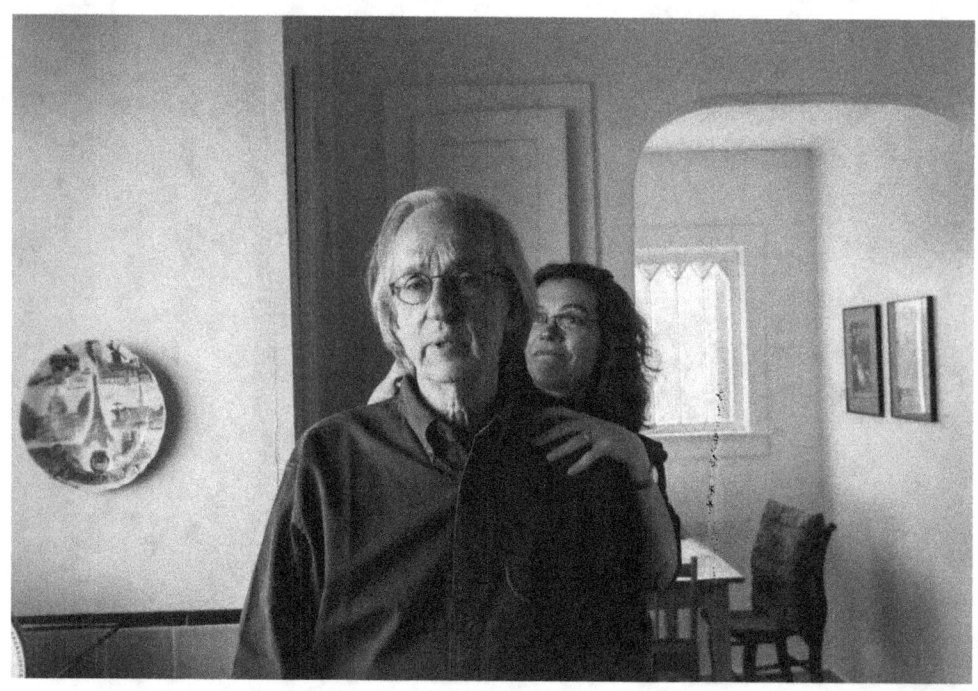

52. Howard S. Becker (sociologist) and Dianne Hagaman (photographer). Santa Barbara, California, 1997.

Words 3

35. Hitchhiker. Nome-Teller Road, Alaska, 1997.

Jean Malaurie, who had, in 1975, published in *Terre Humaine*, his great humanistic ethnography series; a French translation of my *In the Life: Varieties of the Criminal Experience* (1972); and, in 1985, a translation of Diane Christian's and my *Death Row* (1980), phoned from Paris to ask if I could meet him in Nome in two weeks. I said, "Sure."

One day we went to Teller, one of the two towns you could drive to from Nome. Jean had a particular affection for Teller. It was where Italian aviator and Arctic explorer Umberto Nobile, had, in 1926, landed his airship *Norge* in the first flight over the North Pole. Nobile intended to land at Nome, but strong winds forced him down further up the Norton Peninsula. Jean, who was the first European to reach the Magnetic North Pole on foot and who, in presatellite days, did a lot of important Arctic mapping, identified with Nobile. Jean wanted to show me a small monument at the place Nobile's airship had touched down.

Teller is small: a few streets, a few hundred residents, a few boats for hunting and fishing, a short runway on a nearby hill. The marker wasn't where Jean remembered it. While he went off looking for it, I photographed sealskins drying in the sun near a hunter's cabin. After a while, Jean turned up, much relieved: "They're restoring it," he said. "When they're done, they'll put it back." He again showed me where it had been, and we headed back to Nome.

On the way, we picked up a hitchhiker who said he was going to Nome to get a plane to Anchorage the next day so he could be with his sister, who was about to have surgery. We began talking in English, then he and Jean realized that the two of them could communicate in their separate dialects of Yupic—the hitchhiker's Alaskan, Malaurie's Greenlander. They told stories, sang songs, occasionally told me what they were saying. We stopped so the hitchhiker could smoke and Jean could drink from an Arctic stream.

A little after midnight two nights later, when I was coming back from watching the Aurora fifteen miles on the Council Road away from the town's lights, I saw the hitchhiker walking unevenly down the middle of the Front Street. I stopped the car and asked why he wasn't in Anchorage. He'd gotten drunk, he said, and he'd gotten rolled for all his money, so he'd missed the plane. Any chance I could lend him twenty bucks until the next time we met?

36. Flute player. Oaxaca, Mexico, 1970.

We were staying in a second-floor room of an old hotel a few blocks from the Zocalo. It was a big, square place, with all the rooms opening on to a central courtyard.

The first night I heard, coming over the roof, the sound of a flute playing a tune I didn't know in a scale I couldn't identify. Not only was the music strange, but so was its location: first, it seemed to come from the Zocalo, then it paused, resumed from a different place entirely. The third night, I went out to find the musician. When I left the room, the sound seemed to be coming from directly in front of the hotel. By the time I reached the street, the night was silent and the street was empty. Then, a few minutes later, I heard it from somewhere else. I followed the sound, but as I drew close, it went to silence again. I found him the third time: a blind man playing one of the black pottery flutes from San Bartolo Coyotepec.

I saw him only once during the day. I realized immediately why he walked the Oaxacan streets at night. During the day, the sound of that small flute was drowned out by traffic, by all the noises of a busy town; he could be heard only by people close to where he stood. But at night his music occupied the air.

37. Mrs. Esrie Vickers. Big Flat, Arkansas, 1964.

On my way to Texas for my first prison recordings, I stopped off in Mountain View, Arkansas, to visit Glenn Ohrlin, a rodeo bronc rider and singer. Glenn took me to a meeting at the courthouse of the Rackensack Folklore Society, presided over by singer and songwriter Jimmy Driftwood ("Battle of New Orleans"). Solo singers performed from the witness box; groups performed in front of the judge's bench.

A day later, at his house in Timbo, Jimmy told me that before I moved on, I should visit two great old-time ballad singers, Uncle Billy Sutterfield and Mrs. Esrie Vickers. He told me where to find them and said he'd get one of his sons to drive me to their places, which were not easy to find.

I spent an afternoon talking with and recording Uncle Barry. Before he started, he said, "I reckon I'm the best singer that ever puckered lip around here."

The visit to Mrs. Vickers didn't work out so well. Bing Driftwood and I went to her house and her son said we'd find her down at the post office. I asked where the post office was. He pointed to a building slightly to the left of across the street. Big Flat was very small.

She said she'd be happy to sing old-time ballads for me, but just not right now. "Come back tomorrow, sonny," she said.

"I have to be in Huntsville, Texas, tomorrow," I said.

She said that was too bad because she could sing ballads tomorrow, but not today.

Something bad happened with Jimmie's sons. In 1967, while he was in Europe concertizing, James and Bing got into a fight and killed each other. Jimmy never accepted it: he was always going on in later years about the guy who'd murdered them both. The last time I saw him he said, "They'll get that guy yet."

38. Magda Cordell McHale (artist). Buffalo, New York, 1997.

Almost every time I saw Magda she was wearing a stunning piece of jewelry I'd never seen before. She told me that they all had been made for her by her husband, John McHale, one of the inventors of Pop Art, who died in 1978. I loved her cigarette-whiskey voice. She was always smart and a delight to talk about anything with, but there was a sensuality to her voice itself: I'd have listened to her read the telephone directory. At the end she stopped talking—or seemed to. After a few months of silence and not long before she died, her friend Alex Bitterman realized that she had abandoned English, but not German or her native Hungarian. He spoke to her in German, and she burst into enthusiastic conversation.

39. Diane Christian (professor, filmmaker, and author) and Elsa Dorfman (photographer). Buffalo, New York, 1974.

In the mid-1960s, Elsa and I spent a huge amount of time in Gordon Cairnie's Grolier Bookshop on Plympton Street in Cambridge, Massachusetts. She took wonderful photos of the poets and other regulars who frequented the store (which was, for her, like a trout fisherman's favorite spot: you go there, you wait, they show up). The photos all had her inked comments at the bottom: all of us got prints or postcards of them.

In 1980, Elsa began using Polaroid's 200-pound 20x24 camera. Her style was the same, but now the pictures were in color and the people in them had to come to her. The subjects weren't just her longtime poet friends, like Allen Ginsberg, Peter Orlovsky, and Robert Creeley, but even more famous folks like Julia Child and Faye Dunaway, and paying sitters she didn't even know.

In 2016, she and I were involved in unrelated projects that shared the same name: she was the subject of Errol Morris's documentary, *The B-Side: Elsa Dorfman's Portrait Photography*, and I began working with New York's Wooster Group on a play based on my 1964 recordings in Texas prisons, *The B-Side: "Negro Folklore from Texas State Prisons": A Record Album Interpretation*.

40. John Gallagher. Saltville, Virginia, 1965.

On my way to Texas for my second recording of Black convict work songs. I stopped off in Saltville, Virginia, to visit banjo player and balladeer Hobart Smith, whom I'd met at the Newport Folk Festival a year earlier. I also visited Hob's cousin, John Gallagher, who was a pretty good guitar picker.

John lived in a house above a beautiful field of grass beyond which was a dark lake. He told me it was "the muck dam" from the nearby Olin-Matthiessen chemical factory. A few years later, the dam broke and caused all kinds of environmental hell.

That day, we sat on his porch and talked music. He told me he had bad arthritis in his hands, so the only guitar he could play was the cherry-red six-string Gibson he is holding in this photo.

He gave me a twelve-string guitar, which, he said a Black itinerant musician named Blind Lemon had given him in 1917. The back was cracked. "My brother hit someone over the head with it," John said. "It don't matter for the sound."

He was right. What matters most for the sound are the top and the neck. Twelve-strings in perfect condition are hard to tune, but this one had a slightly bent neck, so the only way to tune it was by harmonics or ear. I offered to pay him for it, but he refused. He said he got it for nothing so it wouldn't be right for him to sell it, especially because he wasn't playing it anyway.

41. Melvin "Sam" Holmes (police officer). Saltville, Virginia, 1965.

The guitar John Gallagher had given me was on the backseat of my car when I went to the Saltville gas station for an oil change. Sam was hanging out there: a southern cop in dark sunglasses looking at me and my Massachusetts license plates. He said, "What's that on your backseat?"

"A twelve-string," I said.

"Can I try it?" he said.

"If I can take your picture doing it," I said.

"Deal," he said. We talked about how difficult it was to tune and play a twelve-string with a bent neck. I showed him how I tuned it with harmonics. He said, "How long you here?"

I said, "I'm leaving Monday morning."

He invited me to a Sunday picnic at his dad's house. I went. Everyone played and sang. The next day I headed west.

42. Jean Ritchie and Rev. Frederick Douglas Kirkpatrick (musicians). Newport Folk Festival, Sunday morning gospel concert. Newport, Rhode Island, 1968.

The Sunday morning concerts were one of my favorite parts of the Newport Folk Festivals. It was always called the gospel concert, but any performer on the three- or four-day program who had any religious song could take part. Jean was a traditional singer from Berea, Kentucky; Kirk had been one of the leaders of Deacons for Defense, a Louisiana group famous for breaking up a 1964 Klan rally.

From 1966 on, those concerts were moderated by a Catholic priest. I asked Ralph Rinzler, the Newport Board member who introduced him, how that came about. Ralph said he'd seen the priest in the audience before one Sunday concert and asked him to moderate. The priest told Ralph that he had no special knowledge; he was just there because he liked the music. Ralph told the priest, "That's all you need." He gave him a list of the performers, led him to the lectern at the edge of the stage, and the music came forth.

43. Joan Baez and Mother Maybelle Carter (musicians). Performers' tent, Newport Folk Festival. Newport, Rhode Island, 1965.

The Carter Family are still the elders of country music. Joan Baez is still performing. Maybelle performed at Newport two years later with her cousin Sara, who had been lead singer on most of the Carter Family (Sara, Sara's husband A.P., and Maybelle) recordings in the 1920s and 1930s. Maybelle's daughter June was there, too, along with June's husband, Johnny Cash. Moments like those abrogated time.

44. Rachel Jackson. Eden, New York, 1973.

45. Rachel's son, Samuel Caico. Buffalo, New York, 2017.

For most of the time I've known him, Sam has loved improvising costumes and inhabiting roles.

46. Kate Millett (writer). Hailey, Idaho, 1977.

Kate was best known for her book, *Sexual Politics* (1970). She did a great deal more than writing it.

She was one of the commentators on a talk Diane gave on Wonder Woman at the Institute of the American West that year. The two things I remember of that panel are Kate saying, "To get a woman hero, you have to go to a comic book," and journalist and satirist Paul Krassner looking at Kate and Diane and saying, "I have womb envy."

47. Michael McClure (writer). San Francisco, California, 1982.

Michael was one of the last surviving Beats. He was the only friend I had who said, "My play was arrested." When he said that, he was referring to his 1965 play, *The Beard*, in which Billy the Kid gives head to Jean Harlow. Every time promoter Bill Graham put it on, the San Francisco police would arrest everybody in the company for public obscenity. It's now regarded as one of the decade's classics.

He was the second person I knew who owned a home computer, an early Apple (the Mac debuted in 1984). The first Apple-owning friend lived in Detroit. She didn't have a clue what to do with it. She used words I didn't know, like "cursor" and "mouse." She kept moving the cursor around the screen. I asked what the cursor did. She got stuck on that one. Then, on this visit a few months later, Michael took me to his garage and proudly showed me his. "What can you do with it?" I asked. "Everything!" he said. He showed me some of the things he was up to. Shortly thereafter, I got my first computer, a DEC Rainbow. It, like the Apple, ran on floppy disks. My first hard disk was the size of a cigar box; it had a capacity of five megabytes and cost about $1,000. For years, every time Michael and I met, we'd talk about writer friends and computer gear. Then the surviving writer friends dwindled and the computers in our lives became ordinary.

48. Timothy Leary (LSD evangelist). Sun Valley, Idaho, 1977.

I first encountered him at a drug conference in Buffalo in spring 1969. When he appeared in one of the Institute of the American West conferences in Sun Valley, he said everything I remembered him saying eight years earlier—only this time, he wasn't stoned. I think.

49. Michael Lee Jackson and Irving Jackson. Fords, New Jersey, 1965.

Michael, would have been three then, my father fifty-seven. Michael is now fifty-nine, the same age my father was when he died.

I know these dates and numbers, but I look at photographs like this and those dates and numbers mean nothing. One of the last things my mother said to me was, "You can't stop time, Brucie, you know that, don't you?" I said that I did.

I did know that, but now, at eighty-five, I understand it. Photographs capture time, like insects in amber. They capture it, they have their own form, but no more. You need words, memory, for the rest. That's what this book is about.

The older people in my father's family—his sisters—always called him "Itzie." I long thought that a family diminutive of the name I knew him by, "Irving." Nothing of the sort. A distant cousin on a family genealogical mission sent me his parents' death certificates. The son on those documents, born the same year as he, was "Yitzak"—"Isaac" in American. What I heard as "Itzie" was "Yitzie," a reasonable diminutive for those Belorussian Jews who landed on New York's Lower East Side in 1890. I don't know when or how he became the "Irving" I knew.

When I was young, we sometimes visited the few relatives who still lived in those cold-water tenements. Now, I'm a member of an avant-garde theater company, the Wooster Group, based in the same neighborhood. Michael has been to several performances of *The B-Side*, their play based on some of my early work. A second play, *Untitled Toast*, should open about the time this book is published.

I look at this photo of Yitzie and Michael and I like it as a photo. I look at their hands and imagine what they might be saying to one another and thinking about. And, in another room in my mind, all those decades I just told you about inhabit it or are invoked by it.

50. René Girard (philosopher) and Diane Christian. Buffalo, New York, 1971.

René was giving a seminar on the book that would make him famous in the US academic world: *Violence and the Sacred* (published in France in 1972, in the US in 1977). Diane, then two years out of the convent, and René had a lot in common. The seminar was given in French. Diane's French then, as now, was far better than mine. After each session, I'd try to figure out what I'd just heard while she was discussing with him whatever had caught her attention. A few years later, René went to Stanford, and then back and forth to France, where he was made a member of the Académie Française, the members of which were identified as "The Immortals." He was the only one of my friends to have been so designated.

51. Diane Christian and James Card (film preservationist). Canandaigua, New York, 1995.

Jim created the film exhibition and collection program at George Eastman House/ International Museum of Photography. He was one of the great film preservationists.

He lived in Rochester, but he had a converted chicken coop in Canandaigua, where, in the warm months, he would invite small groups of his friends for screenings of rare film prints. The building had three parts: living quarters, a screening room, and a storage area that held his private film collection and a beautiful Alpha Romeo that never, in the years I knew him, was able to fire up.

He rescued Louise Brooks, his childhood silent film love, from drunken obscurity in New York and brought her up to Rochester, where she wrote the articles that would comprise her great film memoir, *Lulu in Hollywood* (1982). They were, for a time, lovers.

Once, he told me, they had a falling out and he decided he would murder her. She always smoked in bed. His idea was to line her bed with magicians' flash paper and some volatile liquid that, when it burned, like flash paper, left no trace. When a spark fell from her cigarette or she dropped it onto the bed, a fire would erupt and consume her.

They made up so he didn't do it. He did tell her about it. She laughed and said it would be a good plot for a movie. After they stopped being lovers, they continued as friends.

She was, Jim said, always interesting, and she knew it. "She said, 'If I ever bore you, it will be with a knife.'"

52. Howard S. Becker (sociologist) and Dianne Hagaman (photographer). Santa Barbara, California, 1997.

Howie and I met at a drug conference in Buffalo in spring 1969. He's one of the few American sociologists whose early and late work continues to make sense. His genius, I think, is that he has always looked at what was going on rather than finding a theory into which the facts had to be shoehorned. In France, he's still considered the most interesting American sociologist. Dianne is a former newspaper photographer who wrote a wonderful book, *How I Learned Not to Be a Photojournalist* (1996). Some of Howie's books are *Outsiders: Studies in the Sociology of Deviance* (1963), *Art Worlds* (1982), *What about Mozart? What about Murder* (2015), and *Evidence* (2017). We still talk or Zoom every week.

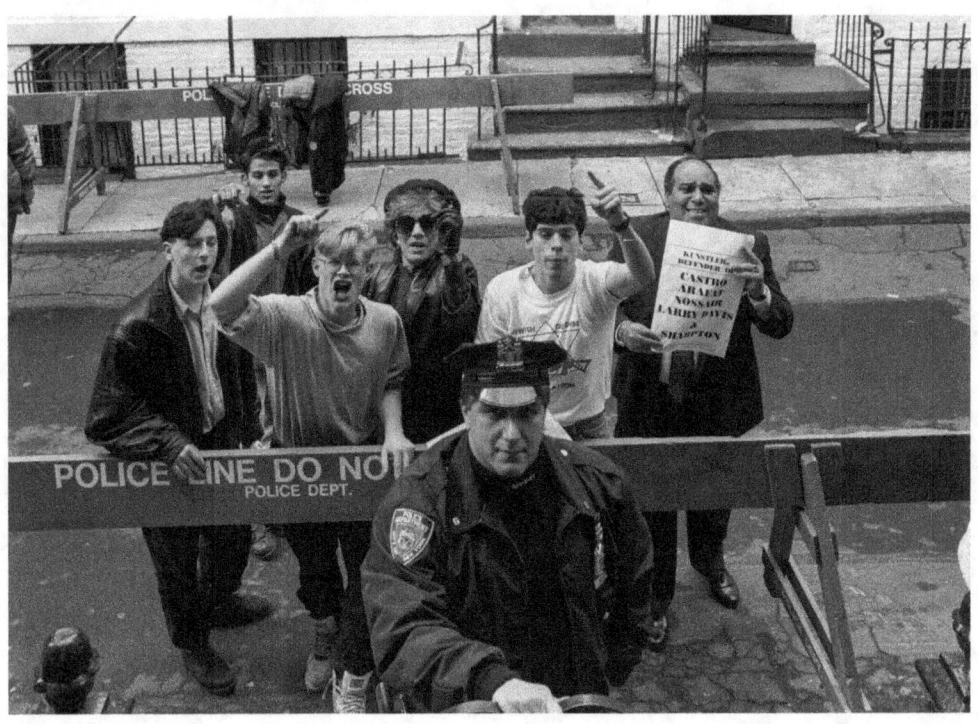

53. Demonstrators in the street outside Bill and Margaret Kunstler's house. New York, New York, 1992.

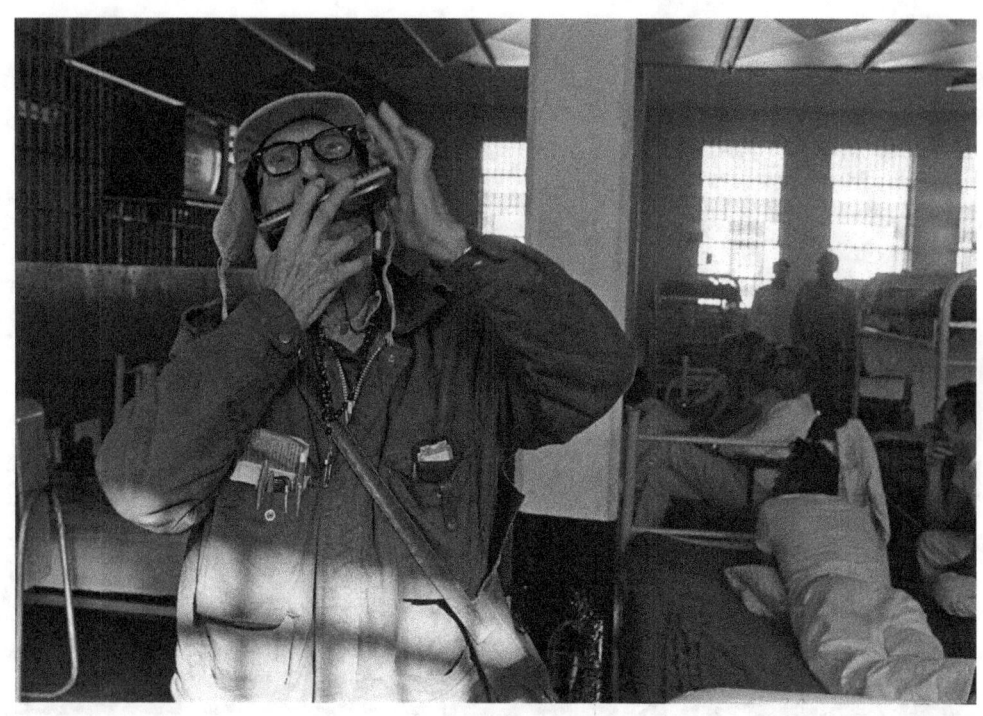

54. Prisoner with harmonica. Cummins prison farm, Varner, Arkansas, 1974.

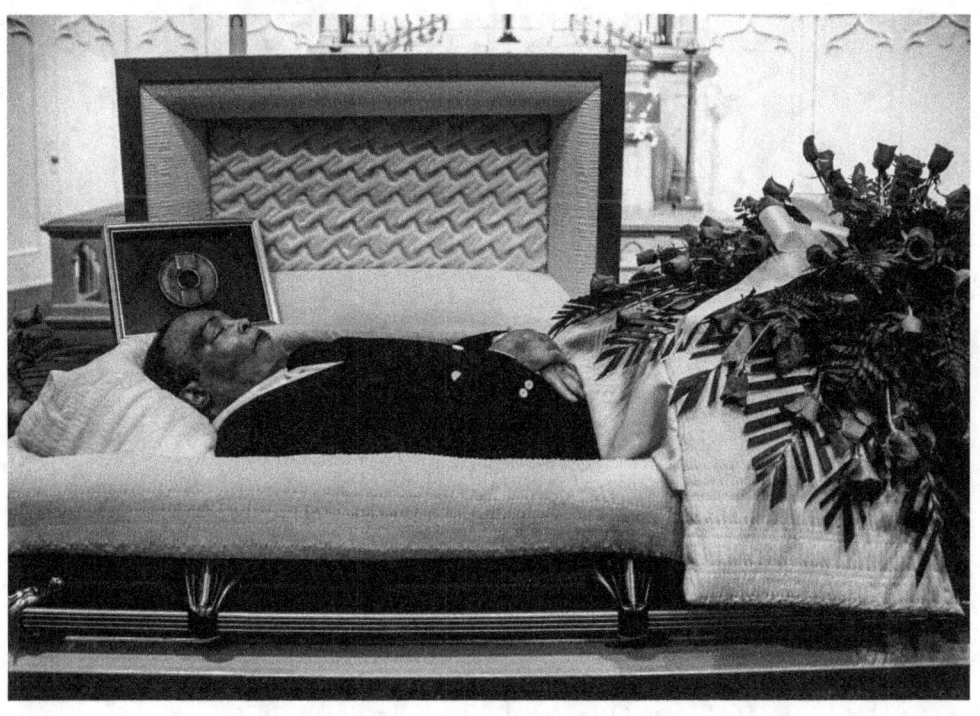

55. Herbert X. Blyden (Attica Brother and civil rights activist). Buffalo, New York, 1997.

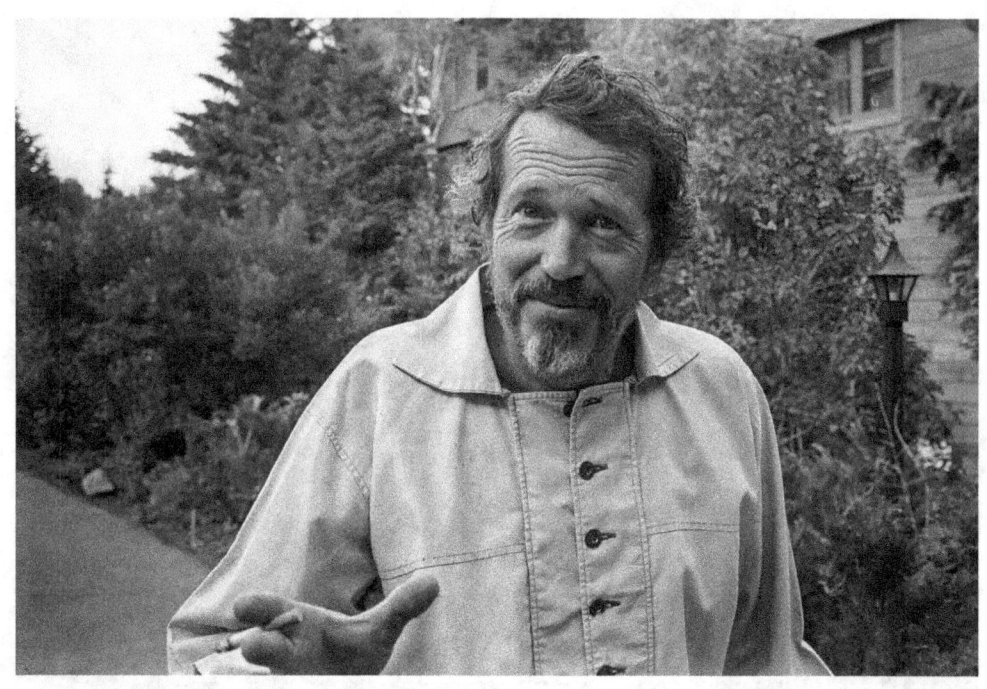

56. Warren Oates (actor). Sun Valley, Idaho, 1976.

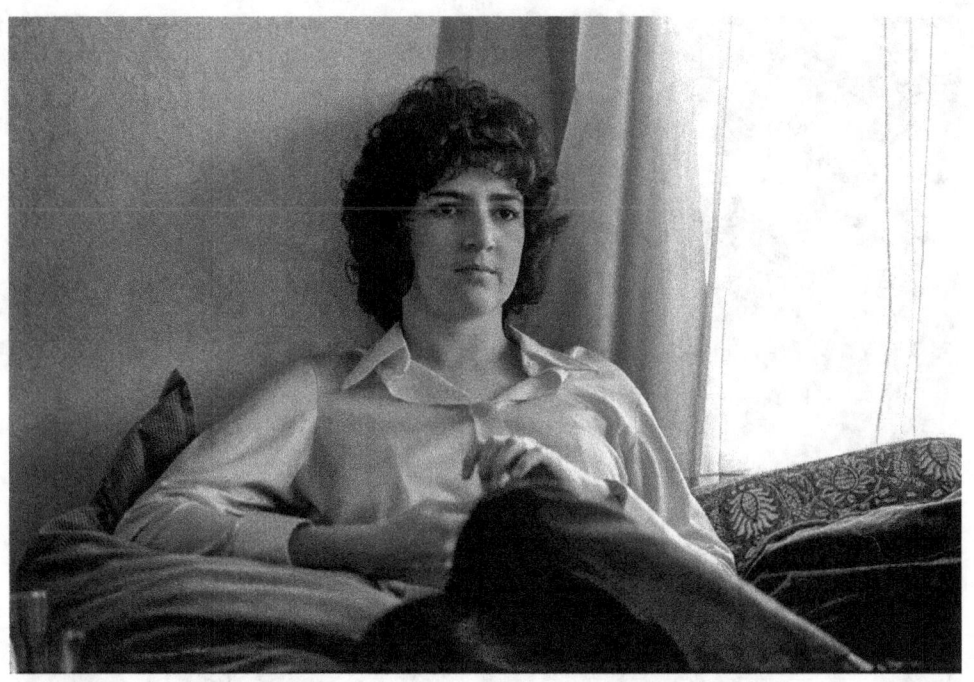

57. Judy Sullivan (sex therapist). Buffalo, New York, 1970.

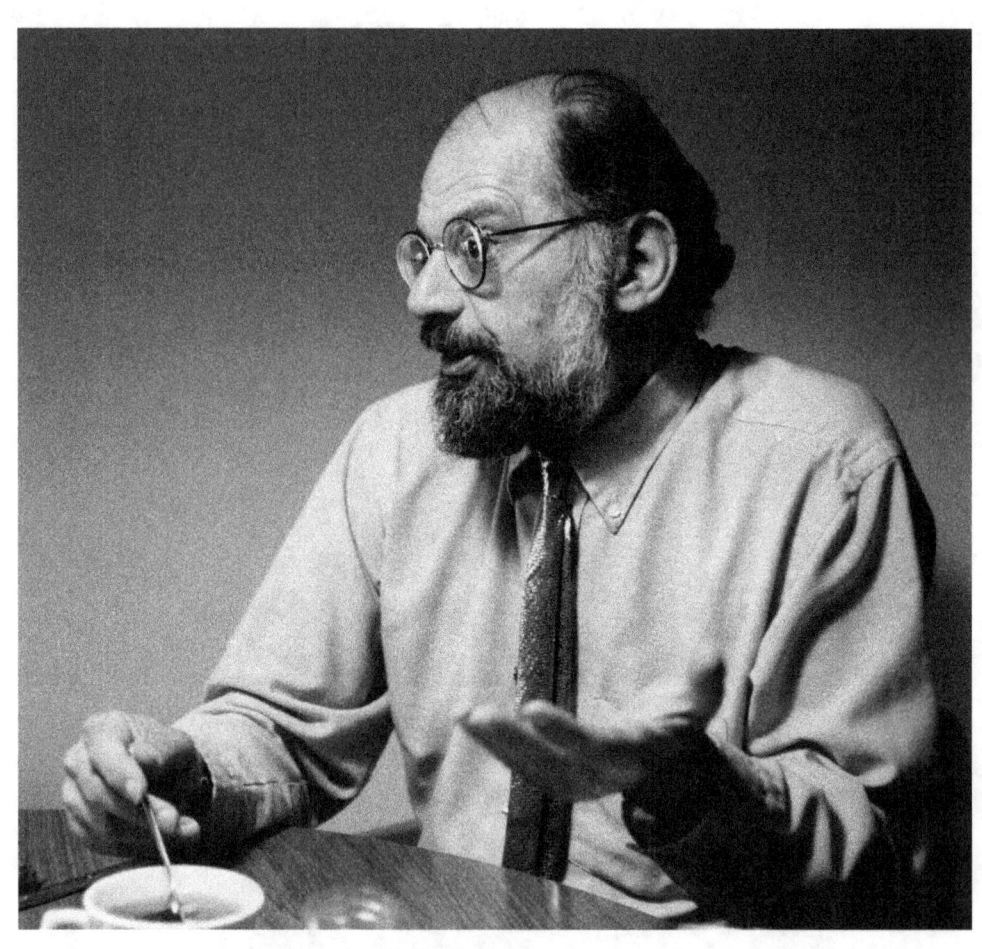

58. Allen Ginsberg (poet). Boulder, Colorado, 1984.

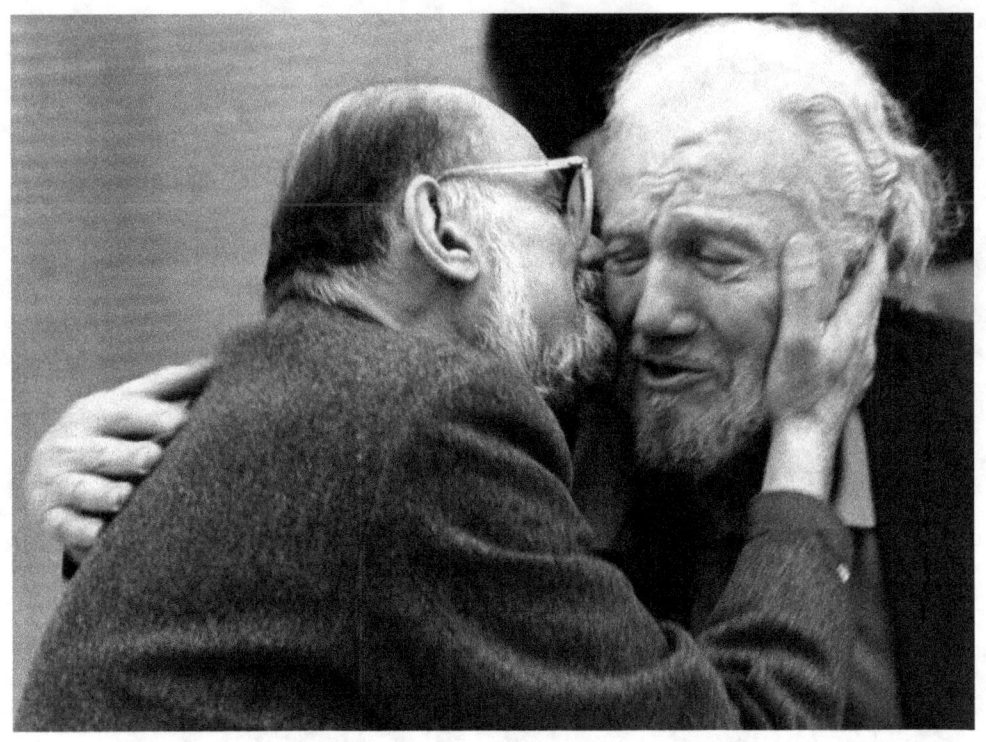

59. Allen Ginsberg and Leslie Fiedler (literary critic). Buffalo, New York, 1994.

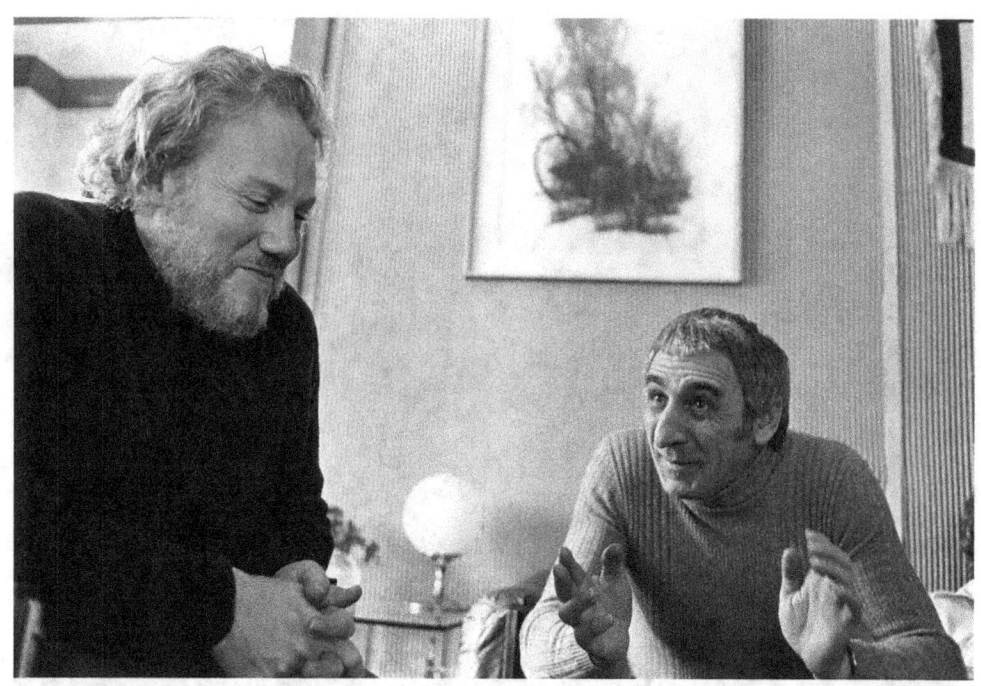

60. Leslie Fiedler and Raymond Federman (writer). Buffalo, New York, 1974.

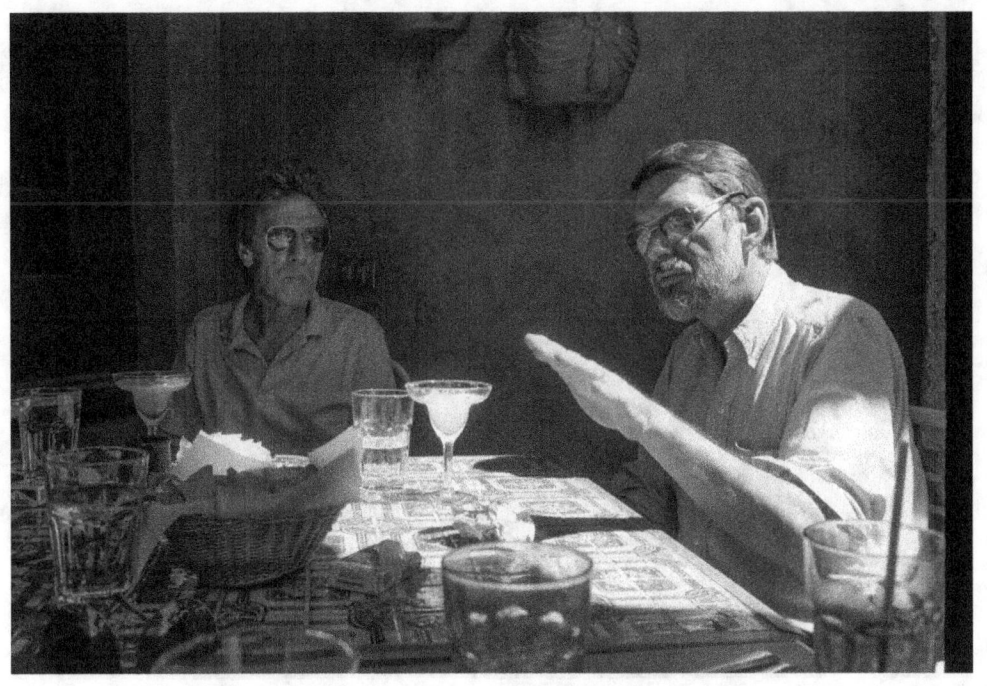

61. Ed Dorn and Robert Creeley (poets). Boulder, Colorado, 1984.

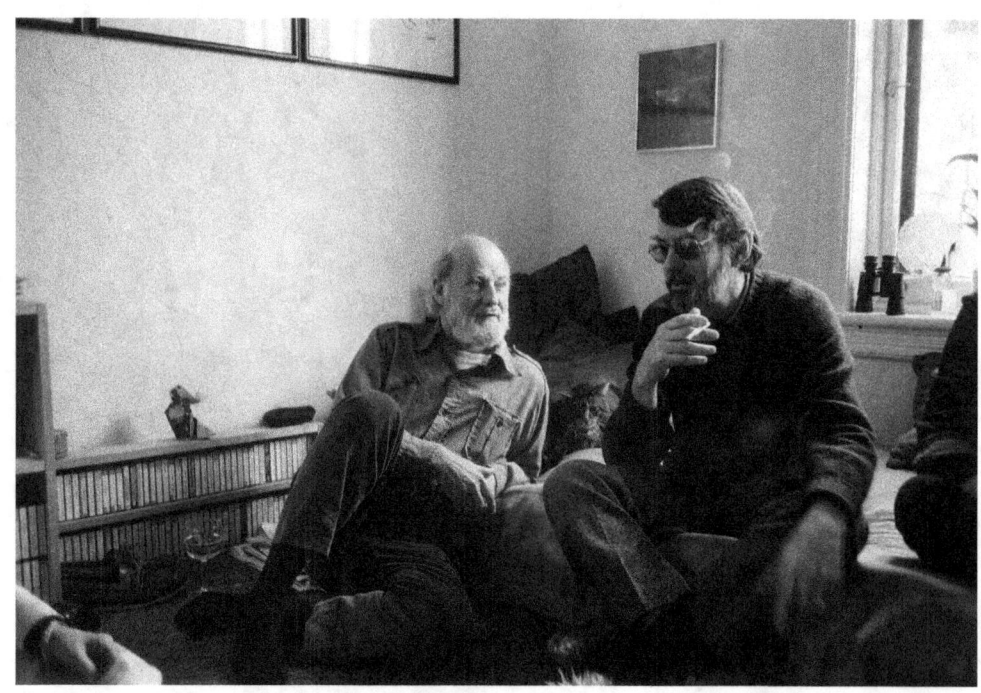

62. Lawrence Ferlinghetti (poet, publisher, and bookseller) and Robert Creeley. Buffalo, New York, 1982.

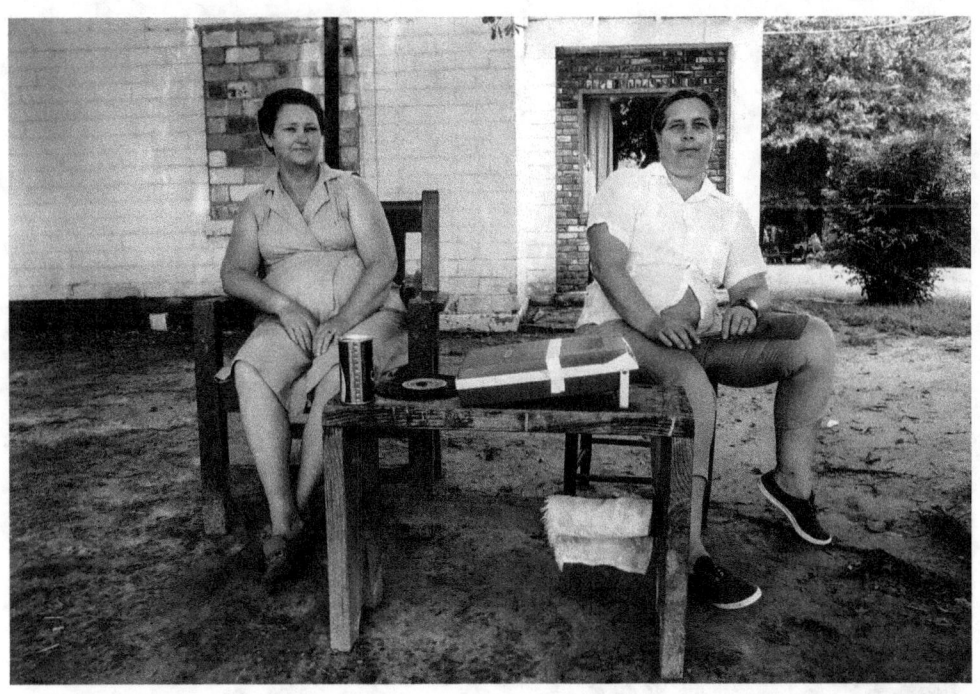

63. Gate turnkeys. Women's Unit, Cummins prison farm, Varner, Arkansas, 1971.

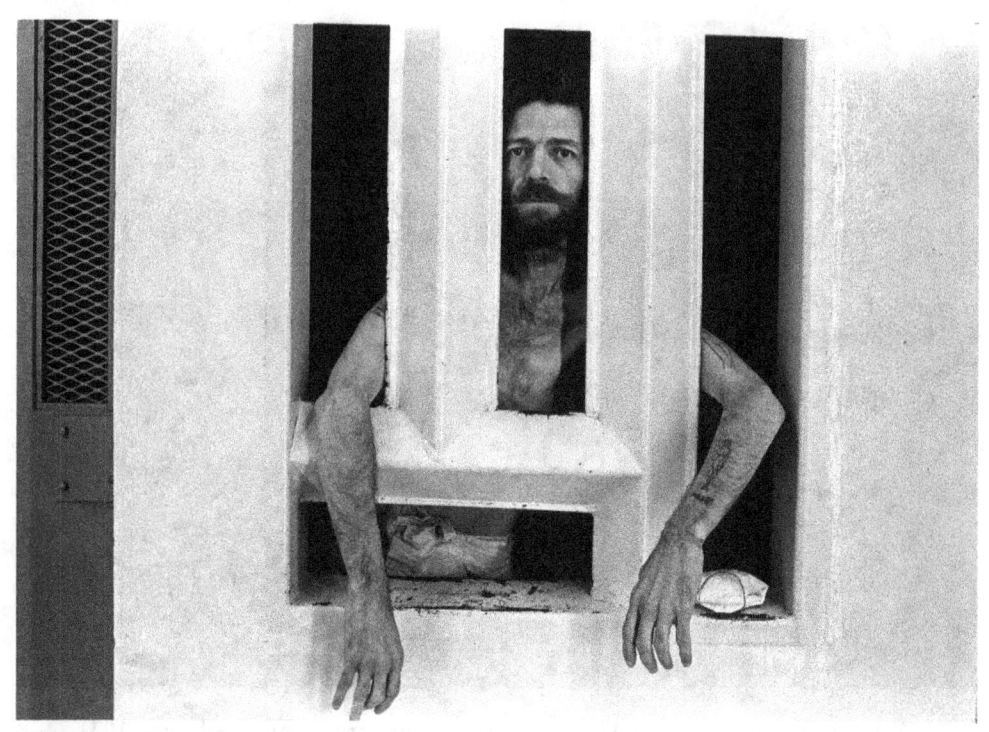

64. Prisoner. Isolation Unit, Cummins prison farm, Varner, Arkansas, 1975.

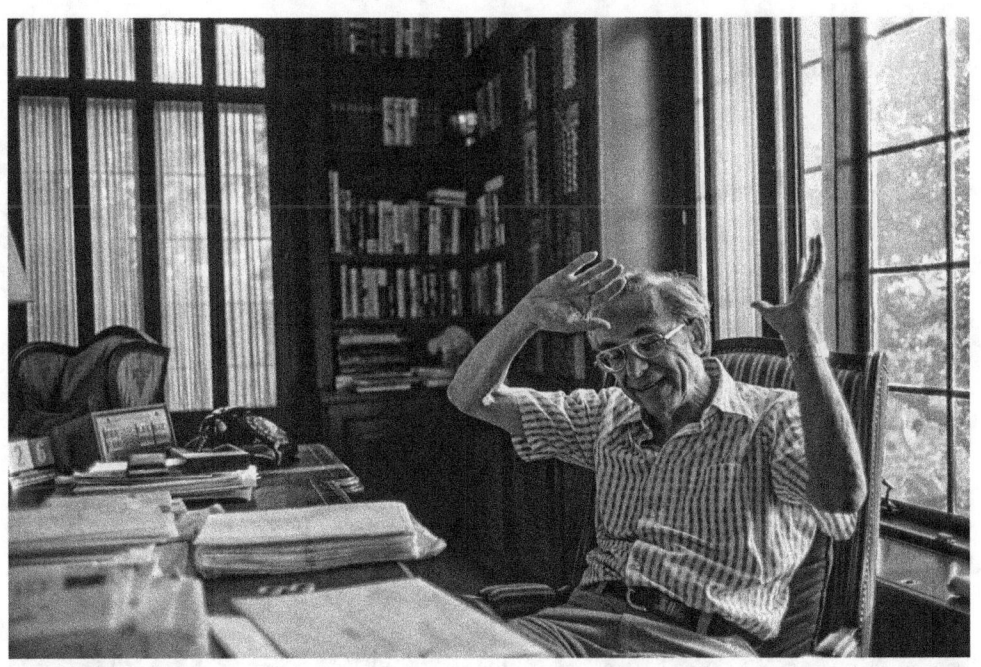

65. David Dortort (TV producer). Brentwood, California, 1977.

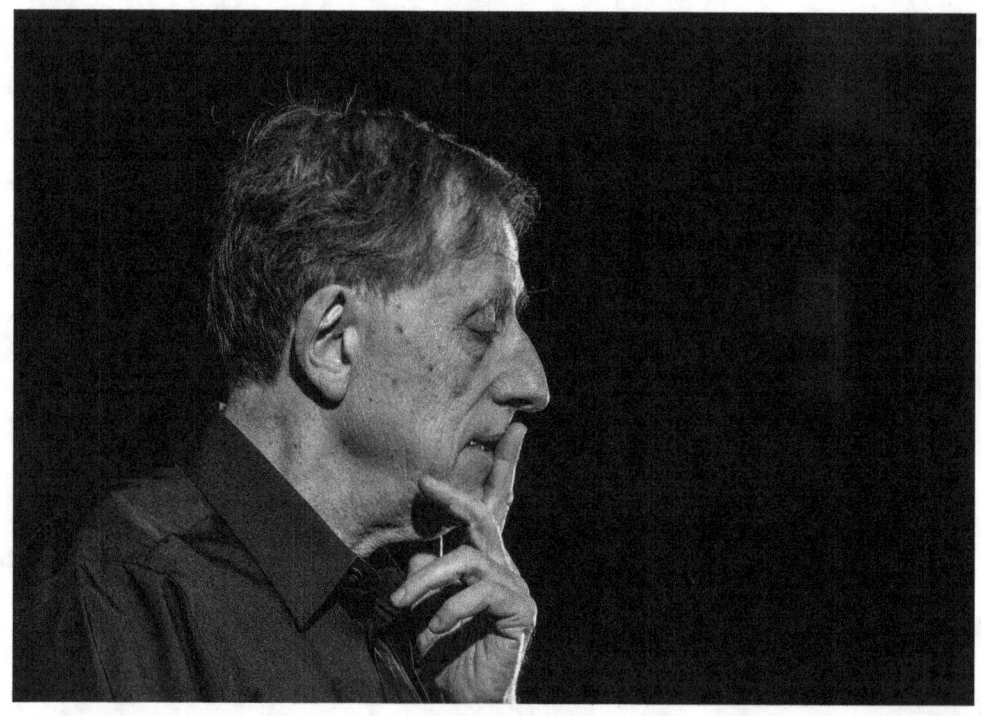

66. Ariel Dorfman (writer) in the first season of Just Buffalo's BABEL series. Buffalo, New York, 2007.

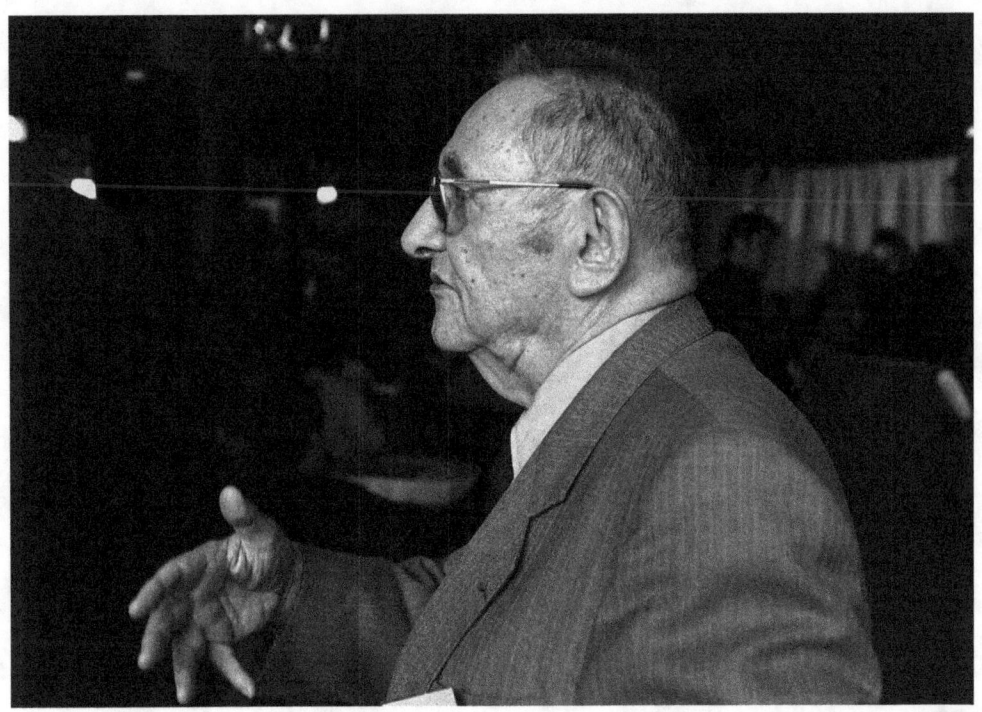

67. Charles Désirat (writer and resistance leader in Sachsenhausen concentration camp). Saint-Malo, France, 1996.

Words 4

53. Demonstrators in the street outside Bill and Margaret Kunstler's house. New York, New York, 1992.

I was going out for bagels and the *Times*. They screamed at me, "Self-hating Jew, self-hating Jew."

I said, "You don't even know if I'm Jewish."

They paid me no mind. They screamed it at me until I turned the corner at Christopher Street. Perhaps they continued after I was out of earshot. The cop at the foot of Bill and Margaret's stoop looked embarrassed to be there, both when I went out and when I came back with the bagels and the *Times*, whereupon they started yelling at me again. They were there because they objected to one of Bill's cases.

I looked at the hatred in their faces and thought of the Nazi *Jugend*. The language was different, but not the hatred. Were it not for the cop, and the other cops elsewhere on that street. I had no doubt that they would have thrown things to shatter his windows. Later, some did.

54. Prisoner with harmonica. Cummins prison farm, Varner, Arkansas, 1974.

Every time I saw him—winter, spring, summer, fall—he had all those garment layers: field jacket, zippered sweatshirt, shirt, undershirt, and hat. Always, there were the pockets full of pens and note cards.

This time, I asked, "Why the small log-log duplex slide-rule?"

He lowered the harmonica and said, "Without it, I couldn't design helicopters."

55. Herbert X. Blyden (Attica Brother and civil rights activist). Buffalo, New York, 1997.

I met Herbert in the Bronx House of Detention for Men in December 1971. He'd been one of the most eloquent spokesmen of the prisoners in the Attica Uprising four months earlier. He was in BHD because of his earlier involvement in a New York City Tombs jail event. I was interviewing him for an article for *The Nation*.

We didn't meet again for twenty years. We became good friends during the Attica prisoners' civil rights class-action trial in Buffalo in 1991.

The lead attorney for that trial was Elizabeth Fink. Herbert had his own attorney, which drove Liz quite crazy. Herbert got to sit at the lawyers' and clients' table, inside the bar, and he didn't have to kowtow to her. The only other Attica leaders who got to sit at that table were lead plaintiff, Akil al-Jundi, and legendary jailhouse lawyer, Jerry Rosenberg (referred to as "Jerry the Jew" by everyone who knew him in Attica), who had a law degree he'd earned in prison and who was defending himself. Liz didn't like Jerry, either.

One time while we were waiting for the judge to come in, Herbert said to Akil, "Bruce and me been knowing one another a long time. I knew him when he was young." He was referring to when we'd met in the Bronx jail in 1971.

I said, "Herbert, we're the same age."

"Yeah," he said, "there is that."

Another time, he, Akil and I were in the elevator after a trial day. The courtroom was on the fifth floor of the Buffalo federal courthouse. They got to talking about another Attica prisoner. The elevator stopped and three white lawyers got on. It was a slow elevator. Herb and Akil talked a bit more about the Attica prisoner, then Herb said, "You can take the nigger out of the jungle, but you can't take the jungle out of the nigger."

Akil bobbed his head and said, "Thass right. Thass right." I'd never previously heard him pronounce "that's" like that.

The three white lawyers pressed themselves against the back of the elevator until the next time the door opened, whereupon they all fled. When the doors closed, Herbert and Akil began talking in their usual voices.

He fell to metastasized prostate cancer. If he'd had decent medical care, maybe they'd have caught it earlier. He didn't. Diane and I had a birthday party for him not long before he died. His once-powerful body was by then bone-thin. When I visited him in hospice later, he was bloated with edema. He told me he'd stopped taking pain killers: they made him sleepy and stupid; he'd rather be lucid and in pain than sleepy and stupid. Every time I left, he'd remind me to bring more mangoes and papayas when I next visited.

In the coffin is his Kunstler Medal for Criminal Justice, which he treasured.

56. Warren Oates (actor). Sun Valley, Idaho, 1976.

I'd given a keynote talk on gunfighter Westerns at the Sun Valley Institute of Arts and Letters conference celebrating seventy-five years of Westerns. Peter Fonda chaired the session; the discussants were Clint Eastwood, Henry King, Delmer Daves, and others. It was infinitely more fun than any academic conference I'd ever attended.

After it, Warren said, "I wish I could write like you, man."

I said, "I wish I could act like you."

Warren said, "So, there we are."

He's wearing the shirt he wore in Monte Hellman's *The Hired Hand* (1971), which we'd screened the previous night.

57. Judy Sullivan (sex therapist). Buffalo, New York, 1970.

Judy was the second wife of a classicist, John Sullivan. John had three wives, all named Judy. "It's so much easier that way," he said when I commented on it.

I'd met John in Austin at Billy Lee Brammer's place in 1966. I'd heard about him from Billy Lee's wife, Dorothy, and two other women in the group, for maybe two years. All described him as incredibly sexy. One time at Billy Lee's, I got into a conversation with a short guy with a Liverpool accent. Dorothy came over and said, "You two finally met! Wonderful." *This* was the "incredibly sexy" guy?

John was then between Judy One and Judy Two. In 1972, he came to Buffalo as dean of Arts and Letters. Judy Two was with him. Judy had become part of Billy Lee's circle after my time there. We told Brammer stories, and sometimes people with connections to Brammer's scene would be in town, so we'd tell them again. Then, she and John broke up. Not long after, John married Judy Three.

For a while, Diane and I lived in a house diagonally across the street from them. Sometimes we'd see John getting into his Mercedes sedan, going to work at the university, a thermos mug filled with a martini in hand. At the university, the word was, if you have any work needing to get done in the dean's office, get it done early in the day. John took a job at University of California, Santa Barbara in 1978. He died of throat cancer in 1993. We talked on the phone a week or so before he died. I had difficulty understanding something he said and asked him to repeat it. "I seem to have this little problem," he said.

Judy Two stayed in Buffalo for several years. She told us she had become a "sex therapist." We asked what the work entailed but she never got more specific than, "I help men with their sex problems. I seem to be good at it."

She moved to Dallas, where, she would tell us in her occasional phone calls, she had more clients than she could handle. For a time, she was occupied with her mother's estate in Texarkana. She would call and tell us about the latest family squabble.

Then she called and said, "I'm in this place."

"What place?"

"I'm not sure."

"Where is it? Dallas? Texarkana."

"Dallas. I think it's in Dallas."

"Why are you there?"

"They say I don't remember things."

"What things?"

"I can't remember."

A few months later, I got a letter from a relative of Judy's in Texarkana. Judy had died in a Dallas nursing home. In her possessions there, they found only one photograph of her. They wondered if I knew who the photographer was. They wanted to give credit in the family's memorial brochure. The letter included a Xerox of this photo.

58. Allen Ginsberg (poet). Boulder, Colorado, 1984.

Every time I saw Allen, he picked up our conversation where we'd left it last time, no matter how much time had intervened. At a 1990 poetry reading, he said, "I saw your friend."

"Which friend?" I said.

"The one we were talking about."

We hadn't seen one another since the day I'd taken this picture, six years earlier.

Allen and Diane had a running conversation about Blake that went on for twenty years. He would just pick it up where it had stopped last time, as if it they'd paused so someone could refill a glass or go to the john.

We'd met at the drug conference at the University of Buffalo in spring 1968. Abbie Hoffman was there, and so were Jerry Rubin and Hugh Romney (aka Wavy Gravy) and the Merry Pranksters; there were researchers and political people; there were musicians and writers.

Even Tim Leary was there: he sat onstage in a full lotus and free-associated while his young wife Rosemary tried to keep their infant son from being too disruptive. Leary kept losing his train of thought and Rosemary whispered in his ear or people in the audience yelled out cues to get him going again. One time he paused and didn't even seem to be missing the train: he just grinned loopily out at the world. After a while someone yelled, "So what's the name of Rosemary's baby?" Leary furrowed his brow, not remembering that either, grinned as if he'd figured something out, then took off on an entirely new tack.

There was a party that night at Leslie Fiedler's house. Mike Aldrich, the organizer of the conference, asked me to drive Allen to Leslie's house, along with Peter Orlovsky and San Francisco psychiatrist Tod Mikurea. When we were in the car, Allen said he had to stop at the motel to make a phone call.

"Make it from Fiedler's why don't you?" Orlovsky said.

Allen said the call was to a *Playboy* editor about his upcoming *Playboy* Interview; he had to look at the page proofs, which were in the room, so he could dictate the final corrections. (Like all the artists I know, Allen was perfectly disciplined when it mattered.) When we got to the motel, he said it might take a few minutes, so we had all better come on up.

We all took off our coats. Allen found the big *Playboy* envelope, he looked over the pages and he made his call. We all put on our coats, we got to the door, Orlovsky opened the door, and that was when Allen said to the psychiatrist, "What's your name again?"

"Tod Mikuriya."

"Tod Mikuriya. That's an odd name," Allen said. "Where does it come from?"

"My mother was German; my father was Japanese."

"*Mik-ur-ee-ya.*" Allen's intonation requested translation.

"It means 'of the royal kitchen' or something close to that. I guess some ancestors on my father's side were officials on the emperor's staff or maybe they washed pots in his kitchen."

"And *Tod* is 'death' in German," Allen said.

"Yes. It's 'death' in German.

"So, your parents named you 'death in the royal kitchen.' What a burden that must have been to grow up with."

It was a long moment before Mikuriya responded. Then he started to talk. He talked faster and faster: words spilled out, poured out, came out so fast they seemed to be pushed out by the words in queue behind them.

Many of us have bits about our names. Descendants of East European Jews like me have explanations about how we got the anything-but-East-European names we now bear. I once heard the very WASP John Updike say, immediately after being introduced to Ipswitch neighbors he hadn't met before, "I suppose you're wondering about my name. It has a very long history . . ."

But that's not what Tod Mikuriya was doing that night in the University Manor Motel in Buffalo, New York. He was doing something he'd never had the occasion to do before. I don't know if he'd even done it with himself in the privacy of his own brain.

Allen sat on one of the beds and he motioned Mikuriya to sit on the other. They faced one another, their feet maybe two feet apart. Orlovsky, my wife, and I stood near the door, still unsure of what was going on. Then it became clear that Allen was not going to interrupt Mikuriya; it was equally clear that Mikuriya was going to keep talking until he was done. The three of us took off our coats and found places to sit.

Allen listened to Mikuriya with eloquent intensity. It was real, it was sincere, it was total, and it was, I'm certain, something Mikuriya had never experienced before in his life. I surely hadn't.

I have no idea how long Tod talked. He talked until he came to terms with being named Death in the Royal Kitchen, he talked until he was shriven, until he said what he'd needed to say for so long and had never, until that moment found a place where and a person to whom it was safe to say it. During all that astonishing monologue, Allen never gave one sign of disinterest, impatience, party lust. It was like one of those movies or a play where two people are talking and the lights on everyone else in the room fade to just this side of darkness. They're there, those other people, but they're not moving, they're not making a sound, and they're irrelevant.

When Tod was done Allen got up and said, "Let's go to Leslie's house," which we did. When we got there, someone said, "We were all wondering what happened to you," and Allen said, "We got to talking," and no more was said of it.

59. Allen Ginsberg and Leslie Fiedler (literary critic). Buffalo, New York, 1994.

Diane and I organized a celebration for Leslie at University of Buffalo's Center for the Arts, "Fiedlerfest." Most such events happen after the guest of honor is dead. We thought it would be good to do it while the guest was still around and could have a voice in the program.

Leslie wanted his old friend Allen Ginsberg; he wanted Camille Paglia, whose writing he admired but whom he'd never met; and he wanted Buffalo poet Ishmael Reed.

During a break, I kept trying to get a photo of Allen and Leslie together, but every time I raised the camera to my eye, a local writer named Alan DeLoach would rush from wherever he was in the large atrium and plant himself between them and throw his arms over the shoulders of both. His ability to know those moments I was going to shoot and to interpose himself was preternatural. I gave up on the shot. Then, just before we went back into the theater to resume, Allen put his hands on

Leslie's head and kissed him. I took the photo without even raising the camera. There wouldn't have been time. There wasn't even time for DeLoach to see it happening.

60. Leslie Fiedler and Raymond Federman (writer). Buffalo, New York, 1974.

A brunch at the small house Diane and I had our first few years together. Leslie and Ray, in those years, were both writing about their pasts, in a way, creating their presents. I guess I'm doing the same thing right now.

61. Ed Dorn and Robert Creeley (poets). Boulder, Colorado, 1984.

Diane and I were working on a film about Bob (*Creeley*, 1988). This day began with us just hanging out—Bob, Ed Dorn, Ed's wife Jennifer, Diane, and me—having margaritas. Then we went to Ed's house, where we started filming.

Ed and Bob continued the conversation and consumed most of a fifth of bourbon. They talked for maybe two hours. That part of the film takes maybe four minutes. Their talk gets a little loopy at the end of that sequence. If you watch the liquid level in the bourbon bottle, you'll understand why. The liquid level in the bottle marks the real time.

Then we went to Naropa, where Bob was to give a big talk. Allen Ginsberg introduced him. I began filming, thinking, "There's no way Bob can do this." He began with a riff that made no sense whatever. The audience, all tuned to the poets, were fine giving him time to get somewhere. I was sure it wasn't going anywhere but down. Allen sat on a sofa, smiling with delight.

Somehow, Bob *did* pull it all together. I don't know if he was heading there all along or if he sobered up, but he pulled those early apparently random riffs together and folded them perfectly into his final burst of words. The Naropa audience applauded in delight, and Allen nodded in approval.

Later, at a party, Ed refused to sign a release that would let us use the film we'd shot at his house earlier that day. It was a matter of principle, he said. "I will never sue you. I don't like involving the state in my life. Contracts are the state."

"Well, fuck you," I said. "We shot a lot of film today that no one will broadcast because of your bullshit principles. You could have told me this when we were having those margaritas and I wouldn't have wasted my time and that money." We growled at one another and went to other parts of the room.

A while later, Ed came over and said, "Give me the form. Where do I sign?"

That scene, with the diminishing bourbon, is the funniest part of the movie.

62. Lawrence Ferlinghetti (poet, publisher, and bookseller) and Robert Creeley. Buffalo, New York, 1982.

Bob had an endowed chair at Buffalo. For years he used part of the annual stipend to bring writers to town. He called the series "Walking the Dog." His wife, Penelope, fed just about all of them.

Many of the visitors, like Ferlinghetti, were Bob's longtime friends. (That's Diane's hand in the lower left of this photo. She still wears that bracelet every day. We got it for a song in London in 1974.)

Sometimes, to give Pen a break, we hosted Bob's visitors. Richard Brautigan was one we did at our house, which delighted me because I'd really liked his *A Confederate General from Big Sur* (1964), *Trout Fishing in America* (1967), and *In Watermelon Sugar* (1968). Diane was delighted because the title poem of his *The Pill Versus the Springhill Mine Disaster* (1969) had annoyed her so much she'd written a counterpoem, and she was thinking of springing it on him.

Brautigan's poem went:

> When you take your pill
> it's like a mine disaster.
> I think of all the people
> lost inside of you.

To which Diane replied, in her book *Wide-Ons* (1981), not long before Brautigan's visit:

In response to "The Pill Versus the Springhill Mine Disaster"
For Richard Brautigan and Pope Paul

> if my pill saddens you
> with thoughts of people perishing inside me
> imagine my anguish
> at the billions of people
> you Portnoys
> have jerked off

I don't know if Diane would actually have said the poem to him. She's extremely polite. None of it mattered anyway: Brautigan arrived very drunk and quickly got drunker, so there was no coherent talk of anything, let alone any recitations of poems.

63. Gate turnkeys. Women's Unit, Cummins prison farm, Varner, Arkansas, 1971.

The women's unit was a former chicken coop inside a one-acre fenced-in area in the 17,000-acre prison farm. Before Judge Henley's decision in *Holt v. Sarver*, the warden lived in a large house adjacent to the fence. Some nights, I was told, a buzzer would sound in the office of the Women's Unit. If it sounded once, they were to send a white woman prisoner through the gate closest to the warden's house; if it sounded twice, they were to send a Black woman prisoner. The gate was still there when I began visiting in 1971, but it was never again opened.

During the years I visited (1971–1975), visitors to the prison would often take lunch at the women's Unit: there were tablecloths, and the food was said to be better than in the guard's dining room in the main building. Visitors were Arkansas legislators, sheriffs delivering prisoners from county jails, journalists, and such.

Diane was with me on five of my last six trips to Cummins. She would have lunch every day with Helen Carruthers, superintendent of the women's Unit. One night, back in our room, she told me that there was a problem: a field lieutenant had taken to sitting at their table and was constantly interrupting their conversation. Helen didn't want to make a fuss about it, because she already had enough problems with the men running the prison; Diane didn't know if it was her place to tell this field lieutenant to move on. I told her I'd take care of it.

The next day, in the cotton field, I said to him, "My wife said if you interrupt her and Helen one more time she's going to kick the shit out of you."

He said, "What?" I repeated what I'd said. He laughed.

"She looks nice and she's polite," I said, "but she's got a black belt in karate, and I wouldn't fuck with her when she was mad."

"I don't believe you," he said.

"I don't care if you believe me or not," I said. "You've been good to me, so I thought I'd pull your coat about this. You can do what you want."

"I don't believe you," he said again, with less conviction. I shrugged and went back to photographing. He never sat at their table again.

Forty years later, he wrote me. A niece had seen a photo I'd taken of him in an exhibit in Little Rock. He asked for a print. I sent it to him. He wrote again, saying he was now retired. He and some buddies occasionally hunted wild boar bare-handed: dogs and knives. Maybe I'd like to come down and join them on a hunt, hang out, take some pictures. Unlike the time Jean Malaurie called and asked me to meet him in Nome, I passed on that one.

64. Prisoner. Isolation Unit, Cummins prison farm, Varner, Arkansas, 1975.

Prisoners got into isolation for one of two reasons: punishment or protection. They'd broken a prison rule or someone wanted to harm or kill them. Either way, it was the worst place to be: solitary confinement, with no contact with anyone other than the guard or trusty who brings and takes away the food tray and checks every now and then to be sure a suicide hasn't taken place or is in progress.

65. David Dortort (TV producer). Brentwood, California, 1977.

David was executive producer of the TV series *Bonanza* (1959–1973). The series ended soon after one of the stars, Dan Blocker, forty-three, died of a pulmonary embolism following gall bladder surgery.

David lived in a very strange house in Bel Aire. It was bracketed by the homes of actor Charles Bronson and director William Friedkin on a cul-de-sac off Sunset Boulevard, just north of UCLA. The house had originally been designed for actor Basil Rathbone (famous for his many radio and screen portrayals of Sherlock Holmes). One side was French Provincial; the other was English Tudor. If you entered the house and walked straight through to the pool and turned to look at the building you'd just exited, what you saw had nothing to do with the building you'd seen on the way in. Halfway through, everything changed: the woodwork, the windows, everything. I remarked on this. David shrugged. "It was done by a set designer. No way they're going to use two sides of a middle for the same thing."

After Blocker's death and the end of *Bonanza*, Dortort told me, he agreed to spend a semester teaching film at UCLA or USC. They'd been after him to do it for years, but he'd always ignored the requests because the TV series took so much time.

"But now I had the time," he said, "and I wanted to get away from the back-biting and pettiness of the TV industry. But you know what? In the university, it was the same backbiting and pettiness. There was only one difference."

"What was it?"

"The stakes are so fucking puny."

66. Ariel Dorfman (writer) in the first season of Just Buffalo's BABEL series. Buffalo, New York, 2007.

He was a cultural advisor to Chilean President Salvador Allende; he barely escaped death the day of Pinochet's coup in 1973. A lifelong human rights activist, he is perhaps best known for his play about torture during the Pinochet regime, *Death and the Maiden* (1990), which was made into a film by Roman Polanski (1994). He and

Diane got into a long discussion about the Sumerian Descent of Inanna (1900–1600 BCE). In an email, he referred to it as "the first torture story."

67. Charles Désirat (writer and resistance leader in Sachsenhausen concentration camp). Saint-Malo, France, 1996.

Jean Malaurie invited three Terre Humaine authors to take part in a panel on the Terre Humaine series at the *Étonnants Voyageurs* book fair, which that year was in Saint-Malo, a small city on the Brittany coast, an hour's drive south of Mont Saint-Michel and the invasion beaches in Normandy.

He had also invited to Saint-Malo Patrick Declerk, a psychiatrist whose *Les Naufrages* (about the *clochards*, the street people of Paris) was soon to come out in Terre Humaine. My two books in the series were about criminal life in the US (*Leurs prisons*, a translation of *In the Life: Versions of the Criminal Experience*) and getting by on Death Row in Texas (*Le Quartier de la mort*, a translation of *Death Row*, written with Diane Christian).

The third Terre Humaine author at Saint-Malo was Charles Désirat, a lifelong political activist and coauthor of *Sachso*, a moving and horrifying book of personal recollections by French deportees to the Sachsenhausen concentration camp.

Charles had been a militant communist before the war, for which the French police imprisoned him in January 1941. He soon escaped. He was recaptured, and in 1943 was sent to Sachsenhausen. Incarceration in one of the Nazis' concentration camps was no reason to stop the work he'd been doing outside: he led the Resistance group within the camp until he and the few other survivors were liberated by a unit of the 47th Russian Army on April 22, 1945. He returned to France and was reunited with his wife, who had been imprisoned in Ravensbruck.

In August 1945, Charles organized the association of former French prisoners of Sachsenhausen—*L'Amicale des anciens déportés d'Oranienburg-Sachsenhausen et de ses kommandos*. In 1964 he helped create the more inclusive *Comité international du camp d'Oranienburg-Sachsenhausen*. He was that organization's president for thirty-five years. He was also director of *Secours populaire*, an important French relief organization.

Somewhere along the way the French government decided it was better to honor him than to lock him up: they made him an *officier* in the Legion of Honor and awarded him the Croix de Guerre (with palm), the Medal of the Resistance, and the Medal of the Deportation.

Sachso was published in Terre Humaine in 1982, under the collective authorship of "Amicale d'Oranienburg-Sachsenhausen." It sold 100,000 copies.

The morning of our second day in Saint-Malo, Malaurie, Charles, and I walked on the stone pavement above the beach. The two of them shared Resistance memories. Malaurie took us to lunch at a pleasant place and later we went to the Terre Humaine panel. Malaurie spoke for a long time, then he introduced Patrick, Charles, and me. Someone asked me a question. Before I could respond, Malaurie answered it—at great length. The same thing happened with the second question. As I recall, I got to say nothing. Neither did Charles nor Patrick.

Afterward, there was a screening of *Death Row*, the documentary film Diane and I had made in 1979, about men waiting to be executed in Texas. The version with a dubbed French soundtrack that had been broadcast on French TV never arrived, so they projected the original English language version I'd brought with me just in case. Patrick provided a running translation for the entire sixty-minute film. Much of the film is in demotic English, and a lot of it is mumbled in noisy prison rooms. There was an overflow crowd, so they screened the film a second time, and Patrick again translated the soundtrack on the fly. I don't think he'd seen it before. It was an astonishing performance.

After the first screening, while the first audience was leaving and the second coming in, Charles said to Jean, Patrick, and me, "Prisons are alike."

The next day, Malaurie was off courting journalists, so Charles and I had lunch together in a big room the conference organizers provided for authors who weren't being taken to local restaurants by their publishers or by publishers hoping to get them to jump ship. At one end of the room were two huge tables covered with massive trays of Channel oysters. There were other tables—ignored by almost everyone—covered with platters of teensy triangular sandwiches.

Charles and I talked about how we'd wasted a grand opportunity by having lunch with Jean Malaurie in that fancy restaurant the previous day. Writers can always have lunch with publishers in fancy restaurants, but how often can they have an unlimited supply of that morning's Channel oysters?

We filled plates with a dozen oysters each, then sat down at a table. A waiter immediately delivered a baguette and a chilled bottle of Chablis. We ate our oysters, drank the wine, and talked about prison. When we were done with the oysters, I said, "Une autre douzaine?" He nodded. I got us another dozen each. We continued talking our way through the second plate of Channel oysters.

After a while I said, "Plus?" Some more? He shook his head. He told me they were excellent but at his age he couldn't manage any more. (I now know that he would have been eighty-eight when we had that lunch, though he looked and acted nothing close to it.) I fetched another dozen.

When I sat down with the plate he said, "Quel homme!" I said it had nothing to do with being "quel homme [what a man!]." Rather, it was about the rarity of such oysters where I lived and the excellence of them now. He grinned as I finished the third dozen, then we finished the wine and walked around Saint-Malo talking about prison things until it was time to board the bus that would take us to the train station.

We stood in the bar car and talked all the way on that train ride back to Paris. He lived, he told me, in Cahors, a beautiful town on the Lot River. The town dated back to Roman times. I should come and visit, he said. We could talk, and it was a good place to read and walk and think and write. There was a room with a bed that was fine for me and fine for me and my wife if we didn't mind being close in a bed. I said we didn't mind. In that case, he said, you should bring her, too, and she could also read and walk and think and write. I said I would certainly do that. When we reached Paris, he went to another track where there was a train that would take him home and I got a cab to my hotel.

Over the next few years, we exchanged cards at holidays, and every time I wrote him, I promised to visit. Every time I went to France, I thought about finding a few days to run down to Cahors, but never quite managed to do it. One time, Diane and I were at a conference at Versailles, after which we had two or three free days and I thought we might do it then, but we went to Paris instead, to the usual places, doing the usual things.

In mid-February 2005, I was in Paris for several events around the fiftieth anniversary of Terre Humaine, which at that point comprised eighty-five books. To commemorate the event, Malaurie republished the American classic that defined and abolished postmodernism before the academics came up with the name: James Agee's and Walker Evans's *Let Us Now Praise Famous Men*. He had me write the postface for it.

There was a reception at Bibliothèque Nationale de France marking the opening the following day of a large exhibit about Terre Humaine. The exhibit would be up all spring. The next night President Jacques Chirac hosted a reception in Elysée Palace for Malaurie and about seventy-five Terre Humaine writers. There were also a lot of editors, filmmakers, and heads of French cultural organizations.

I hoped I'd see Charles Désirat at the two receptions. But he wasn't there. It hardly seemed possible that nearly a decade had passed since we'd talked prison and writing over those memorable Channel oysters and on the train back to Paris from the coast. I tried to cook up a good reason why I'd never visited him in Cahors in all that time, but I couldn't think of one. It didn't matter: he wasn't there.

The next day, Wednesday, February 14, Malaurie took me to lunch at Le Café Marly, at the end of the Richelieu wing of the Louvre, just off rue de Rivoli. He suggested I start with the oysters. We ordered, then he began talking about where Terre Humaine would go next. "What we've done thus far," Malaurie said, "is just breaking the ice. Terre Humaine is a great family of authors. We must decide what the family shall do now."

His cell phone went off. He looked at the caller ID on the phone's screen. Most of the time when we were together and he did that, he put the phone back in his pocket. This time, he took the call, and mostly listened.

When he was done, he said to me, "Charles Désirat has died."

He was quiet for a moment, then called someone at *Le Monde* and dictated the obituary they would run the following day. He told the reporter that for his entire life Charles Désirat bore witness for tolerance, peace, and reconciliation.

When he was done, he said to me, "He was one of my closest friends. You two would have liked one another and had good conversations. It's unfortunate you didn't know one another."

"We did," I said. "You introduced us in Saint-Malo in 1996. We ate oysters there and talked on the train all the way back to Paris. He invited me to visit him in Cahors but I never did. Every time I've been in France since then I meant to, but I never got around to it."

"Too bad for you," Malaurie said. "He was a great man. He never gave up. He cared. You should have gone to Cahors."

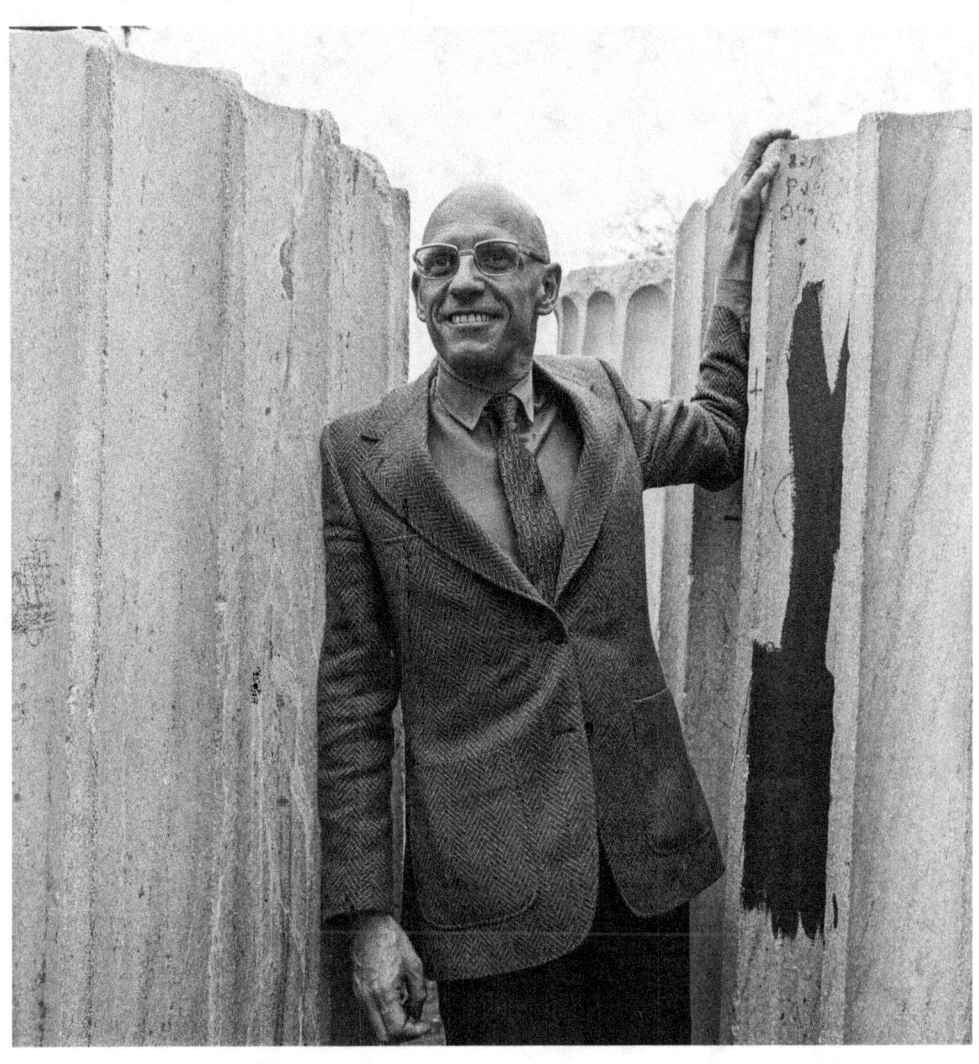

68. Michel Foucault (philosopher). Buffalo, New York, 1971.

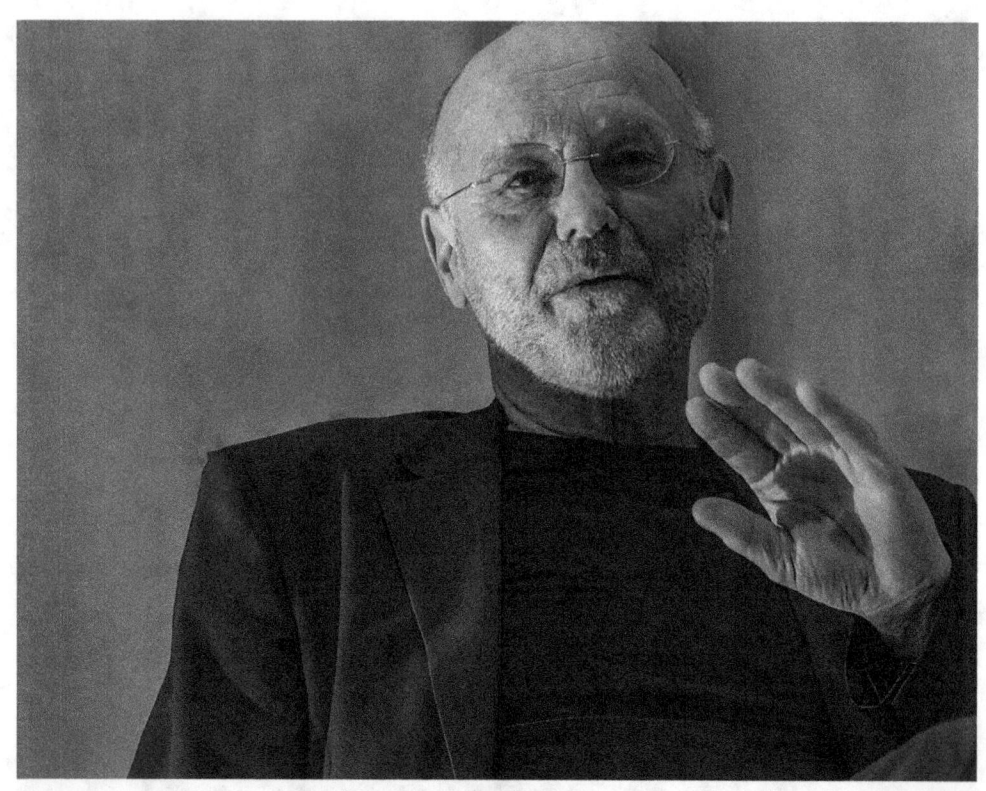

69. Anselm Kiefer (artist). Albright-Knox Art Gallery, in conversation with Janne Sirén about his work. Buffalo, New York, 2014.

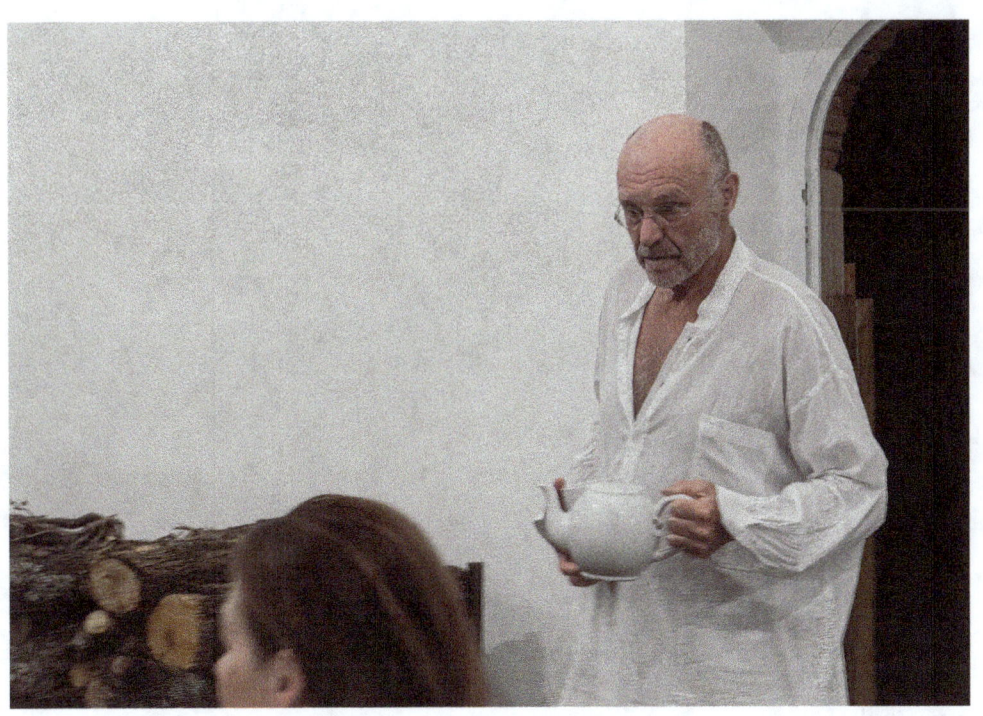

70. Anselm Kiefer. "La Ribaute." Barjac, France, 2018.

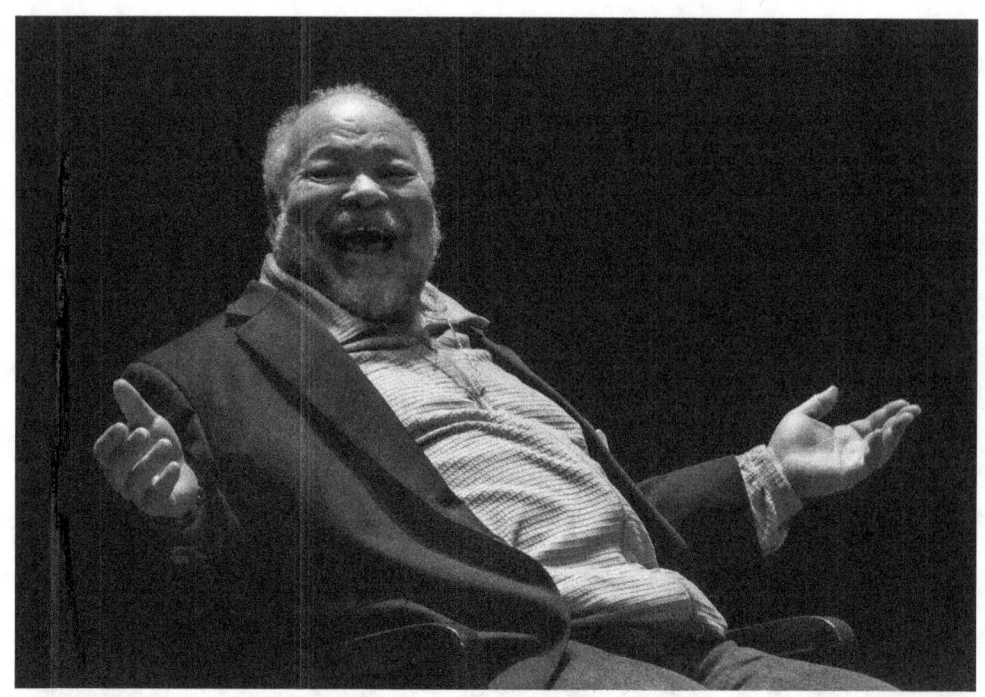

71. Stephen McKinley Henderson (actor). Buffalo, New York, 2015.

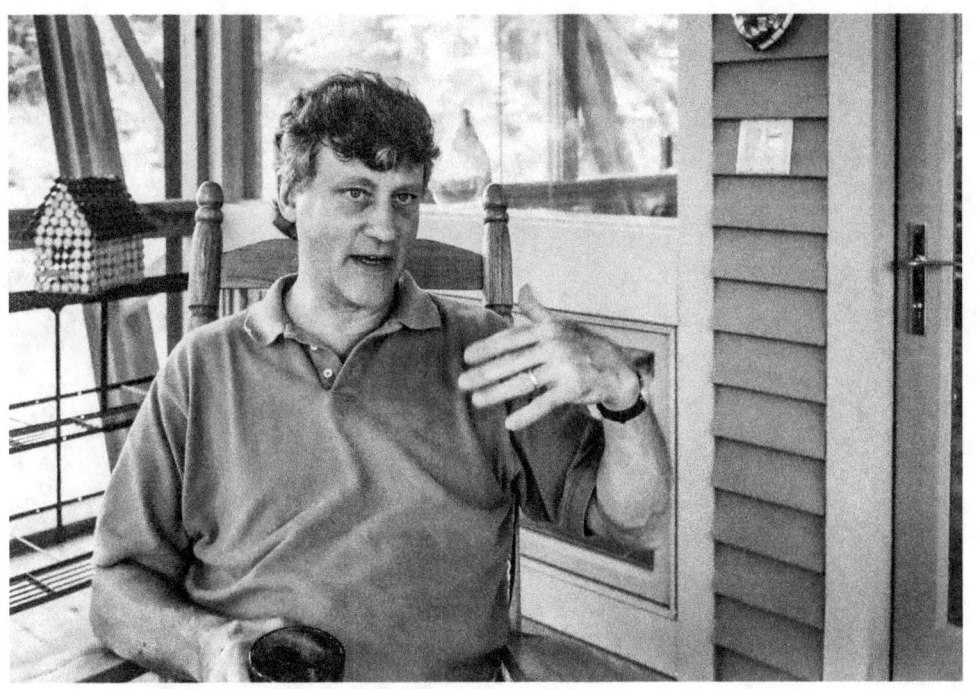

72. William Ferris (folklorist and writer). Oxford, Mississippi, 1997.

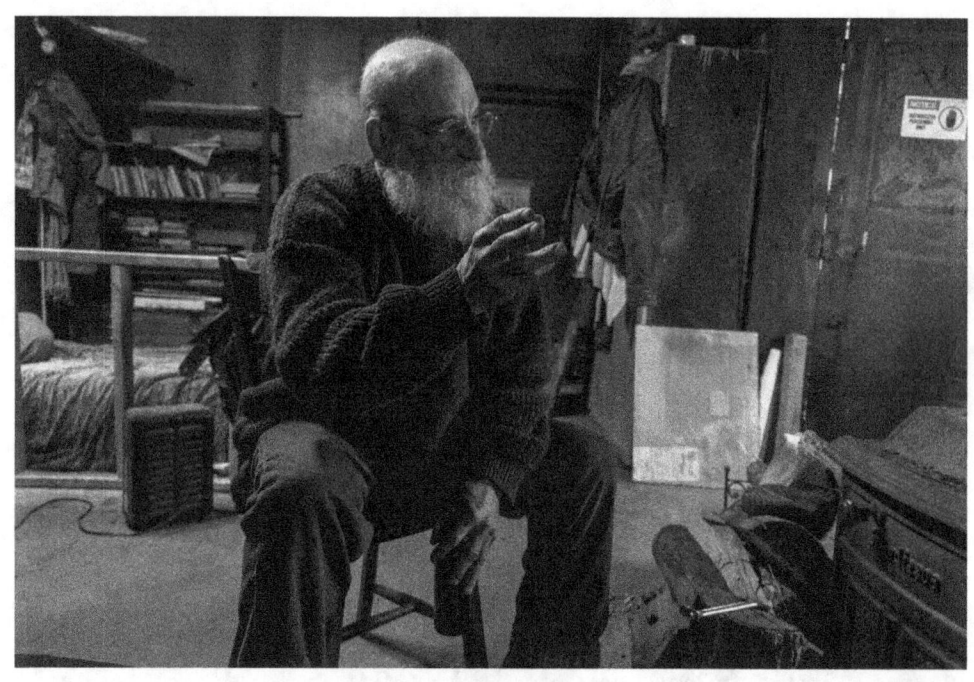

73. Jim Watson. Buffalo, New York, 2017.

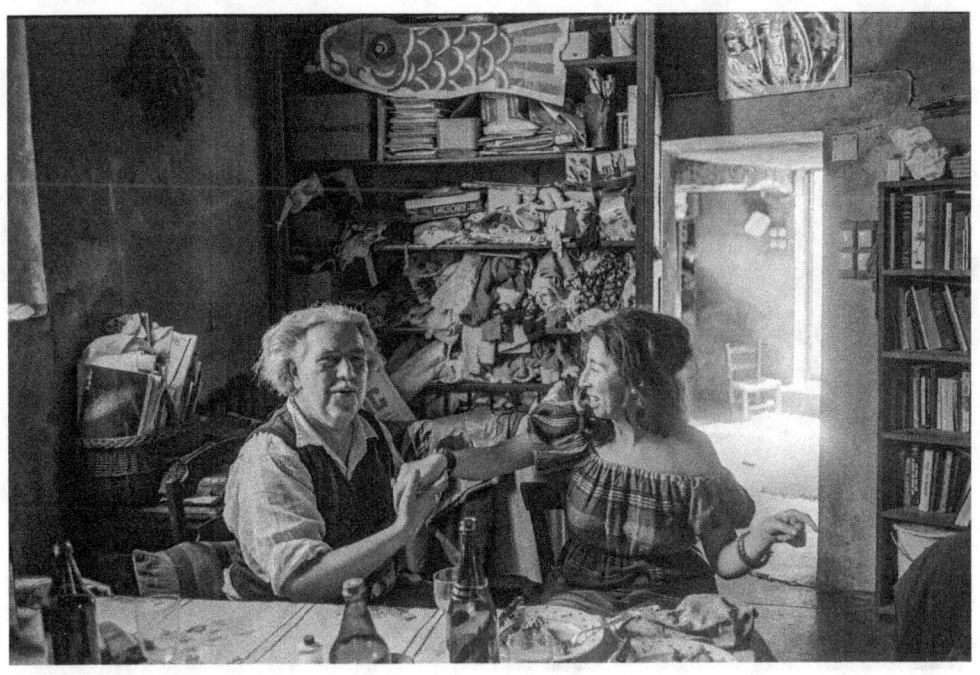

74. Gershon Legman (folklorist, pornographer, and writer) and Diane Christian. Valbonne, Alpes-Maritime, France, 1975.

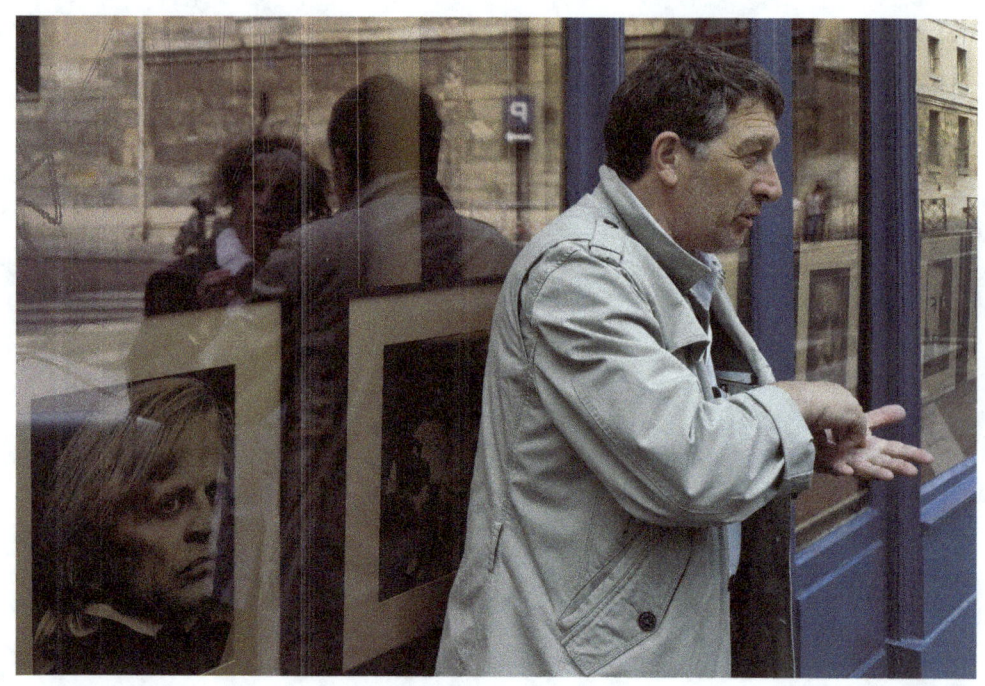

75. Diane Christian and Philippe Lemonnier (photographer). Paris, France, 2010.

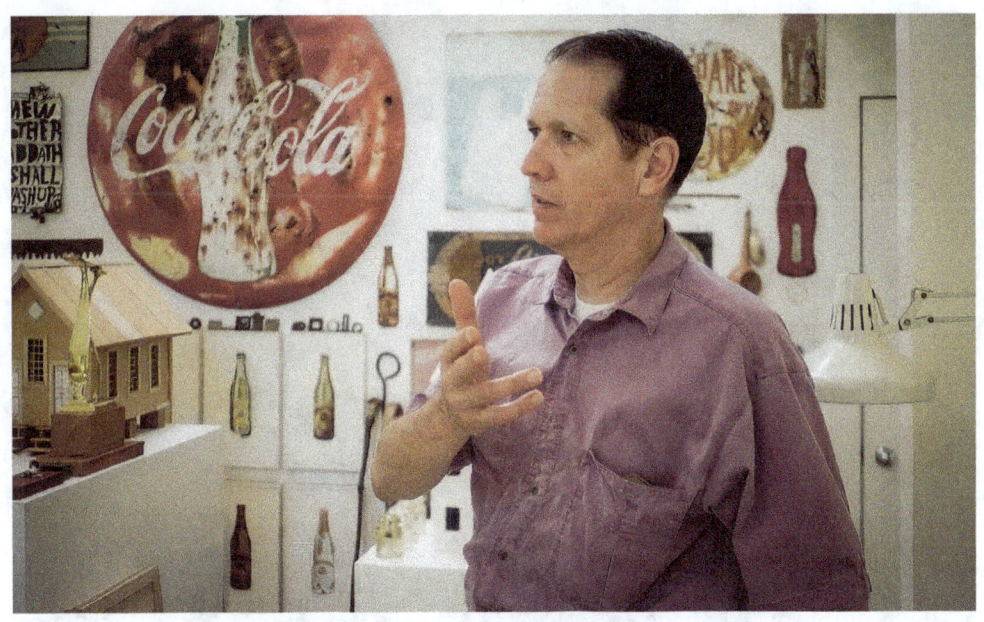

76. William Christenberry (artist). Washington, DC, 1998.

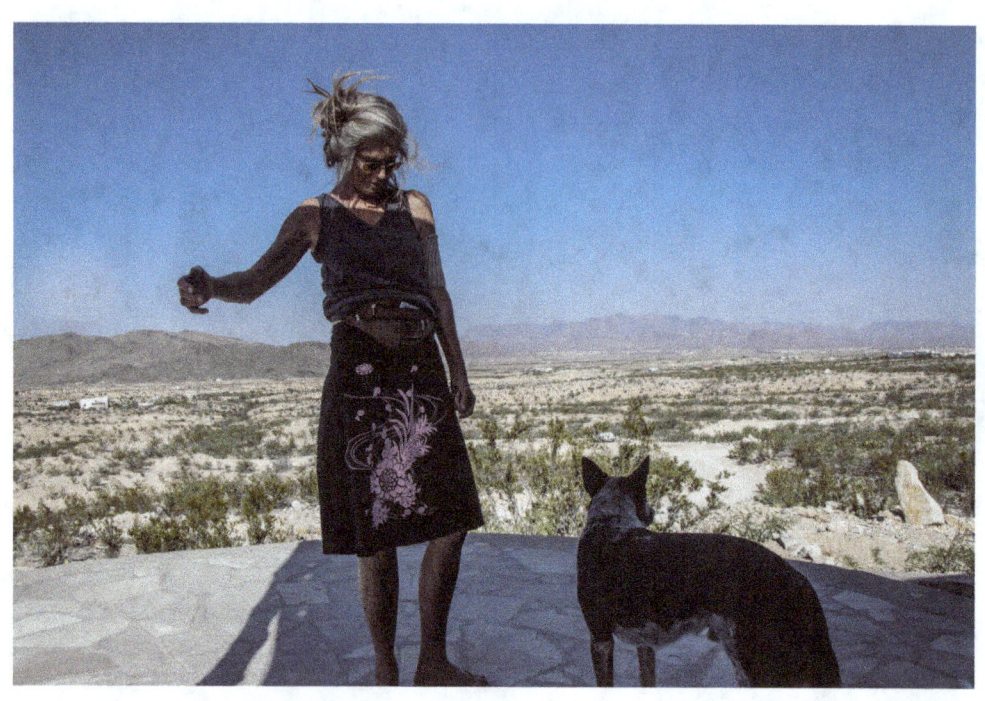

77. Cynta de Navarez (Rio Grande River guide). Terlingua Ghost Town, Texas, 2013.

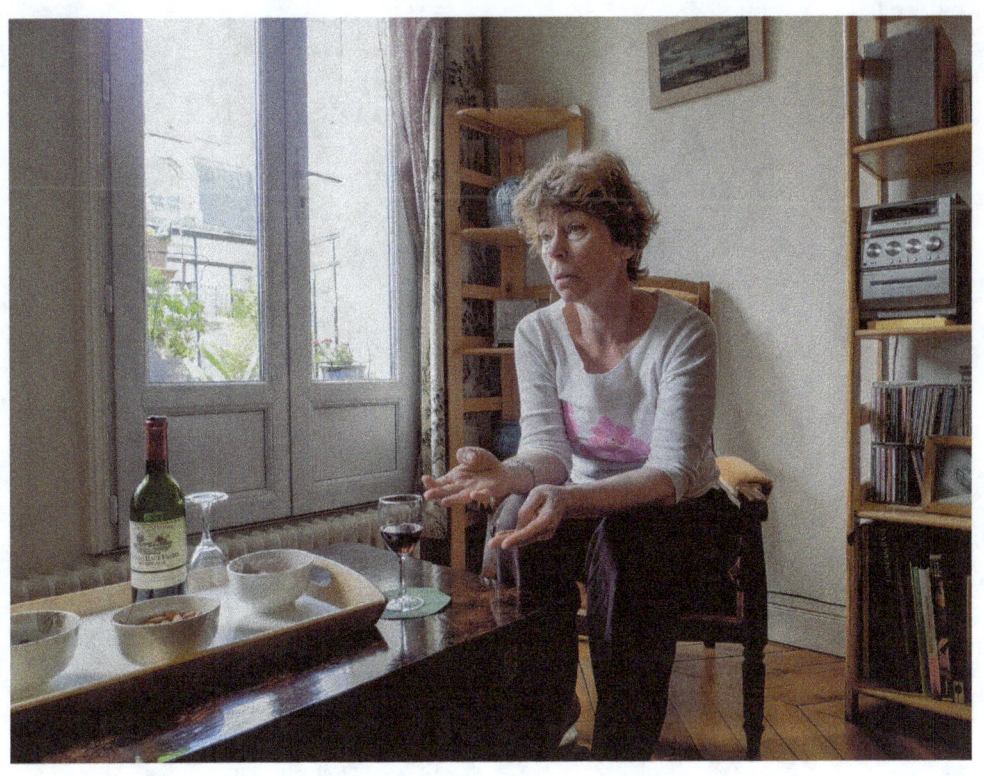

78. Hélène Korn (shiatsu practitioner and poet). Paris, France, 2010.

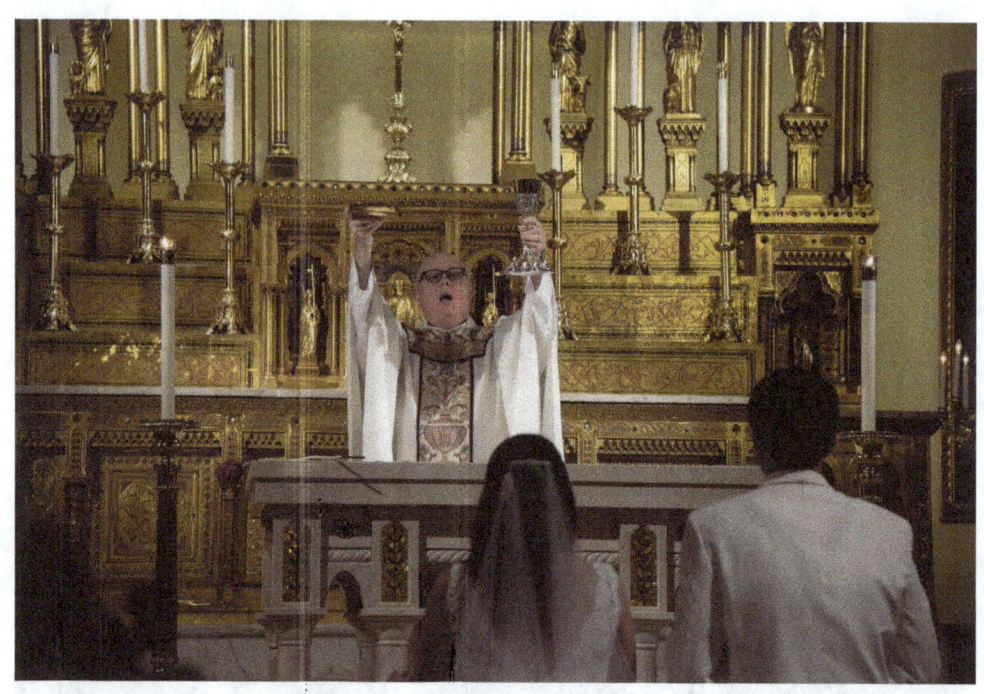

79. Wedding of Lauren Christian and David Oubré. Immaculate Conception Jesuit Church, New Orleans, 2014.

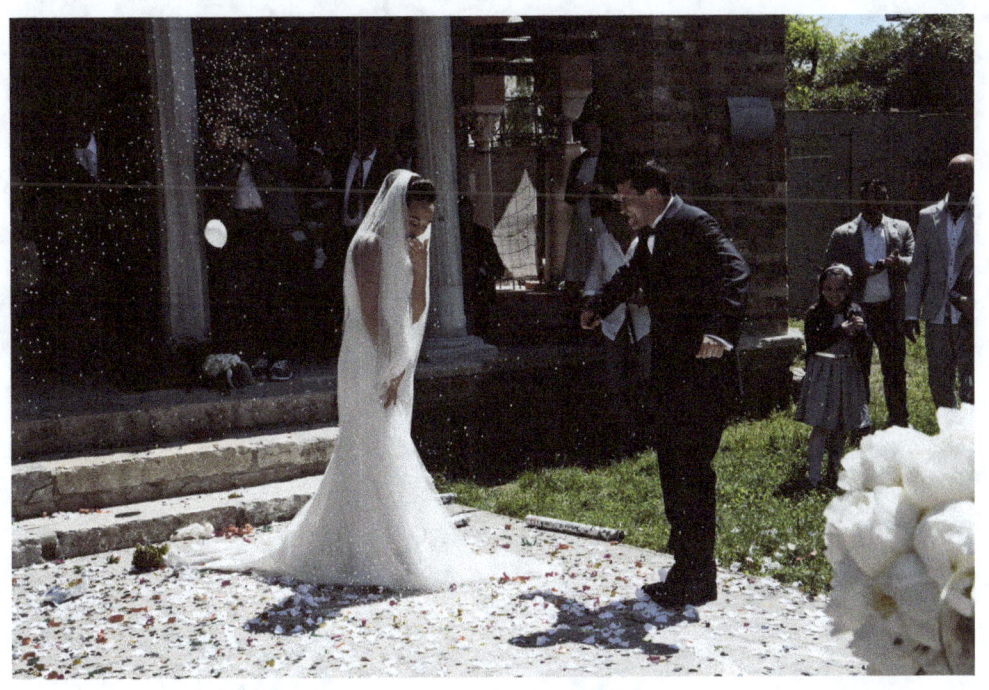

80. Wedding couple in front of the Church of Santa Fosca. Torcello, Italy, 2016.

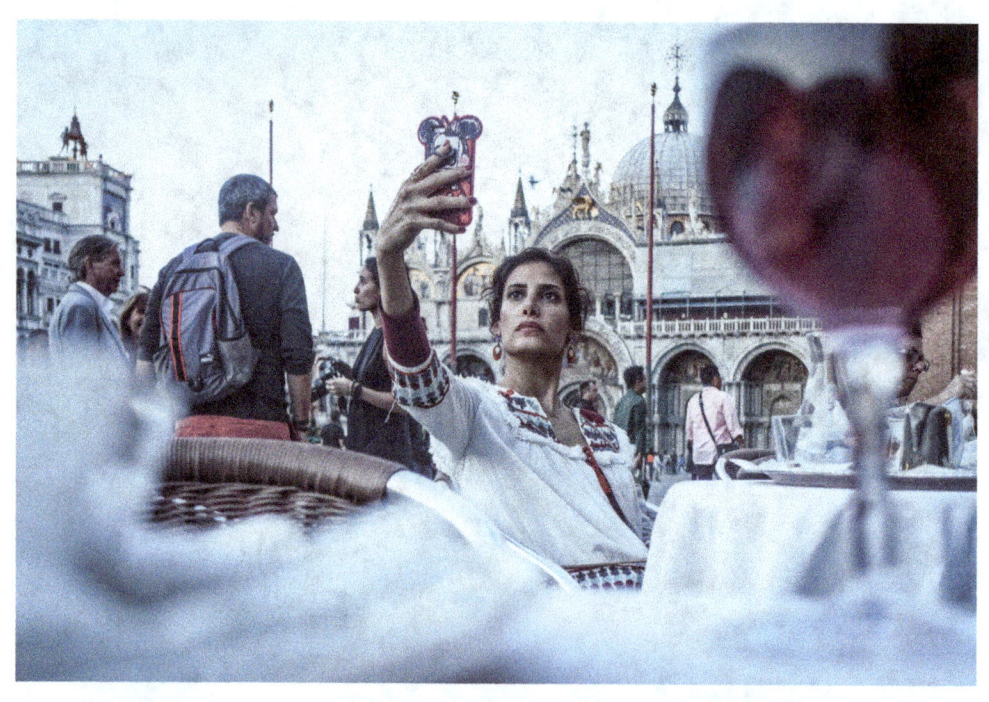

81. Woman taking selfie, Caffè Florian, Piazza San Marco. Venice, Italy, 2016.

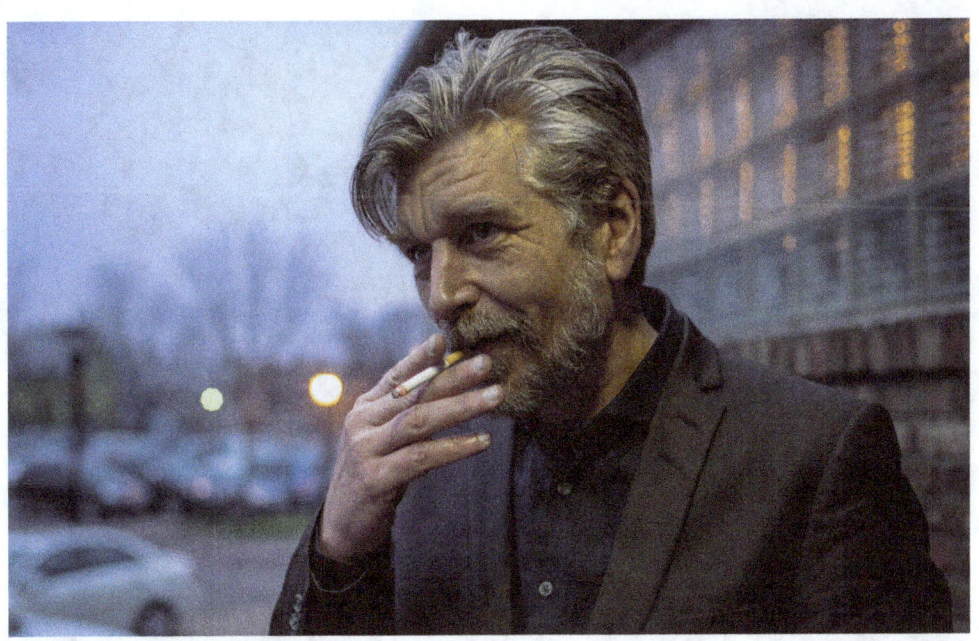

82. Karl Ove Knausgård (writer) on the back steps of Kleinhans Music Hall, before his appearance in Just Buffalo's BABEL series. Buffalo, New York, 2016.

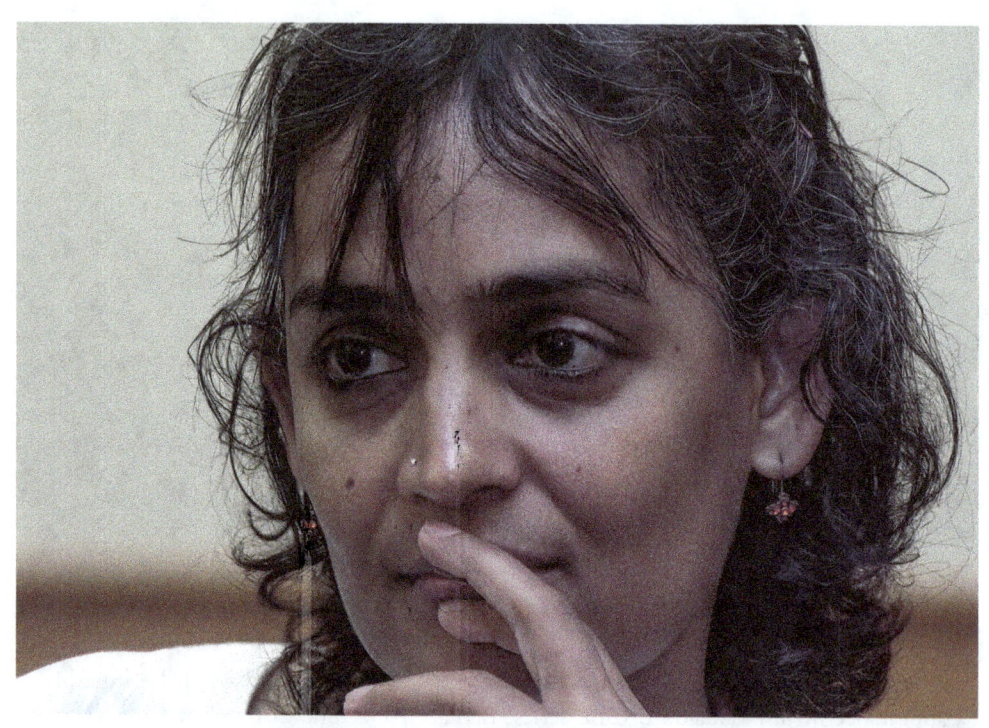

83. Arundhati Roy (writer). Buffalo, New York, 2004.

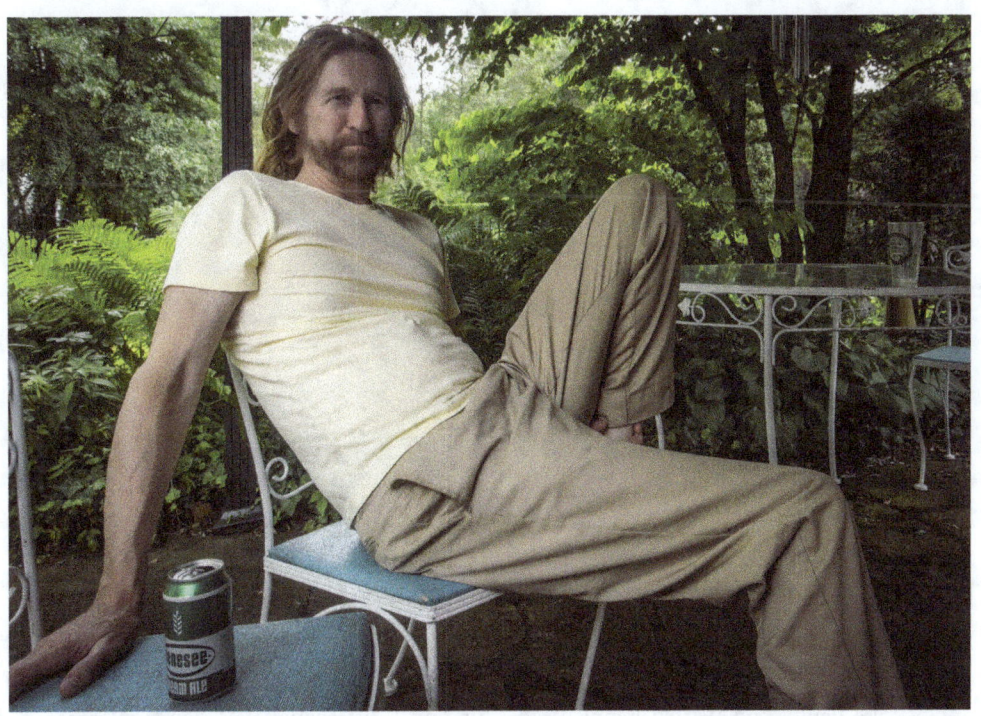

84. Tom Toles (political cartoonist). Hamburg, New York, 2015.

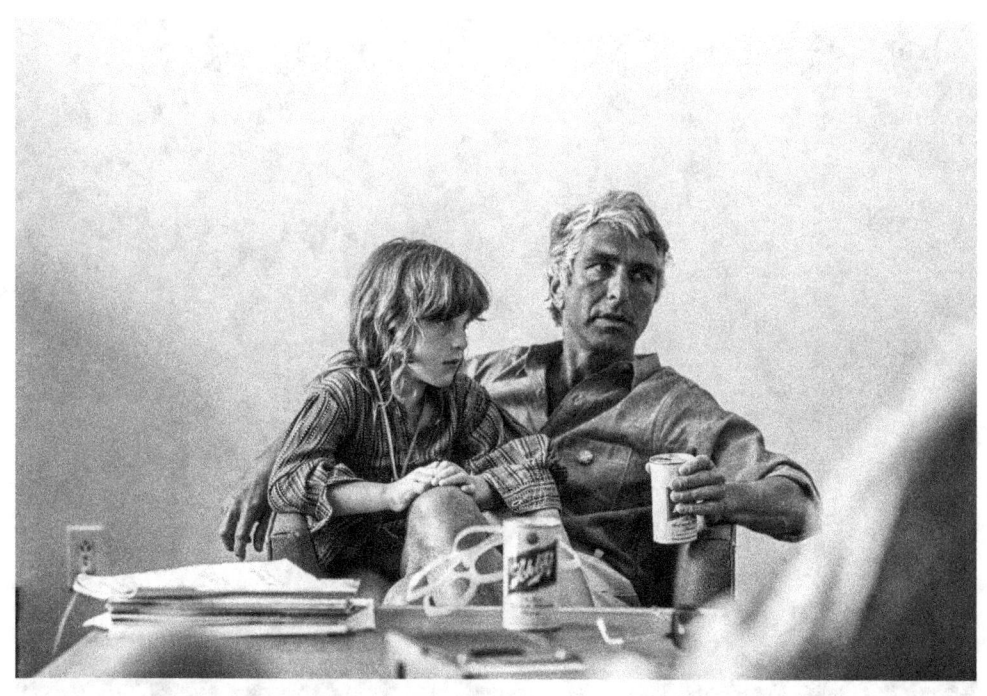

85. Kate Bennis and Warren Bennis (leadership guru). International Design Conference, Aspen, Colorado, 1971.

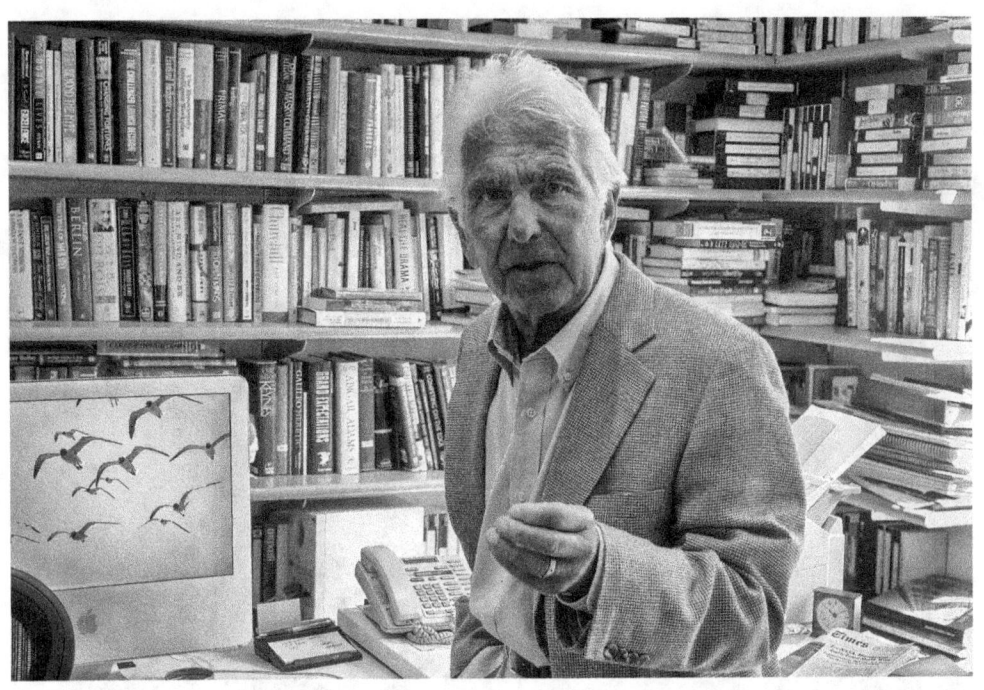

86. Warren Bennis. Santa Monica, California, 2005.

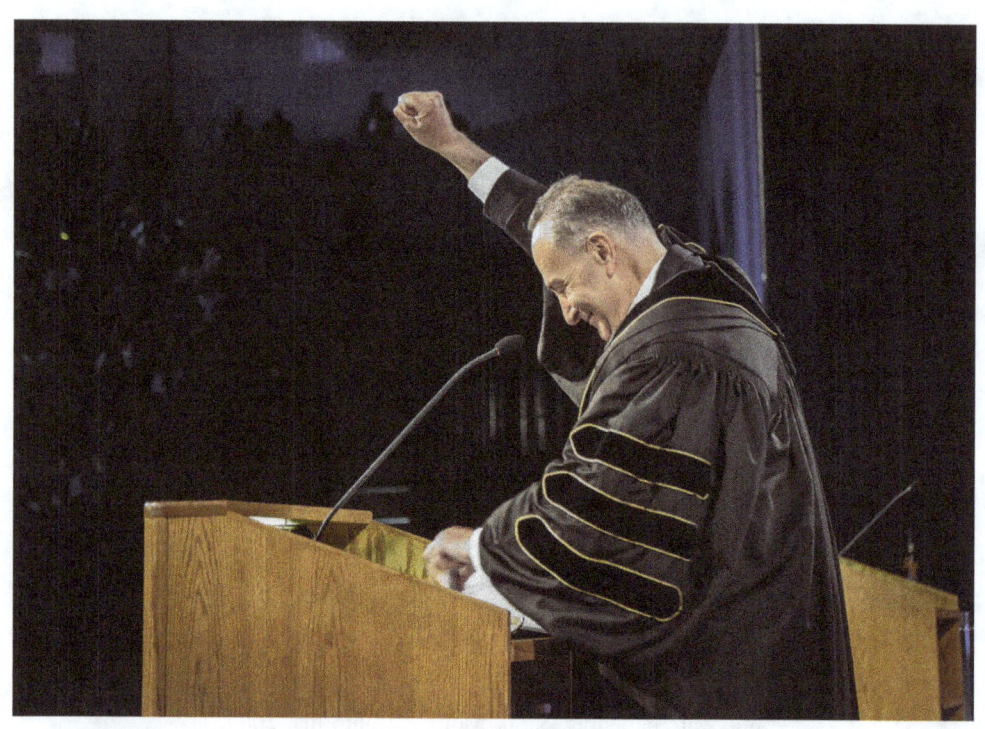

87. Chuck Schumer (US senator). Buffalo, New York, 2001.

Words 5

68. Michel Foucault (philosopher). Buffalo, New York, 1971.

Michel Foucault, Ray Federman, Olga Bernal, and I were walking around the University at Buffalo (UB) campus, and we came upon pieces of columns that had once decorated the front of a now-forgotten Buffalo bank. No one I've ever met knows how those chunks of marble came to be dumped there. Michel and Ray got silly: they posed between the chunks and atop them. Olga watched; I took pictures.

A few years later, Olga retired from her position as professor in the UB French Department, returned to France, and became a sculptor. She made railroad boxcars, like the one in which she was taken as a girl to be a sex slave in a German concentration camp.

The last time I saw Michel was in 1975, in Paris, when he came to an exhibit of my Arkansas prison photos and made dinner for Diane and me in his Rue Vaugirard apartment. He was the first of our friends to die of AIDS.

69. Anselm Kiefer (artist). Albright-Knox Art Gallery, in conversation with Janne Sirén about his work. Buffalo, New York, 2014.

70. Anselm Kiefer. "La Ribaute." Barjac, France, 2018.

La Ribaute, a two-200-acre place a few miles northeast of Barjac, in the Cévennes, an hour's drive north of Avignon, was, from 1992 to 2010, Anselm Kiefer's working studio. In 2021, it became home to Eschaton-Anselm Kiefer Foundation.

It is often referred to as a *Gesamkunstwerk*, a German word that has many translations, ranging from "universal artwork" to "synthesis of the arts." That German word is close but may not quite get it. La Ribaute is all the things Kiefer wants us to see on any particular day. A different day, a different us, a different configuration.

Several buildings that had been a nineteenth-century silk factory comprise his residence, his former working studio, and his children's residence (connected to the main building by an elevated enclosed tubular bridge). There is an inverted ziggurat, an amphitheater, a field of concrete towers, a pond, and a covered swimming pool with a sand beach. There are tunnels and indoor and outdoor earthworks. There are concrete bunkers, large sheds, and vitrines he has built to house his sculpture, paintings, photography, drawings, and calligraphy. The vitrines range in size from a few cubic feet to the huge greenhouses enveloping his sunflower-and-poppy-spouting jet fighter planes. Most of the objects are in structures designed specifically for them: greenhouses, some with clear and some with frosted glass; sheds with wide doors and skylights and some with no doors at all. In all of them, the light is as much a part of the object on display as the object itself.

During the two days Diane and I were there—June 30 and July 1, 2018—several of his *Die Frauen der Antike* (*Women of Antiquity*) sculptures were in the courtyard and scattered through the woods. I've seen pictures of some of those spaces with none of those concrete women in sight. I've seen pictures of some of those sculptures in parade formation in one of the greenhouses.

We were there as guests of our friends, Janne Sirén and Sonja Gallen-Kallela-Sirén. Janne, who is director of the Albright-Knox Art Gallery in Buffalo, and Kiefer were planning some things.

The first day was an event for a few hundred people who spent the day roaming around and the evening at a sit-down dinner in the amphitheater Kiefer designed. The building had a huge hall, where the dinner took place, and other spaces: a beeswax tunnel created by Wolfgang Laib; the inverted ziggurat at the bottom of which were, during the afternoon, live bodies on mats, as if they were people, just hanging out.

Before the dinner, in a huge room that was formerly part of Anselm's working studio, Janne and Anselm spoke, then Laurie Anderson and Reuben Kodhelli performed. One of the reasons for the event was to celebrate the installation at La Ribaute of Laurie's *Handphone Table*.

Our second day was more relaxed. Janne and Sonja took us on a two-hour tour of La Ribaute. Many of the roads, Janne told us, Anselm had carved himself.

Diane's left knee was troubling her, so she stayed in the car most of the time, watching the three of us prowling around and taking photographs of the objects, installations, and one another.

The day ended with a dinner for twenty-one people in the residence. Shortly before it began, there was a cello concert by Reuben. Just before the cello concert, at the top curved stairway, Diane's left patella split in two.

During Reuben's performance, Diane and I sat on the upper steps. Sonja brought us champagne. Someone else brought Diane a bag of ice. The sound, from where we sat, was astonishingly good. Kiefer's two yellow labs braced Diane. At the base of the stairs, people talked. A cat came out of nowhere and attacked a border collie belonging to one of the guests. The terrified dog ran to the far side of the courtyard. Sonja went to comfort the dog.

After the concert, Janne, one of Anselm's sons, and another man ported Diane into the dining room. For the first hour, one of the yellow labs stayed at Diane's feet. At the end of the dinner, one of Anselm's friends, a noted transplant surgeon, examined Diane's knee. It could, he told her, get complicated. Anselm gave Diane a pair of crutches.

The nearest city was Avignon. We had no medical connections there and no notion of what medical facilities we could trust. We had medical friends in Paris, but medicine there is very bureaucratic, and we didn't want to fuss. Our original plan had been to go to Helsinki with Janne and Sonja, so that's what we did. They had good medical connections there. A day later, an orthopedic surgeon in Helsinki saw Diane, took an x-ray of her knee, and told her she needed surgery to wire the patella back in place. He said it should be done in the US because, after the surgery, her leg would be immobilized for weeks.

A day or so later, and thanks to our Amex card, we flew home business class. We needed the space because Diane's leg had to be straight, from the hip on down. We had trip insurance, which covered $565 of the additional $5,000 Finnair fee.

We almost missed our plane from JFK to Buffalo because of the Kiefer crutches. We made a mad dash (Diane in a wheelchair) from the international terminal to the Jet Blue terminal. When we went through security at the Jet Blue terminal, the TSA people found the crutches suspicious. They looked all right, and the scanning device showed nothing untoward about them, but, when shaken, they made a light rattling noise.

TSA decided to disassemble both. They spent a very long time disassembling them.

When they finally succeeded, dirt and tiny pebbles spilled out, stuff that had gotten into the aluminum tubes through the small height-adjustment holes. I wanted that La Ribaute dirt and those La Ribaute pebbles, but TSA kept them, and sent us on our way.

71. Stephen McKinley Henderson (actor). Buffalo, New York, 2015.

Steve, who is perhaps best known for his performances in August Wilson plays, said, in a talk and later in a note, my favorite line about the work. He got it from one of his drama teachers, Lloyd Richards or William Esper: "Don't get it right; get it true."

72. William Ferris (folklorist and writer). Oxford, Mississippi, 1997.

Bill and I have been friends since 1967, when he was a graduate student at Penn and I was a Junior Fellow at Harvard. Over the years, our research has often run on parallel tracks. And recently, we've both done some books and recordings based on archaeology in our own work over the years—finding connections in things only retrospect allowed to be visible.

In 1997 I was preparing an exhibit in Buffalo of Walker Evans's FSA photos. As part of it, Diane and I visited many of the places Evans worked during that period, then drove to Austin to look at the Evans material at the University of Texas Harry Ransom Center. On the way, we stopped off in Oxford to visit Bill and his wife, Marcie.

An hour or so before this photo was taken, Diane and I had been in Bill's office at Ole Miss when he got a call from someone at the White House telling him Bill Clinton had nominated him to be chairman of the National Endowment for the Humanities. When we went back to Bill's house to celebrate, Marcie was having a meeting in the living room, so we sat on the porch and talked a while, then crossed the road to St. Peter's Cemetery and visited William Faulkner.

73. Jim Watson. Buffalo, New York, 2017.

In his shed at Silo City, a group of then-derelict grain elevators. Jimmy knew every inch of all of them. Several times, when I was photographing the elevators, he saved my life: "Bruce: don't step there. It won't hold you."

Rick Smith, who owned the property, met Jim at Buffalo's oldest bar, Swannie House, and jokingly referred to him as "Swannie Jim." The name stuck; more people in town know him as Swannie Jim than as Jim Watson.

Rick noticed that during the summer, vandals were stealing some of the exterior copper gutters on the buildings. He hired Jim to be caretaker during the warm months. Jim stayed in that shed with no running water and electricity from a small generator off and on, then moved in permanently. He stayed until the property started being repurposed for condos, a bar, and exhibition space. A lot of people were there now, so Rick had to install fences to keep them away from places where they could get into trouble, particularly the bar customers wandering around late at night. "It's something else here now," Jim said to me. "The interesting part left. Those fences!"

The conversation reminded me of a verse in cowboy song recorded by John A. Lomax early in the twentieth century.

I'm going to leave
Old Texas now.
They've got no room
for the longhorn cow.
They've plowed and fenced
all over my range.
And the people there
they look so strange.

74. Gershon Legman (folklorist, pornographer, and writer) and Diane Christian. Valbonne, Alpes-Maritime, France, 1975.

Diane and I went to Paris for a week in 1975, for events connected with the publication of the French translation of *In the Life: Versions of the Criminal Experience* (1974) and an exhibit of some of my prison photos at Galérie Quatorze Juillet in Place Bastille. Then we drove to Rome, with stops at Vézelay, Nice, Avignon, St. Tropez, and Florence. On the way from St. Tropez to Florence, we visited Gershon Legman, who lived outside a small town north of Cannes.

Gershon and I had met only once previously. It was at the 1965 Newport Folk Festival. He was there with folklorists D. K. Wilgus and Ellen Stekert. We were at the back of the audience area while Peter, Paul, and Mary were doing mike checks. He said two things I remember.

The first was: "She's the balls of the group. Without her, they're nothing."

The second was just after the sound got very loud. "Shut the fuck up!" he screamed. The stage was so far away they couldn't possibly have heard him. But that was when they finished the sound check, so they left the stage, whereupon Legman said, "See?"

Though never an academic himself, he was the person, more than any other, who made research into erotic folklore and erotic verbal behavior academically respectable. He was enormously helpful to me when I was working on *Get Your Ass in the Water and Swim Like Me: Narrative Poetry from Black Oral Tradition* (1974). Mail from him was always a visual delight: he'd highlight parts of the text in different colors, and he'd curate the stamps on the postcards and letters to fit the content.

He'd written me that they lived in a converted barn. I'd read somewhere that his place had belonged to the Templars, so I expected an elegant barn. It wasn't. It didn't even have running water. It was small and cramped. When we got there, his wife, Judith, said, "Gershon's in his *atelier*. I'll let him know you're here." She buzzed him on an intercom. A few minutes later he came through some high grass. Diane and I gave them the chicken, wine, and a tin of cookies we'd brought. We chatted for a few minutes. Then Gershon said, "Let's go over to my *atelier*. Diane can stay here with Judith and have girl talk."

I knew Diane was as interested in seeing where he worked as I, so I said, "Diane has a Ph.D. from Johns Hopkins. She doesn't do girl talk." Gershon looked annoyed.

Diane gave me a look I interpreted as saying: "Go ahead. I've been through this before." Gershon and I went off through the high grass.

His study was a house, a regular house, with running water, electricity, a huge number of books and LP records, and a grand piano. We talked for a while. Two of the children came and went. Then we went back to the barn.

Judith, Diane, and one of the sons were sitting at the table. Something was wrong. Nobody was saying anything or looking at one another and the boy seemed to be crying.

"What's going on here?" I said.

"He bit me," Diane said sweetly, "so I bit him."

I asked how that came about.

She and Judith had been conversing in French, Diane said. She noticed Judith's French seemed studied. She'd asked if French was Judith's native language. "No," Judith said, "I'm from California."

"Then why are we talking in French?" Diane said, in English.

"Gershon thinks we should."

Diane continued the conversation in English and so did Judith.

The boy, Daniel, was very annoyed. He had trouble following what they were saying. "I *forbid* you to speak English. Speak French."

Diane and Judith told him English was a fine language, which he should speak also.

"If you don't speak French," Daniel said to Diane, "I will bite you."

"If you bite me," Diane said to him, "I will bite you back."

"We continued in English," Diane said to me. "Then he bit me. So I bit him."

75. Diane Christian and Philippe Lemonnier (photographer). Paris, France, 2010.

We'd met Philippe when he was photographing Jean Malaurie at a Terre Humaine conference at Versailles in 2002. He made his living as a photographer, but he loves to write books about long walks: very long walks. In books like *La Voyage à pied: Chroniques de la Pérégrination* (2007), he notes, in exquisite detail, the things you see along the way, nearly all of which you'd miss traveling by any other mode.

When we joined him and his wife, Claire, for lunch at La Palette on rue du Seine this day in 2010, we took scores of photographs of one another. Diane gave him *Feuille d'herbe*, a French translation of Whitman's *Leaves of* Grass. "Another walker," she said.

Claire went back to work and Philippe walked with us to a gallery on the river. He and Diane continued, without pause, a discussion they'd begun in the restaurant. Occasionally, one or both of them got so involved in the conversation they stopped walking and focused on the talking. I took several photos of that encounter, my favorite of which is this one, with Diane in reflection and Klaus Kinski silently watching.

When we parted at the gallery entrance, Philippe said, "Next time you're here, you'll stay with us in the banlieue. You'll see a part of Paris that doesn't exist in the places you stay. We'll go out with our cameras." We vowed to do that.

It wasn't to be. By the next time we got to France, he had moved south, to Die in the Dröme. When we went to Barjac in 2018, we thought we'd borrow a car and drive over and visit them there. Then, as you know, Diane's patella split and the journey took a different turn entirely.

76. William Christenberry (artist). Washington, DC, 1998.

Bill was a painter, sculptor, and photographer. He is credited with convincing his friend, William Eggleston, to shift to color in 1964 or 1965. Bill worked for years with a simple Kodak Brownie camera. Then, Bill told me, Eggleston returned the favor. He turned up at Bill's studio one day with an eight-inch-by-ten-inch Deardorff camera. "Some of us think it is time you started thinking bigger," Eggleston said.

Bill had been friends with Walker Evans. He'd grown up in Birmingham, but his family was from Hale County, Alabama, where, in 1936, Evans and James Agee had done their work for *Let Us Now Praise Famous Men* (1941). For decades, Bill had photographed the same buildings in Hale County again and again, looking at time. Walker went with him on one of those trips. Walker, Bill told me, would regularly ask him to stop the car, where upon he'd get out, run over to a barn with a few tools he'd brought with him, and steal a sign advertising something. Evans loved those signs. After a while, Bill fell in love with them, too, so he started his own thievery. The wall behind him displays some of his favorites.

He told me all this not long before Diane and I made the trip through Alabama and Mississippi retracing Evans's route when he worked for the Farm Security Administration (FSA) in the mid-1930s. I was then preparing for a large exhibit of Evans's FSA photographs I was curating. Bill got me hooked on the barn signs, so in the car I had the tools I thought I'd need to steal them most efficiently.

But I didn't see any. On the whole trip, not one. Diane and I continued on to Austin, Texas, where I looked at the Evans holdings at the Harry Ransom Center. I met a Time-Life photographer there researching a project. I told him about my failed sign-stealing plan. "You're too late," he said, "they're all in Hollywood. Companies that rent period items for feature films have scraped that area clean. The only place you'll see them now," he said, "is at the movies."

"And on Bill Christenberry's wall."

"Yeah. There, too."

77. Cynta de Navarez (Rio Grande River guide). Terlingua Ghost Town, Texas, 2013.

I stayed in Cynta's guest house twice when I was photographing in the Big Bend and that part of northern Mexico. She'd been a river rafting guide on the Rio Grande until she was hit by an affliction her doctors couldn't diagnose. While they were figuring it out, some of her muscles atrophied. It got to a point where, if she fell, she couldn't get up. She couldn't work on the river.

One early evening when we were sitting on her porch having a drink, a beautiful Empress Leilia butterfly settled on a wicker chair between us. We fell silent. After it flew off, we resumed our conversation. Her dog, Baxter, slept at her feet. The same thing happened the next evening. A few days later, I was back in Buffalo. Cynta texted me: "That butterfly came by last night to visit you again. She hung out for a good while with us."

One dreary Buffalo September day, I wrote Cynta about missing the desert view from her porch. She responded:

> Sorry my friend, it's absolutely glorious here. Yes, there is just the first hint of winter in the air; the vultures are gathering to fly south, there are tons of mice trying to find good homes in our houses and I saw two rattlesnakes on the road last night. Besides that its greengreengreen and cool in the mornings (71 degrees with kickinthehinder sunrises) and then 80 or so at night (with kickinthehinder sunsets). Shadows and brilliant shooting orange or yellow light, and the Clouds! Okay, okay, it sucks.

Another time she wrote:

> We got an inch and a quarter of rain last night. It was fantastic.
> Baxter and I just sat there and soaked it up for hours.

It may have been only a 20% chance of rain but holy shit we got
    carwashed around here.
It was magnificent.
Now the roads are all textured with flow lines from the floods,
the plants are smelling sexy
and the frogs are starting their season of serenade.
They say it will happen again tonight.
Well, I'm tanned, rested and ready . . . bring it on.

And on another:

You know, if someone has never tasted chocolate, you just can't describe
it to them, or, you can try, but they will never get it. Besides the beauty
here, you just can't help respect the place and want to emulate it. Here I do
not feel like a worm; the magnificence of a rain, or a morning, or a lunar
eclipse, as we talked about, is far more important than physical comfort;
that is why people are obese now and let their fellow citizens step all over
them politically; slowly this sugarly life makes us lazy and wormlike. It takes
a dose of someplace raw; like Alaska, I bet, or the desert, to remind us of
what is important. Someplace that still gets too cold, or gets too hot, that
shakes us up and reminds us to be alive every single day! Hot feels great
sometimes, jeez, it could be worse; we could be in Baghdad. The Mexicans
have a dicho: "No hay pedo" (Nobody farted) or, in its real meaning, "hey,
things could be so much worse!" Sometime we all need to be reminded.
Just looking at those guys in your jail photographs put me back in line.
    Onward to the Milky Way

A mutual friend, Charlie Angell, also a river guide, visited her. She sent me a note:

Got to spend yesterday evening with Charlie.
He is not only a hoot, but a fantastic friend.
If he were a dog, I'd just have to keep him.
When she saw this photo, she wrote:
Thank you, thank you.
It shows everything that is my world:
my dog, my desert, my house, my view,
my hair, my sun, myblueblue sky. Everything I love.

Everything that gives me peace everyday.
Everything that holds me in my place now
and takes care of me and makes me who I am.

After years of tests and trials, her doctors decided that her muscle atrophication was from undiagnosed Lyme disease, probably acquired on one of her rare visits to her family in Connecticut. The last time she wrote, she said the meds seemed to be working and she was looking forward to getting back on the river.

78. Hélène Korn (shiatsu practitioner and poet). Paris, France, 2010.

I met Hélène when she was five. Her father, Henri, a neurophysiologist, was then a good friend. Then he turned out not to be. And she, a grown-up now, is part of our family.

79. Wedding of Lauren Christian and David Oubré. Immaculate Conception Jesuit Church, New Orleans, 2014.

Lauren is the daughter of Diane's youngest brother, Robert. The whole family clan went down to New Orleans for a two-day party.

During that weekend, a death-penalty lawyer friend, Billy Sothern, had us to dinner at his house in Tremé and took us to visit Buddy Bolden's grave marker in Holt Cemetery. "He's around here somewhere," Billy said, "but nobody knows where. This was the city's potter's field. They didn't bother with real grave markers."

My own family never had any parties. Diane's family has been having them the entire time I've known them. At the beginning, we were the young marrieds; now we're the elders. The most recent was this summer, at Bobby's son's place in a rural county halfway between Rochester and Buffalo. Lauren and David were there, with their new baby. Enough young kids were there for them to form a kid scene totally separate from the adults: some played soccer, some tooled around on a golf cart driven by an eight-year-old. There was a lot of food and drink, but the main attraction was a 200-pound pig, which had been rotating over a grill for several days.

The only other time I'd seen something like that had been in 2018, at Anselm Kiefer's place in Barjac. During the afternoon concert by Laurie Anderson, three small pigs turned over an open fire amid some of the statues. They were one of the three meat courses at the big dinner.

80. Wedding couple in front of the Church of Santa Fosca. Torcello, Italy, 2016.

Diane and I visited Torcello to study the magnificent eleventh-century Byzantine *Last Judgment* mosaic occupying the entire west wall of the basilica of Santa Maria Assunta. When we came out, a wedding was in progress at the adjacent twelfth-century Church of Santa Fosca. A crowd of exquisitely attired people were on the church steps. This couple emerged and instantly the air was full of confetti, like snow.

81. Woman taking selfie, Caffè Florian, Piazza San Marco. Venice, Italy, 2016.

Her smartphone was in an elaborate Mickey Mouse case. She worked on the selfie for almost an hour. In one of the most beautiful public spaces in the world, she spent all that time looking at herself. And I spent the same amount of time watching her do it.

82. Karl Ove Knausgård (writer) on the back steps of Kleinhans Music Hall, before his appearance in Just Buffalo's BABEL series. Buffalo, New York, 2016.

As I mentioned earlier, I was with most of the BABEL writers I photographed in their afternoon meetings with high school students, the pre-performance receptions, sometimes the dinners, and backstage before the performances began. Most of them were friendly. Poets and novelists are like that: they inhabit a world of words; they like encountering and talking with people. Not Kanusgård. He was by far the coldest of the thirty-five writers I spent time with on that project. I saw him again at the first of the two dinners at Anselm Kiefer's place in Barjac in 2018. We didn't speak. He did a profile of Kiefer that appeared in the *New York Times Magazine* ("Into the Black Forest with the Greatest Living Artist," February 16, 2020). It had several beautiful black and white photos of Kiefer by Pedro Pellegrin. The article was more about Kanusgård than Kiefer, maybe not surprising for a writer best known for his 3600-page, six-volume autobiographical novel titled *Min Kamp* (*My Struggle*, 2009–11). Somebody else wrote a book with the same title.

83. Arundhati Roy (writer). Buffalo, New York, 2004.

The huge turnout for her visit led to the idea for, and initial funding of, Just Buffalo's BABEL series. It was the first time many of the local and federal funding agencies realized there were large audiences for one-off arts events in the provinces.

84. Tom Toles (political cartoonist). Hamburg, New York, 2015.

Tom began his career as a political cartoonist drawing for the University at Buffalo's student newspaper while still a high school student, then for the same paper while a UB student, then for the *Buffalo Courier-Express* until Warren Buffet killed it, then for the *Buffalo News* (where, in 1990, he won a Pulitzer Prize), and, finally and most notably as Herblock's successor at the *Washington Post* (2002–2020). No political cartoonist in the country nailed the Trump years better than he. He continues to be a terrific rock drummer.

University at Buffalo honored him in its Signature Series in 2016. One of the events was Tom showing and talking about some of his favorite cartoons, followed by the two of us in an onstage conversation. Before that event, Tom, his wife Gretchen, Diane, and I had dinner in the Center for the Arts Green Room. I asked Tom if he'd like us to bring anything to drink. "Bourbon might be nice," he said.

That afternoon, Diane picked up a bottle of bourbon. Neither of us knows anything about bourbon, so she asked the liquor store guy for something special. Special it was: Booker's 128 proof! When Tom saw it, he said, "I was joking, but what the hell." We all had some.

When it came time to go onstage, he said, "This can't all go to waste." He poured a significant amount into each of two coffee cups, handed me one, and off we went.

A while later, during our onstage conversation, Tom said, as an aside, "You probably think Bruce and I are drinking coffee. We're drinking 128 proof bourbon." He took a swig, and so did I.

The audience laughed. Tom was one of the funniest political cartoonists in the country. He was, obviously, joking.

85. Kate Bennis and Warren Bennis (leadership guru). International Design Conference, Aspen, Colorado, 1971.

Warren invited me to show some 16 millimeter footage I'd recently shot in a Texas prison farm. It was a high-power event, and I was an amateur in that company. Warren was one of the keynote speakers, and so was Buckminster Fuller.

Richard Wurman, a Philadelphia architect I'd met in Buffalo a few months earlier, was one of the organizers of that year's IDC. Ricky had, not long before, done a wonderful exhibit in Philadelphia called *City/2*. He did graphics showing how much of the city was privately owned and how much belonged to the public: all the land occupied by streets, parks, schools, churches, and other nonprofits. The exhibit graphically demonstrated how much of the city belonged to the people living there. He wore, at that IDC, red-white-and-blue suspenders I admired so shamelessly he took them off and handed them to me. (The elasticity is long gone, but I still have them.)

Bucky Fuller's talk was, for me, the high point of the week. It was supposed to be an hour, but it went on and on, and on and on. I bailed after three and a half hours. It wasn't just that I was by then bored, which I was, but because I was in physical pain.

The room they'd put me up in was maybe a hundred meters from the auditorium where he was doing his presentation. It was hippie time. I'd walked over there barefoot in the early evening sun. A little beyond halfway I began feeling discomfort in my feet. My room—with my shoes—was farther away than the auditorium. So, I continued on.

When I got back to the room after bailing out on Fuller, there were huge blisters on the soles of both feet. The air temperature had been comfortable—maybe eighty degrees Fahrenheit. But at that altitude, an asphalt pathway is significantly hotter than that, enough to cause real damage, which it did. A few days later, I had to go to a wedding in Newark, New Jersey. I was limping from both feet. Limping from one foot or leg you can manage; from two, you're a klutz. I cursed my high-altitude hippiness of a few days before.

86. Warren Bennis. Santa Monica, California, 2005.

Warren and I met one another late Saturday morning, April 29, 1967. At the time, he was on the faculty of the Sloan School at MIT, and I was finishing my fourth year as a Junior Fellow in Harvard's Society of Fellows. In September, both of us would be moving to Buffalo: I as assistant professor of English and comparative literature; Warren as provost of the Faculty of Social Sciences. UB was then divided into seven faculties, each with a "provost," a job that everywhere else was called "dean." A few years later, Warren would be UB's vice president for Academic Affairs and administrative vice president, a job that universities now call "provost."

We met at his house on Boston's Beacon Hill. He'd invited me to brunch because a mutual friend, Norman Zinberg, a Cambridge psychiatrist with whom I taught a graduate seminar that semester, thought we'd find one another interesting. Warren's wife Clurie was at the brunch, and so was Saul Tauster, a poet and attorney. One of Saul's clients was Martin Meyerson, then president of University at Buffalo.

During the brunch, Saul got a telephone call from Aaron Rosen, an English professor then posted as associate provost of the Faculty of Arts and Letters at Buffalo.

One of UB's most famous literary scholars, Leslie Fiedler, had been arrested the previous night on a drug charge. (It was a bogus bust, arranged by the same Buffalo narcotics cop who did the made-for-TV raids on the Road Vultures clubhouse I mentioned earlier. The charges were eventually thrown out by a state court.)

After we moved to Buffalo, Warren and I got to be good friends. Our families hung out. One night, I was at his house helping him with the design for a program of freshman seminars. He, Clurie, and I started wiping our eyes at the same time. Between his house and the University, was a large city-owned golf course. I don't remember which one of us realized it first: Buffalo police were bombarding the campus with tear gas.

The two of us went to the campus radio station, WBFO (which figured in the founding of NPR). The police had not only sprayed tear gas all over the campus, but they'd specifically targeted Norton Hall, the Student Union. They fired gas grenades into all the stairwells, so anyone wanting to get out from the second floor or basement floor had to pass through a closed space full of gas. One of them had blasted one of the front doors with a shotgun: I have photographs of that door with pellet holes in it. We got to the WBFO office. It had its own air-conditioning system, so it was gas-free.

Once there, we watched police lobbing tear-gas grenades into the windows of a women's dormitory across the street. A speaker in the studio was pumping out one of the local radio stations. The Buffalo police commissioner was saying that people were making false charges about his cops firing tear-gas grenades. "Impossible," he said. "We don't have grenade launchers."

Remember Richard Pryor's line in his bit about being caught by his wife screwing their neighbor on the couch: "Who you gonna believe: me or your lyin' eyes?"

Grenade launchers in those days were a simple device that latched on to the muzzle of a shotgun. We listened to the commissioner lie, then Warren got on an WBFO microphone and described what we were looking at.

Martin Meyerson left Buffalo and became president of University of Pennsylvania. Warren was the logical successor, but many local people still called the University "Jew B" because of all the downstate students who'd started attending after University of Buffalo became part of State University of New York, and a lot of Jewish professors like Leslie Fiedler, Warren, Martin, and I came on board. Warren didn't have a chance. He became president of University of Cincinnati, one of the great city universities, and he was the person most responsible for folding it into the Ohio university system, which is why it survives today.

He and I saw one another a bit when he first had that job, then we fell out of touch for several years. In the early 1990s, someone asked me to review a book of some of his essays. I did. It was a snippy review. He wrote me a note about it. I was then doing some work in Hollywood, and we agreed to meet and talk about what I'd written.

He was living in the Santa Monica condo where this photo was taken. The encounter was a little fraught, so we went to a café in Venice, a five-minute walk to the south. We talked for five hours. He invited me to dinner that night, to continue the conversation and to meet his new wife. She was someone he'd been involved with years before and had reconnected with only after he'd relocated to the West Coast and became a faculty member at University of Southern California.

That night, at that dinner, we did what people who have known one another a long time always do: we told stories. Ostensibly, we told them not for one another, but for the new person; in actuality, the new person lets those old stories be retold. In the course of that evening, I learned something important about memory and narrative.

Warren told the story of Leslie Fiedler's arrest, and how he learned of it during the April 29, 1967 brunch. He was there; Clurie was there; Saul Tauster was there. And Martin Meyerson was there, recruiting him for the Buffalo job. I was nowhere to be seen.

When he was done, I said, "Martin wasn't there. It was me. I was there."

Warren said he remembered it as Martin. I pointed out that no one would be hiring someone for a senior academic administrative job in late April. That dance happens in the fall.

Warren realized he'd collapsed two brunches, one in the fall when Martin was talking him into the Buffalo job, the second in late spring when we met in the same room having the same food. His narrative combined two almost identical events, subtracting the least significant person: me.

That's when I understood that the fact that you remember something doesn't mean it happened; it means only that you remember it. (There's a corollary: the fact that you don't remember something or part of it doesn't mean that thing didn't happen or that a part wasn't it; it means only that you don't remember it.)

A few years later, in the same Santa Monica condo, someone else was visiting. Warren told the story again, and once again the least significant participant—me—was subtracted. He finished and looked at me. I said nothing, but I must have had a look on my face that he understood. He said, "I did it again, didn't I?"

We remained close until his death in 2014. When we became friends in 1967, he was a lot older—eleven years: I was thirty-one; Warren was forty-two. By the time he died, the age difference was only one decade. Negligible.

Warren was one of the youngest, perhaps the youngest, lieutenants in World War II. He was in the Battle of the Bulge, one of the horrific campaigns of mutual attrition of the war in Europe. Not long before he died, I asked, "What do you remember of it?"

"The odor of burning flesh," he said. "I can still smell it."

87. Chuck Schumer (US senator). Buffalo, New York, 2001.

For years, University at Buffalo graduation ceremonies coincided with Mother's Day. And for years, Chuck Schumer would show up and give the same speech. He'd make little adjustments: if a campus team or the Buffalo Bills or Sabres had had a good year, he'd toss that in. If his staff found out the students' favorite place for chicken wings had changed, he'd alter that reference. Otherwise, it was the same.

Sometimes his staff let UB officials know he was coming, but even when they didn't, they saved a seat in the front row of the platform for him. The platform party consisted of top University officials, honorary degree and other award winners, and SUNY Distinguished Professors. Most of the time, during the long speechifying and name-reading, we'd all be reading something tucked into our program booklets. But when Chuck gave his speech, many of us recited the lines along with him. We did it in low voices; the audience couldn't hear it, but Chuck could. I once asked his assistant how many graduations Chuck gave that speech at this year. "You mean today or in all?" I found out Chuck was hitting three or four graduations on Mother's Day alone. At each school, he'd find out the name of the favorite bar or pizza joint and fold it in at the appropriate place.

"How many times have you heard that speech?" I said to the aide.

"I couldn't count."

"Don't you go nuts hearing it?"

He shrugged. "It's a pretty good speech, isn't it?"

It was political gold for Chuck: he didn't have to make a political pitch. He could just be an entertaining part of a day on which the 15,000 people in front of him were happy.

One year, in the robing room before the procession into the arena, I said, "You're going to give that same speech again, aren't you?"

"Of course," he said.

"We're going to recite it with you, Chuck," I said, waving toward the rest of the platform party.

"You've heard it before, Professor," he said. "They"—he pointed toward the corridor through which we would shortly walk to reach the large arena already filled with the graduates and their families—"haven't." I made a noise. "But I've changed it," he said.

"I don't believe you," I said.

"I did. But people complained, so I changed it back."

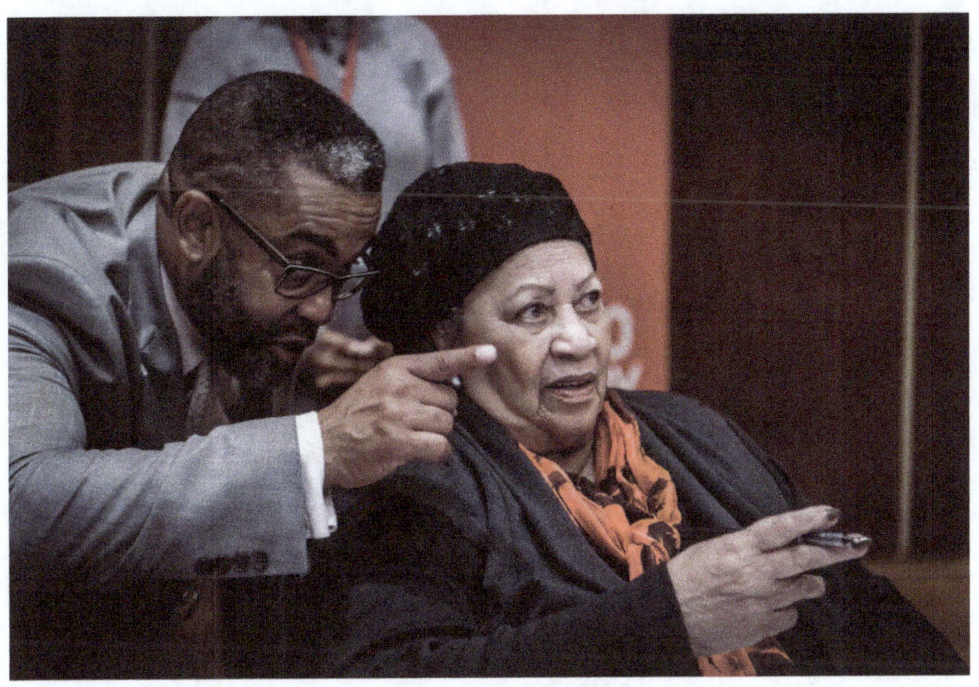

88. Roscoe Henderson III (police officer) and Toni Morrison (writer) backstage at Klein-hans Music Hall, Just Buffalo BABEL Series. Buffalo, New York, 2017.

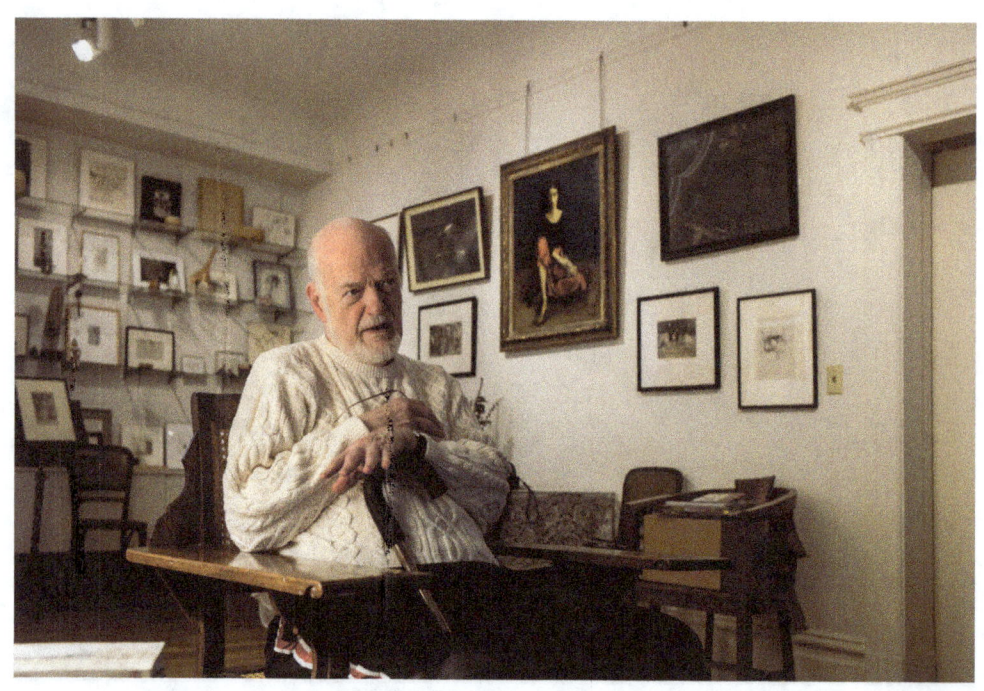

89. Roy "Bud" Johns (writer, publisher, and corporate executive). San Francisco, California, 2011.

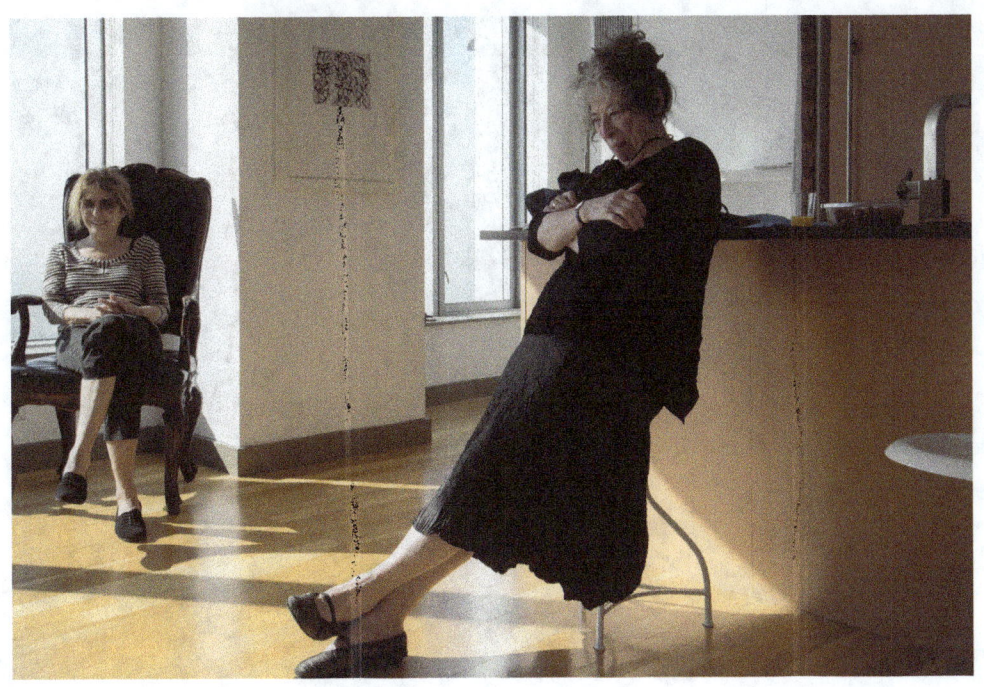

90. Margaret Kunstler and Diane Christian. New York, New York, 2012.

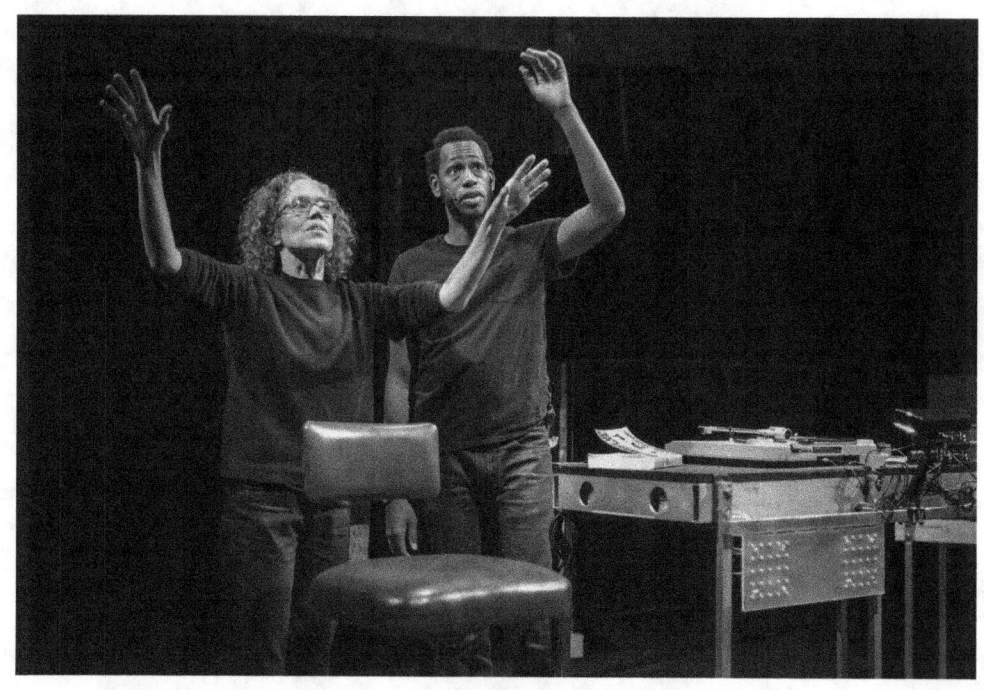

91. Kate Valk (actor and director) and Eric Berryman (actor and dramaturge). Wooster Group rehearsal for *The B-Side*. The Performing Garage, New York, New York, 2016.

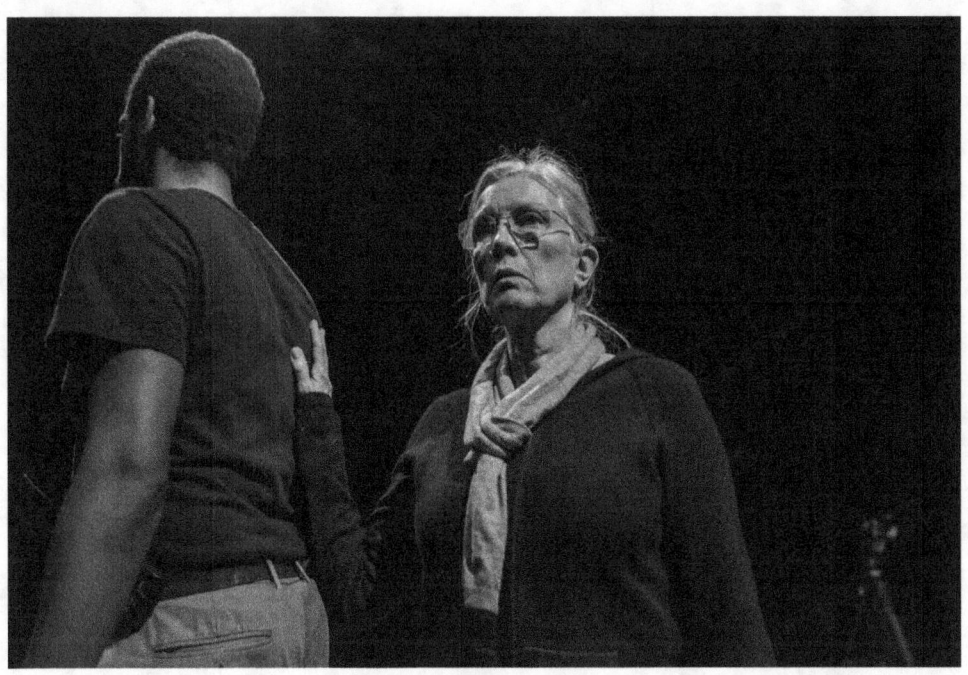

92. Eric Berryman and Elizabeth LeCompte. Wooster Group rehearsal for *The B-Side*. Center for the Arts, University at Buffalo, Buffalo, New York, 2018.

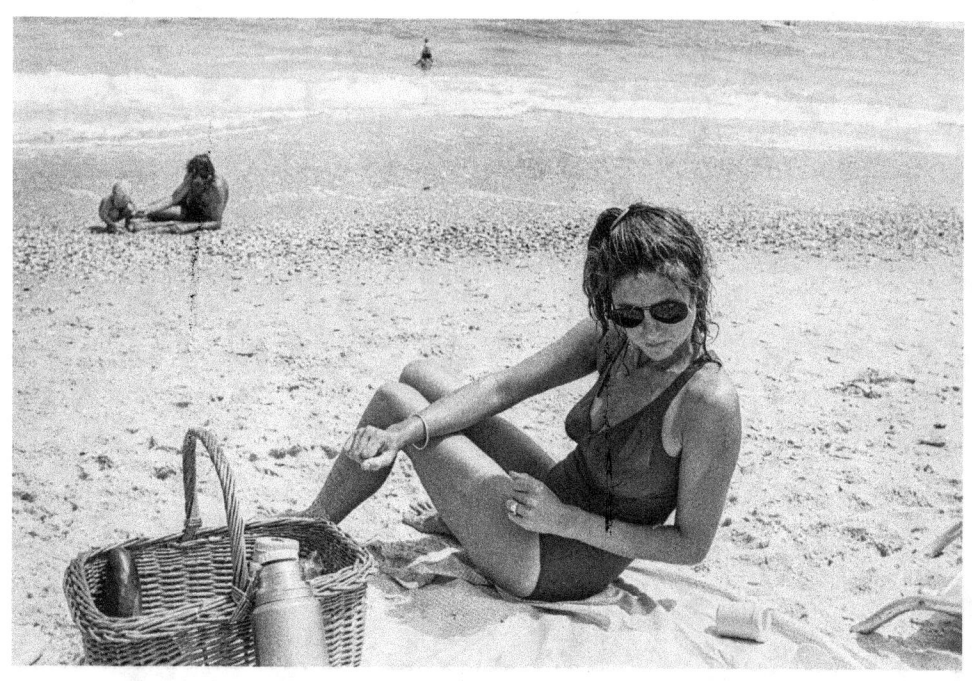

93. Will Creeley, Robert Creeley, and Penelope Creeley. Wilmington, North Carolina, 1984.

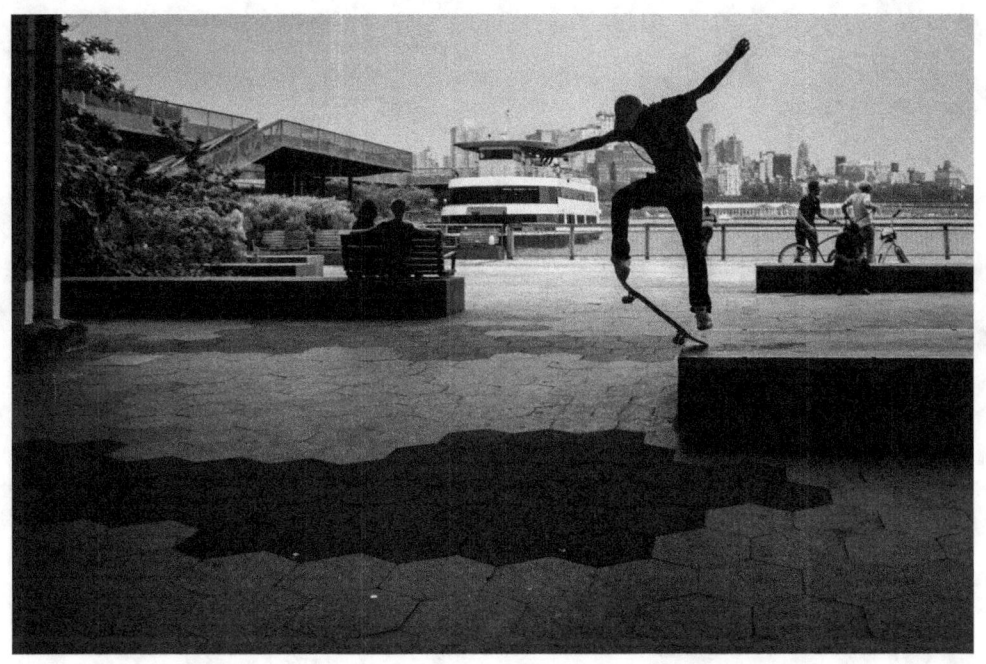

94. Skateboarder near Pier 11. New York, New York, 2016.

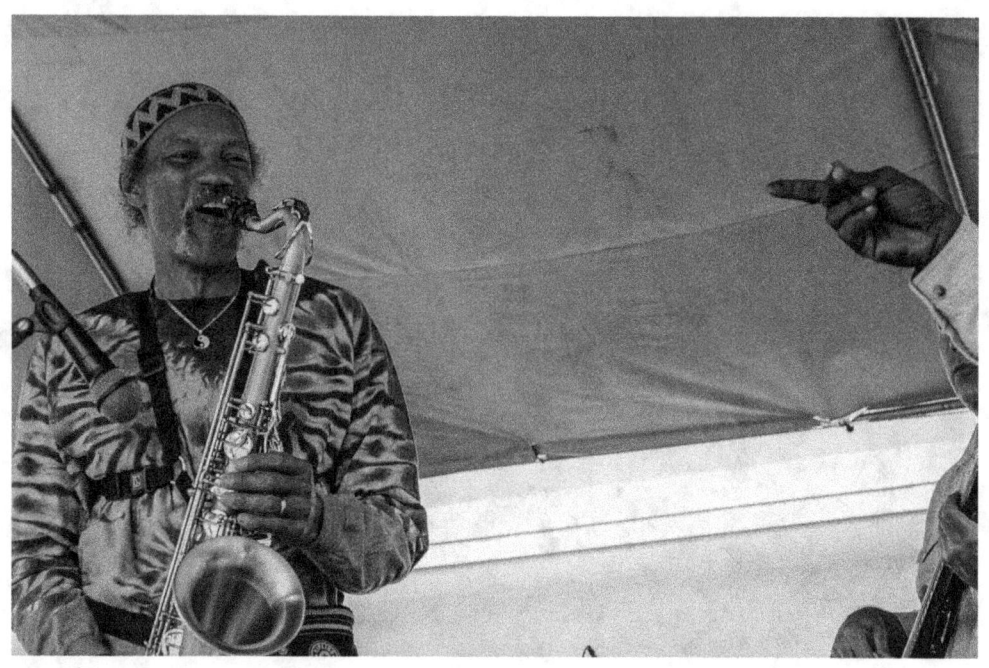

95. Charles Neville (musician). Louisiana State Penitentiary (Angola), Tunica Trace, Angola, 2001.

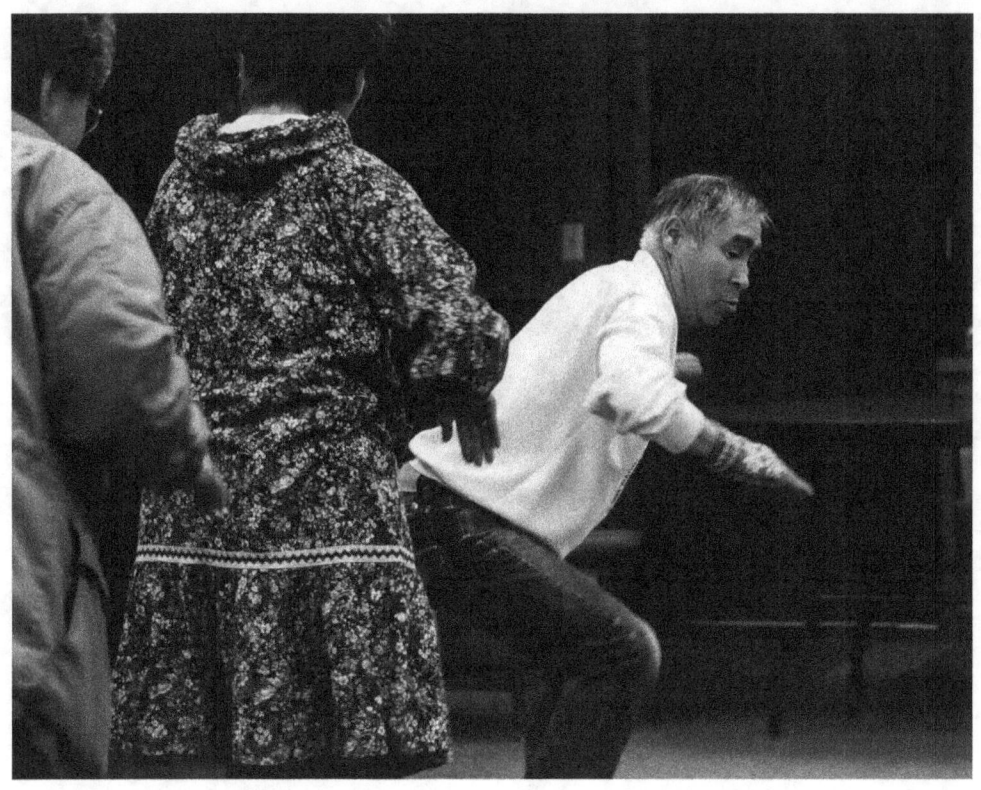

96. Elders teaching traditional dance. Nome, Alaska, 1997.

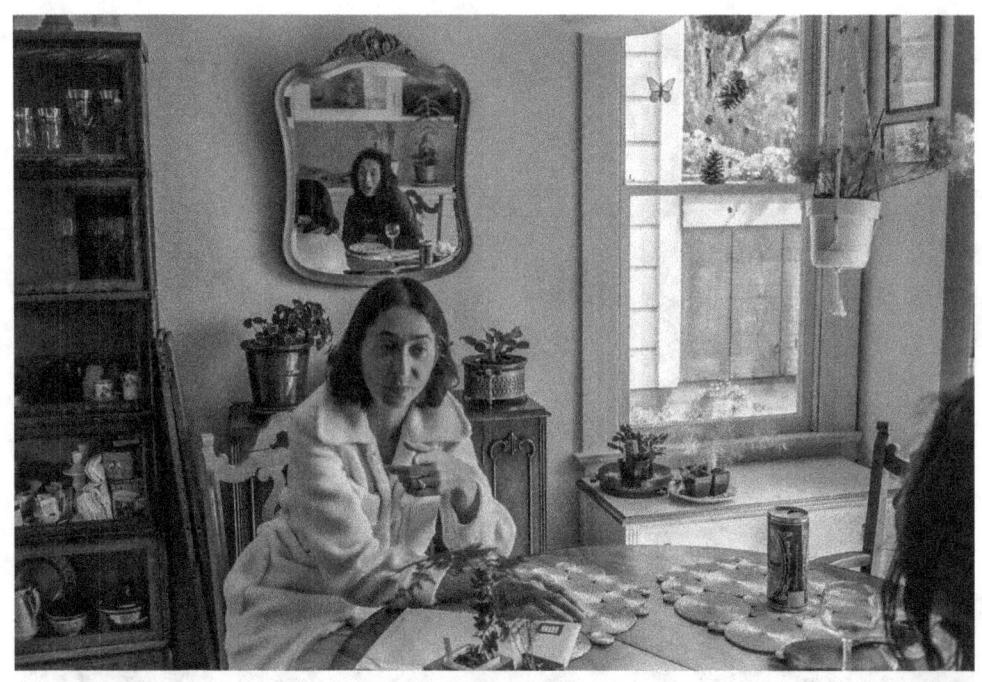

97. Judith Spector Clancy (artist) and Diane Christian. San Francisco, California, 1977.

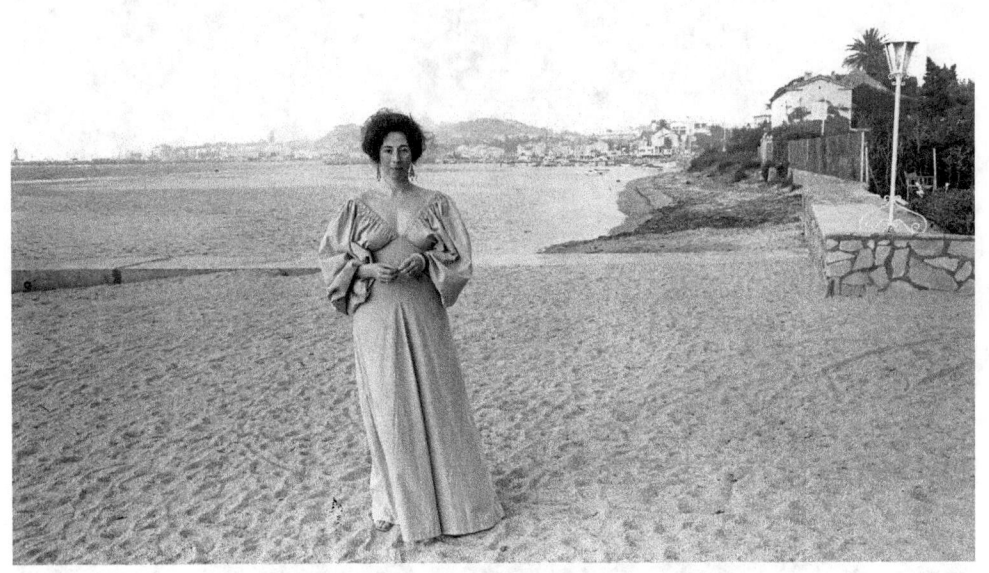

98. Diane Christian. St.-Tropez, France, 1975.

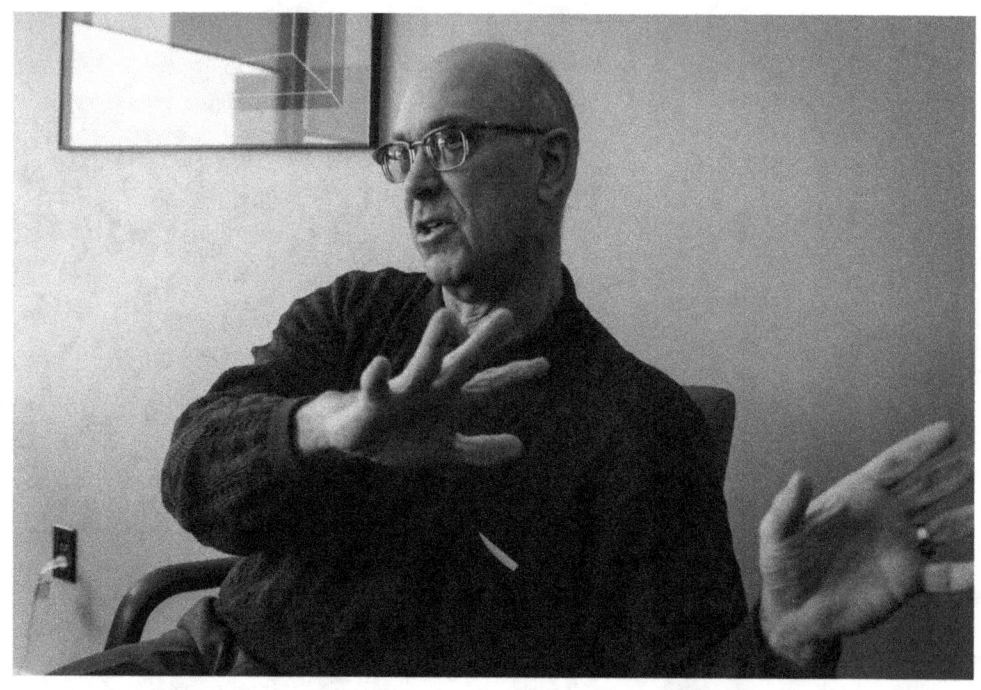

99. David Felder (composer). Buffalo, New York, 2015.

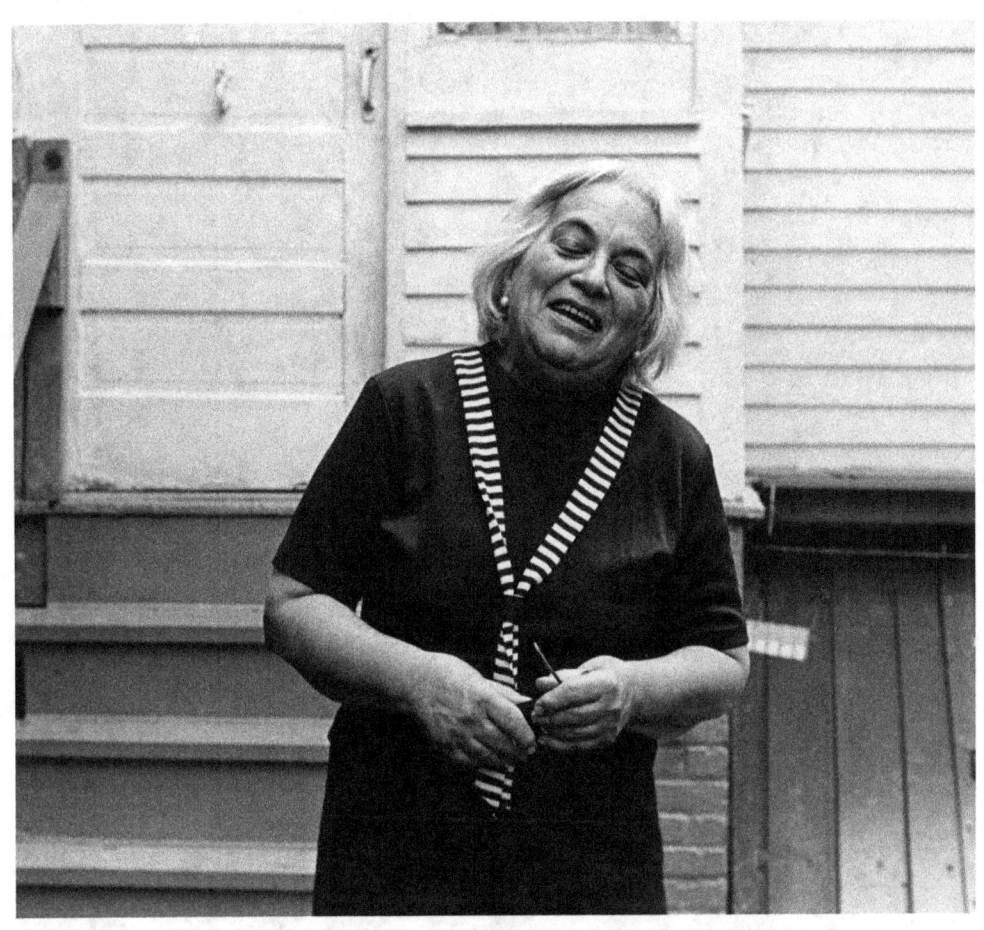

100. Julia Jackson. Edison, New Jersey, 1972.

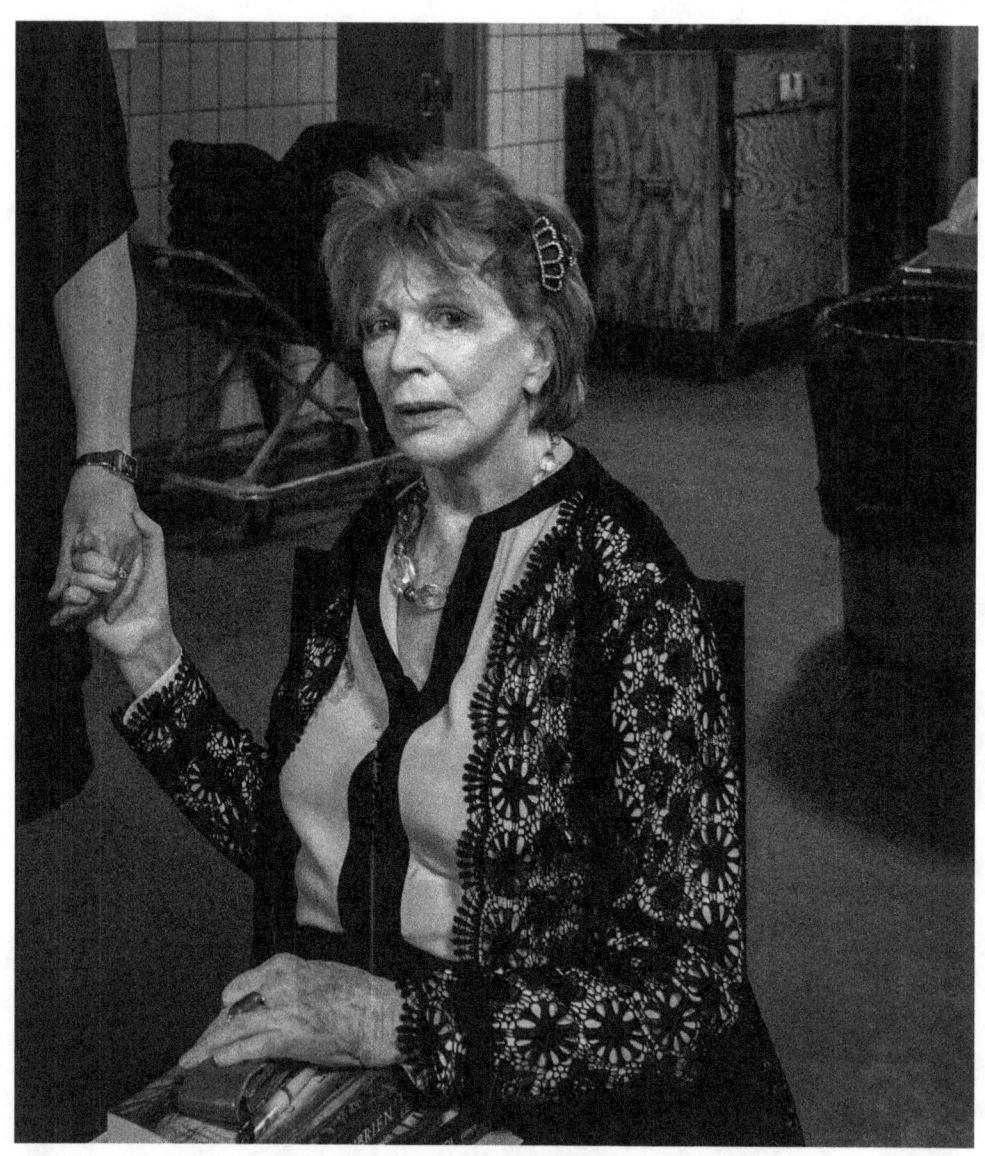

101. Edna O'Brien in Just Buffalo's BABEL series, backstage at Kleinhans Music Hall. Buffalo, New York, 2017.

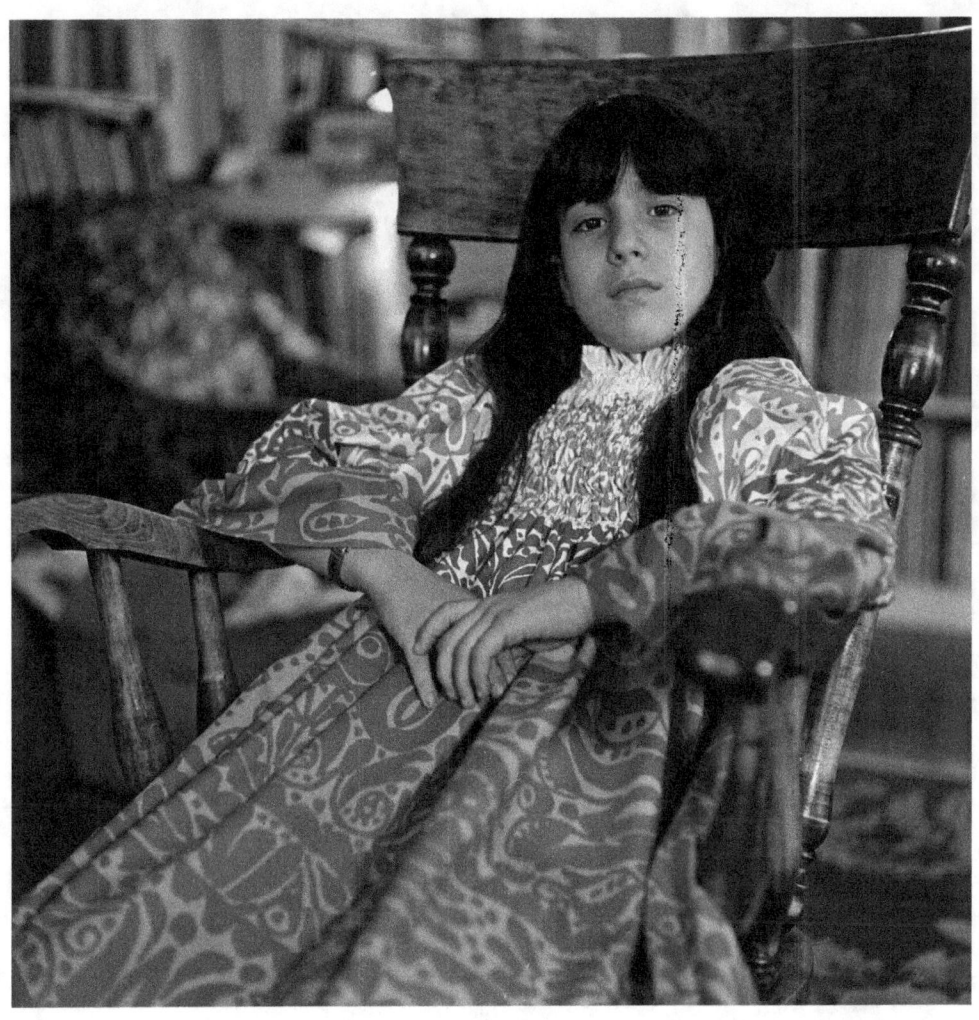

102. Jessica Jackson. Buffalo, New York, 1973.

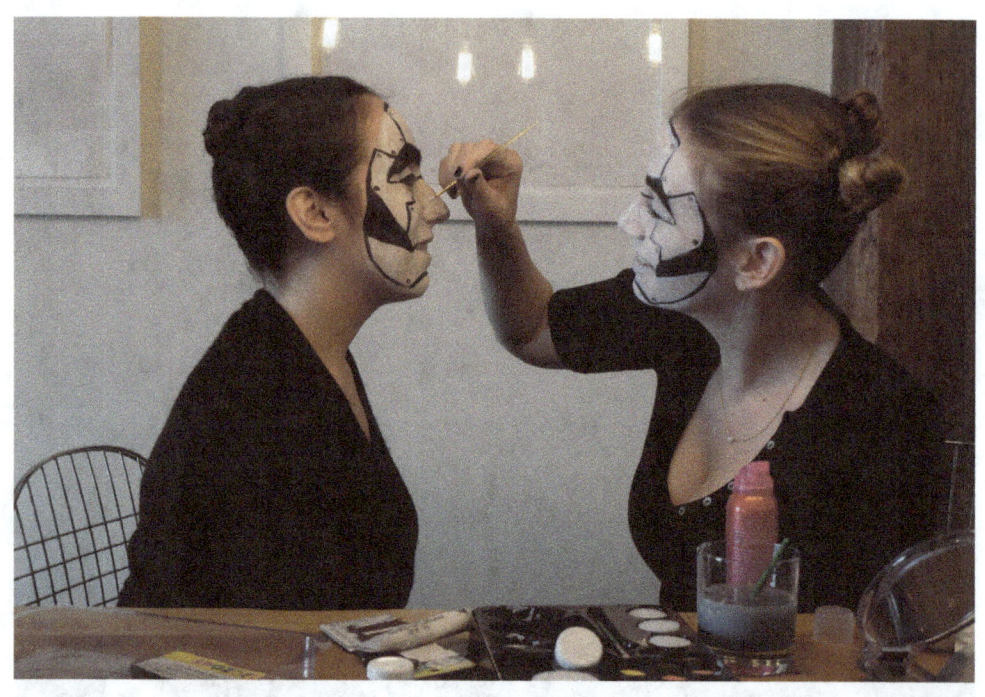

103. Sarah and Emily Kunstler. Red Hook, Brooklyn, New York, 2015.

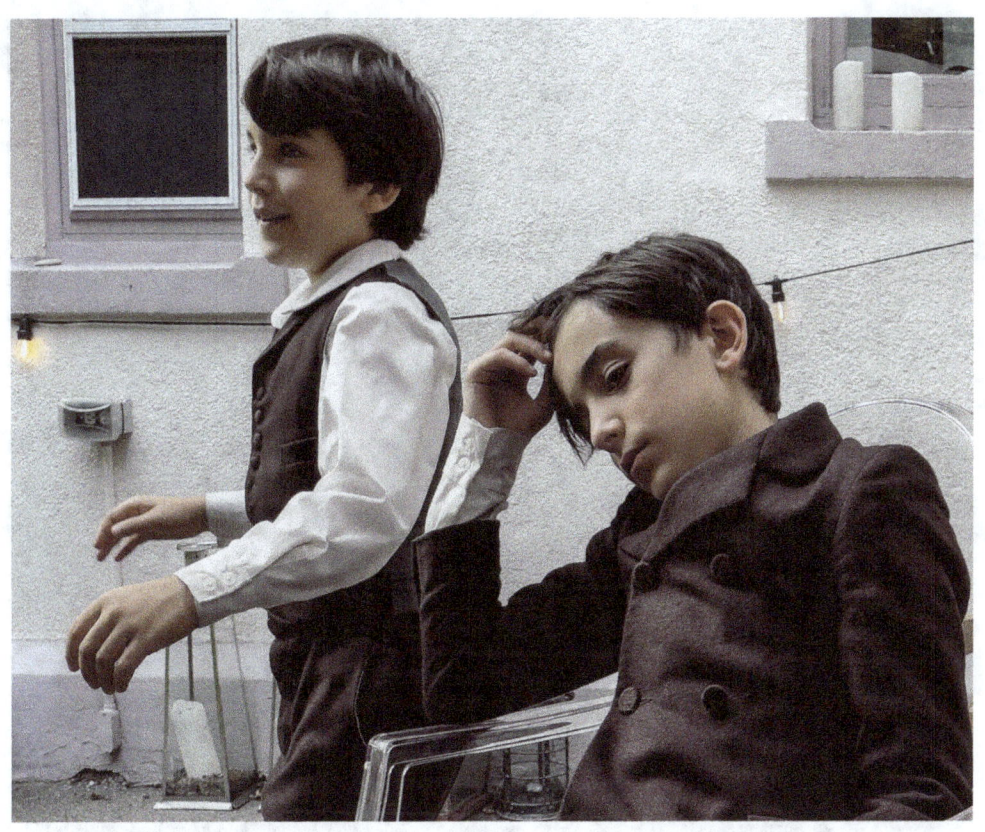

104. Michael and Samuel Caico (actors). Buffalo, New York, 2021.

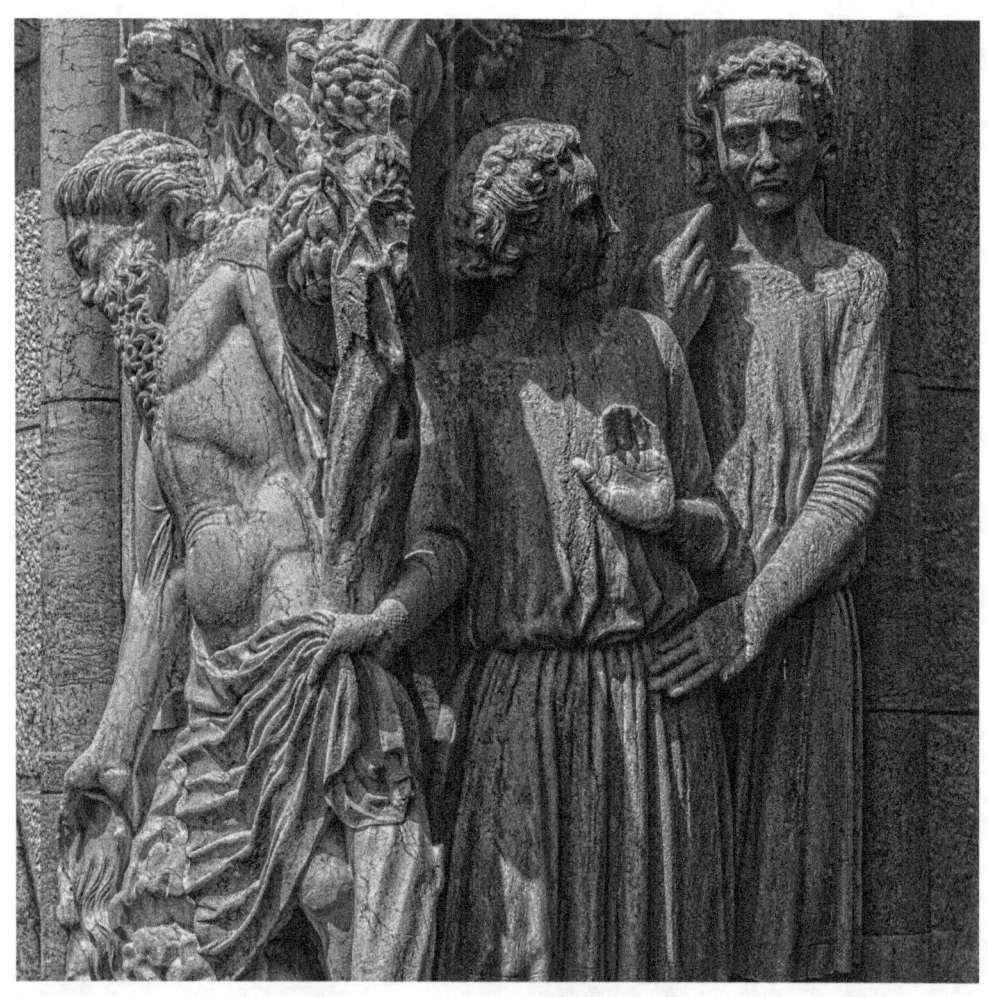

105. Sculpture. Palazzo Ducale, from Ponte della Paglia. Venice, Italy, 2016.

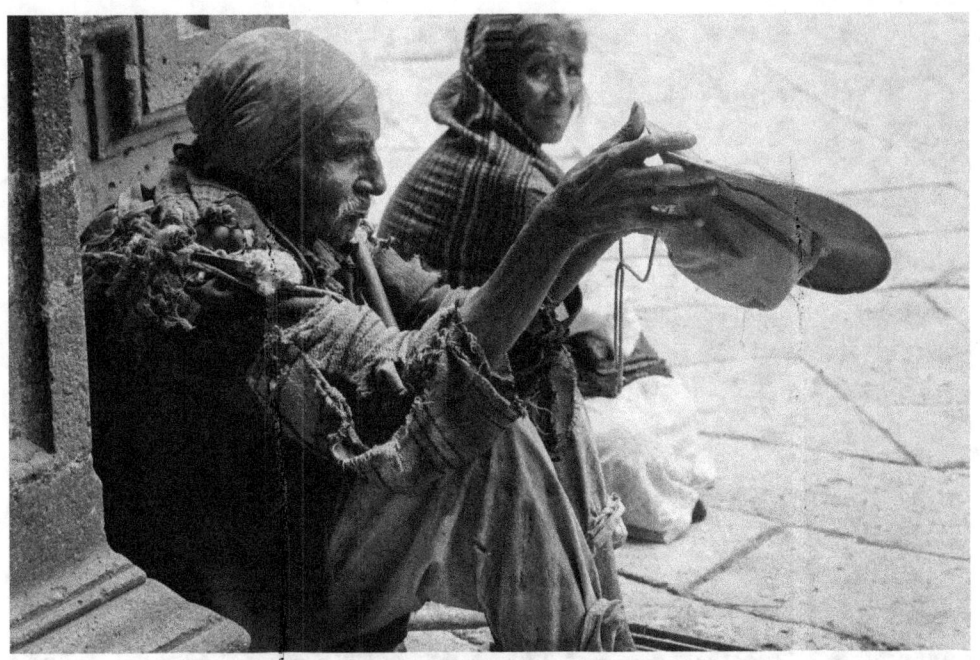

106. Beggars. Church steps. Taxco, Mexico, 1970.

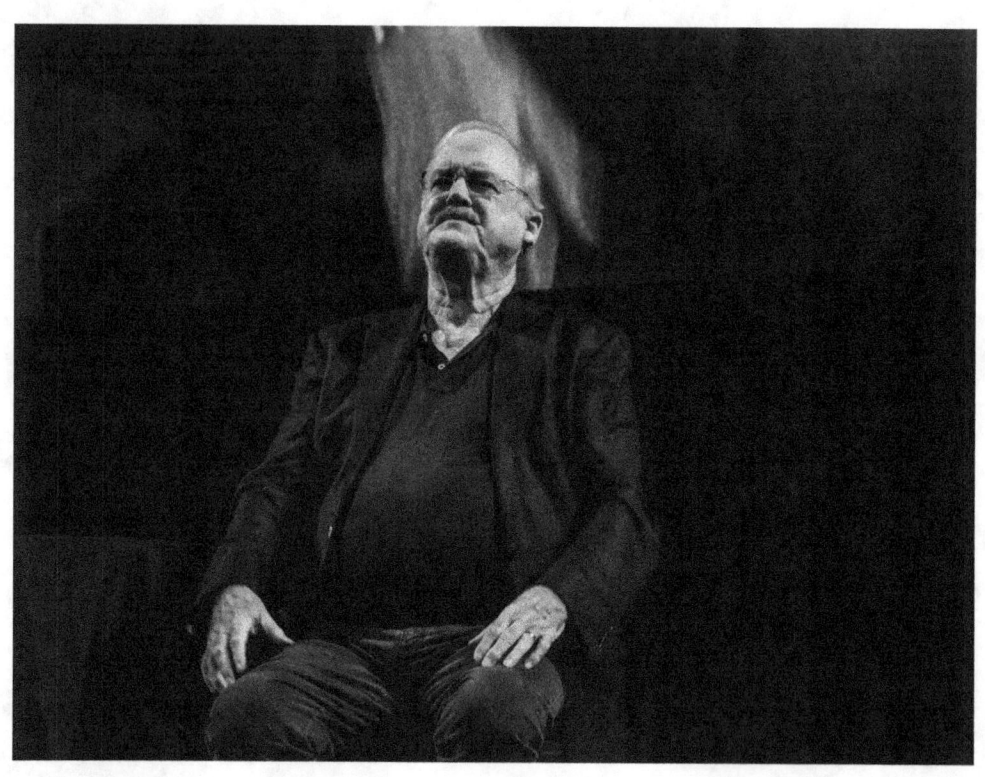

107. John Cleese (actor). Buffalo, New York, 2016.

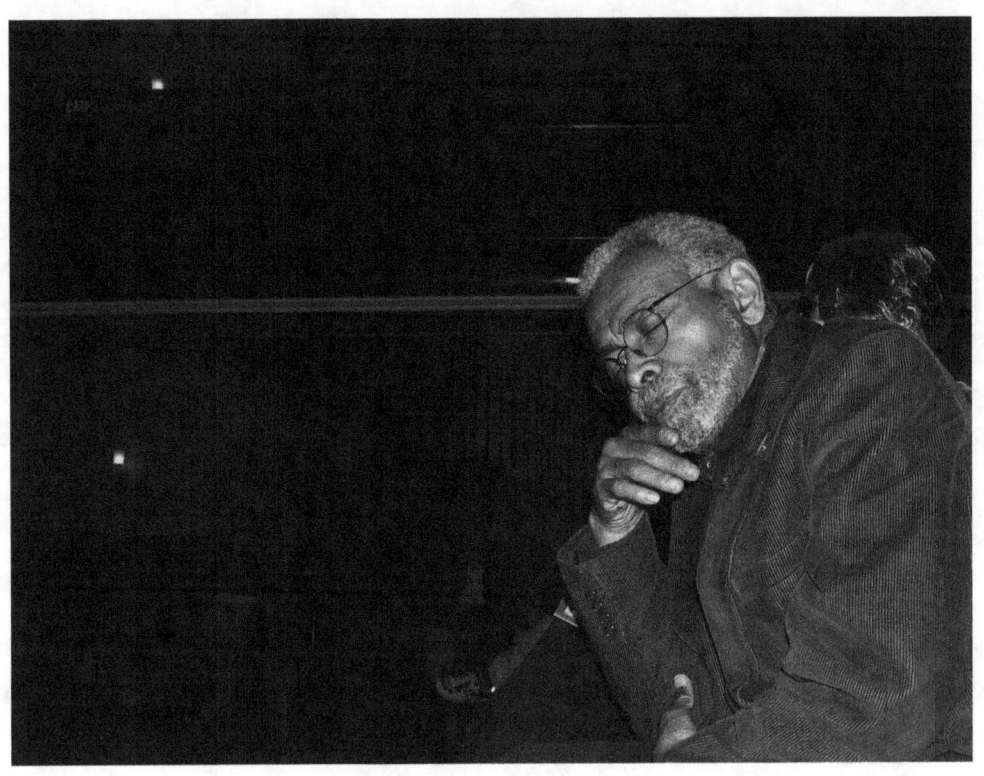

108. Amiri Baraka (writer). Buffalo, 2006.

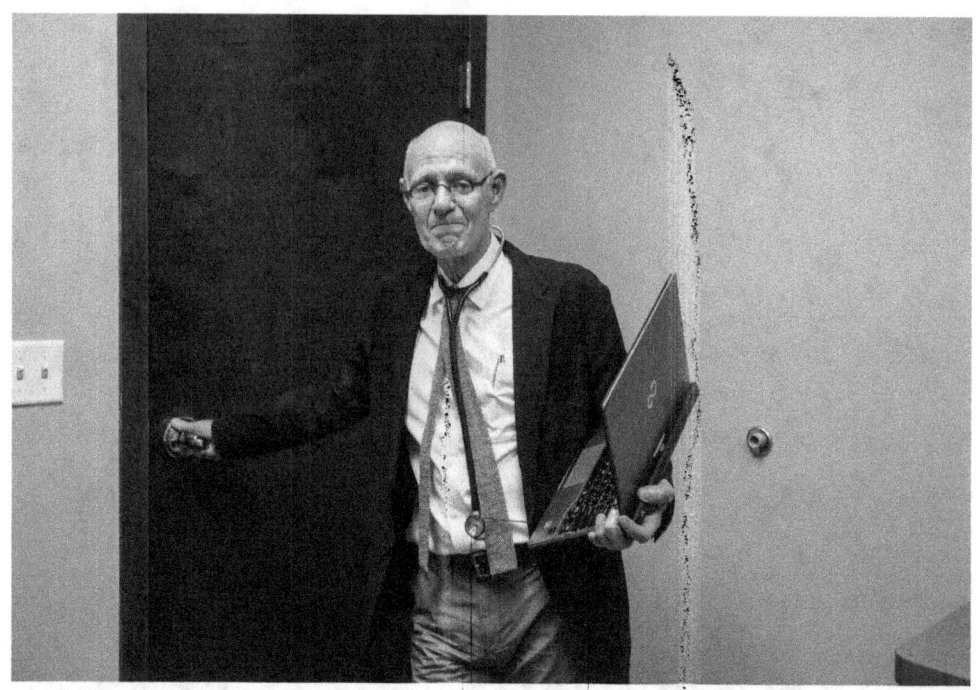

109. Howard Lippes, MD. Buffalo, New York, 2016.

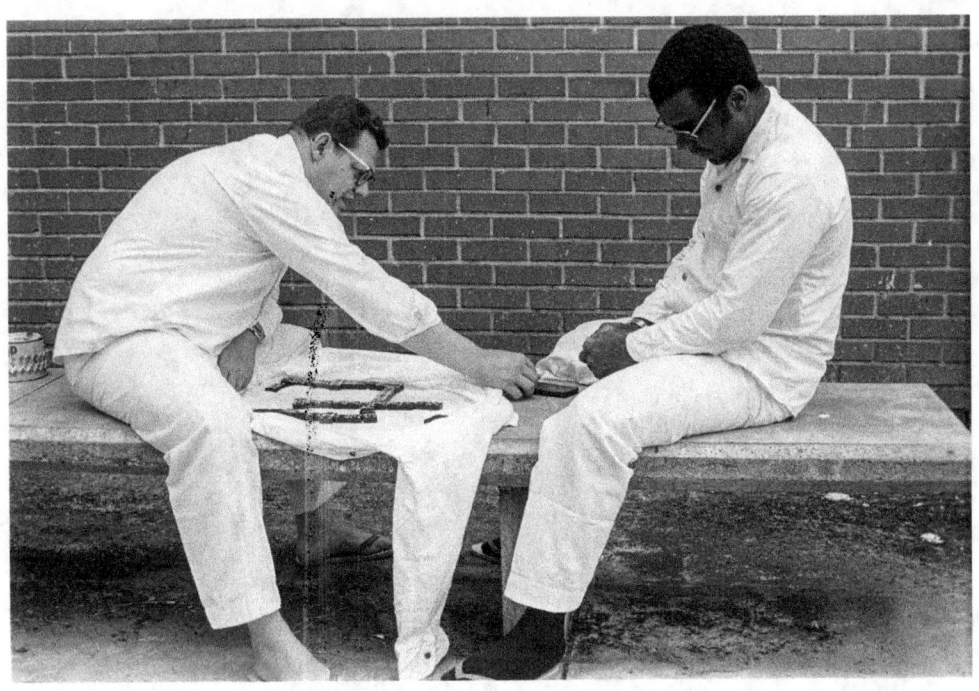

110. Ronald "Candyman" Clark O'Brian and Raymond Riles (condemned prisoners). Texas Death Row recreation yard, Ellis Prison Farm, Huntsville, Texas, 1979.

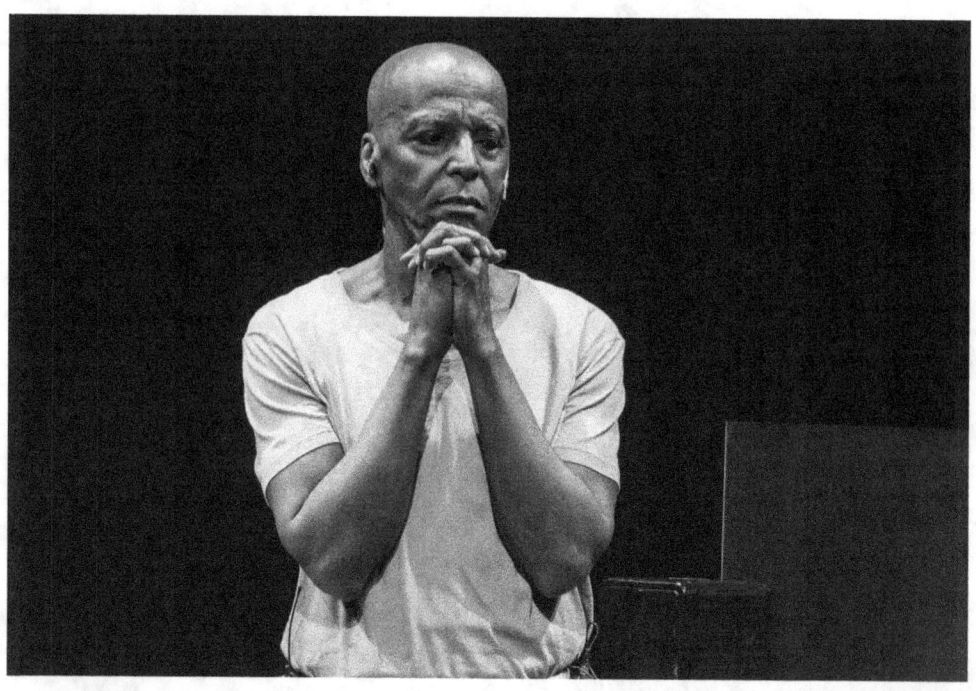

111. Jasper MacGruder (actor). Wooster Group rehearsal for *The B-Side*. Center for the Arts, University at Buffalo, Buffalo, New York, 2018.

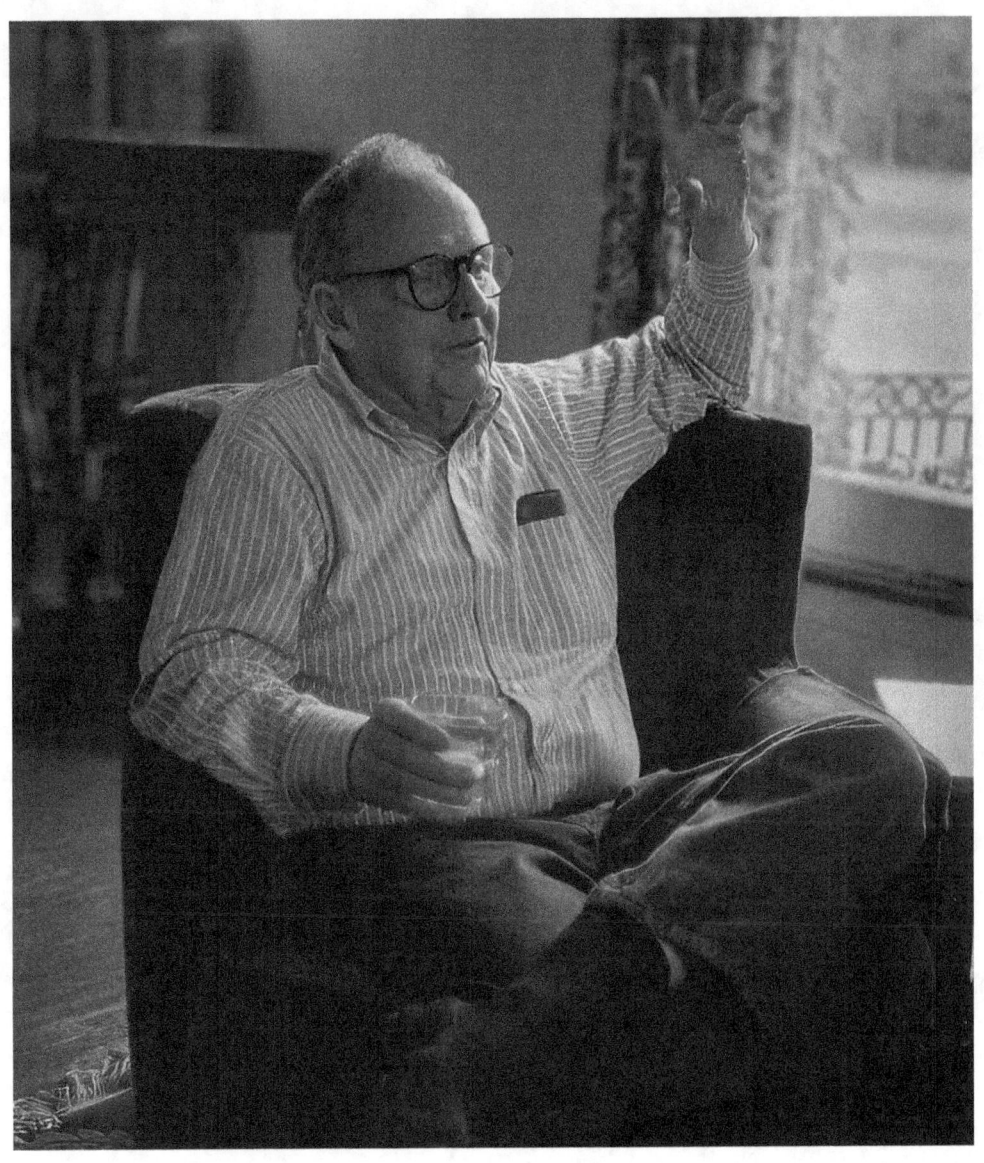

112. Emile de Antonio (filmmaker). Buffalo, 1988.

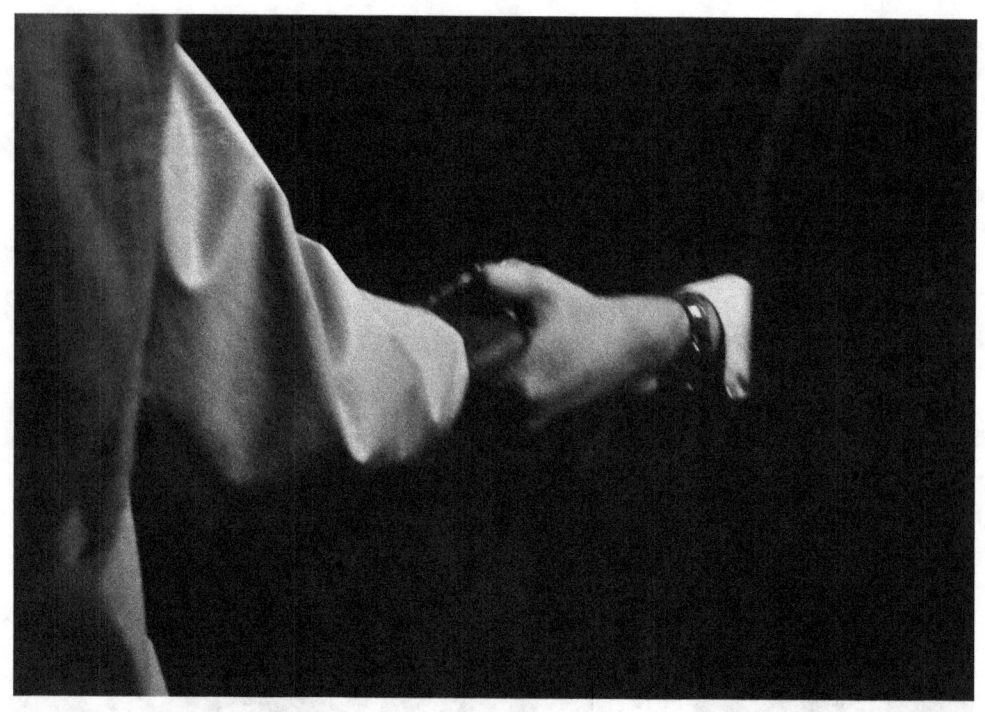

113. Two hands. First Resurrection City town meeting. Washington, DC, 1968.

Words 6

88. Roscoe Henderson III (police officer) and Toni Morrison (writer) backstage at Kleinhans Music Hall, Just Buffalo BABEL Series. Buffalo, New York, 2017.

Roscoe is a Buffalo cop. Sometimes I see him around town, driving his black-and-white. He loves the arts. He is on the board of the Albright-Knox Art Gallery. He would regularly bodyguard the Just Buffalo BABEL visitors. At first, I thought it was because he was helping Just Buffalo out. Then I realized that he loved the books. After every one of the readings, there was a book signing; people would line up for that, and all during it, Roscoe made sure that the author was secure. The last book signed every time was Roscoe's.

More people lined up for Morrison to sign their books than any other BABEL writer—about one thousand of them. "She was wonderful," Roscoe told me later. "She signed every book and chatted with everyone who came up to her." He mentioned two other writers in the series who had gotten tired and cut it off. "Not her," he said, "not her."

89. Roy "Bud" Johns (writer, publisher, and corporate executive). San Francisco, California, 2011.

After a long career as a newspaper reporter, Bud became director of corporate relations for Levi Straus & Co. While he had that job, with Levi's backing, he invented a sport: Ride and Tie. He also led Levi's engagement in the annual conferences held in Sun Valley by the Sun Valley Center for the Arts and Humanities and then the Institute of the American West. The first of those was in 1976. That's when Bud, his wife, Judith Spector Clancy, Diane, and I became friends. One of the things Bud and I bonded over was that we both had been stationed at the same Marine Corps air station, Cherry Point; he got out the year I went in—1953.

Judith died in 1990; Bud died in 2019. The Moses Soyer painting of a young ballet dancer over his left shoulder was the first piece of art he bought, and it remained his favorite until his death. The first time Judith came to his house, in 1971, she saw the painting and said, "That's my painting."

"Don't be silly," Bud said, "it's my painting. I've had it for years."

"It's mine," Judith said. "I'm the girl in the painting. I was Moses Soyer's model." They married soon afterward.

The last time I saw Bud, he said, "I have something for you." He wasn't doing well and we all (Bud, Diane, Frances Moreland, whom he married in 1992, and I) knew it was perhaps the last time we'd see one another. He got a bag from a closet and took out a Nikkormat camera with a well-brassed 50 millimeter lens.

"Eddie gave this to me just before he died," he said.

"Eddie" was photographer Eddie Adams, who won a Pulitzer in 1969 for his photo of Saigon police chief General Nguyễn Ngọc Loan shooting a Vietcong prisoner in the head. Eddie and Bud had been friends since they were stationed together at Cherry Point.

"It's one of his Vietnam lenses," Bud said. "I said, "Why are you giving it to me? I'm not a photographer." Eddie said, "You'll know what to do with it.""

Then Bud gave me Eddie Adams's 50 millimeter Vietnam lens.

90. Margaret Kunstler and Diane Christian. New York, New York, 2012.

I don't think there are more than one or two times since we became friends with Bill and Margaret during the 1975 Attica felony trials that we've visited New York City and stayed anywhere but with them. At first it was in an apartment they had on Grove Street. Then, for many years, it was their house on Gay Street, a wonderful one-way one-block-long street between Christopher and Waverly that got almost no traffic. It was a few blocks from Washington Square and near all the main subway lines. After Bill's death in 1995, Margaret rented out the Gay Street house and lived in smaller rentals. This was an apartment with a wonderful view high up in the Frank Gehry building near the World Trade Center. Then it was a condo in Red Hook in Brooklyn above the Fairway Market. A ferry to Wall Street had a pickup just a two-minute walk from her front door. It was a perfect location when we were down for rehearsals and performances with the Wooster Group at their base, the Performing Garage, on the lower East Side, very close to where my grandparents landed in 1890.

91. Kate Valk (actor and director) and Eric Berryman (actor and dramaturge). Wooster Group rehearsal for The B-Side. The Performing Garage, New York, New York, 2016.

92. Eric Berryman and Elizabeth LeCompte. Wooster Group rehearsal for The B-Side. Center for the Arts, University at Buffalo, Buffalo, New York, 2018.

This is a very New York story.

Eric Berryman, a twenty-eight-year-old actor, was a tea apprentice in SoHo, one of the jobs he was juggling until his acting career took off. This day in 2015, he overheard a conversation among some women at a table. They were talking about a Wooster Group play, *Early Shaker Spirituals: A Record Album Interpretation*. One of the women was the actress Kate Valk, who'd directed the play. Another was Francis McDormand, who is in it. Eric told them he had another old LP they might consider. He told Kate that he was in the middle of composing an email to her about exactly that.

The LP was an album of my recordings from my first visit to Texas prisons in 1964: *"Negro Folklore from Texas State Prisons."* It had been released in 1965. Eric, a vinyl fan, had come across it on a website. He'd bought it and had become ensorcelled by the work songs, blues, toasts, and recitations on it. He had sent me a few emails about parts of it he couldn't quite understand. Then we talked on the phone. And then he encountered Kate.

I was delighted with the conversations for several reasons. One was, it was great that this LP I'd recorded and edited a half-century ago had currency for this kid who was now my age when I'd done the recordings. Another was, Eric was the first person I'd encountered who realized that the 1965 Elektra album wasn't simply a collection of black performances from Texas prisons, but rather a coherent work with a structure.

Through much of 2016, we talked, we had meetings, there were rehearsals, and then on Wednesday, November 9, 2016 (the night after the election), Wooster put on the first of eight work-in-progress performances. The play then went to Taiwan and Korea. It opened in New York at the Performing Garage on October 25, 2017. The *New York Times* named it one of the ten best plays of the year, as did the *Washington Post.*

It's a three-actor play, with Eric in the lead, joined by Philip Moore and Jasper McGruder. Eric does a riff on how the play came about, then he, Philip and Jasper channel every track on the album, with Eric occasionally reading comments from my liner notes to the album or my book on the work songs, *Wake Up, Dead Man: Afro-American Worksongs from Texas Prisons* (1972). The material was recorded on Texas prison farms (some of them former slavery plantations) in 1964, but the performances and presentation are very much in the present. It's like being in two time zones at once.

The performances seem casual, almost conversational. They're not. Every word, every movement is considered and designed. Kate and Wooster guiding genius Elizabeth LeCompte tune and tweak the performances every time, in rehearsals and in what they call "Notes" before performances: things from the previous performance that might go this way or that, everything from where Eric puts down the teapot to the lighting and sound design. The phrase I heard most during rehearsals and Notes was, "Let's try it." Wooster is an environment of continual creation. Through it all, the three performers remain absolutely faithful to the original recordings: when one of them coughs, it's because someone on the original recording coughed.

It's been a delight for me. The lively academic department I joined in Buffalo in 1967, when I was thirty-one, was arguably the most avant-garde English department in the country; it now is neither. Wooster made me an associate member of the company 2017: at the age of eighty-one, I became a member of the most honored avant-garde theater company in the country. Sort of arriving where I started.

Wooster is now in rehearsal with a second play conceived and acted by Eric: *Untitled Toast*. This one is based on my 1974 book and companion LP, *Get Your Ass in the Water and Swim Like Me*. It was to have had its first public rehearsal performance at the University of Texas Arts Center in September 2021, but the resurgence of the Covid epidemic shut down just about all public performances of anything.

A New York story, as I said: it's not rags to riches—off-Broadway is artistically rewarding, but the pay isn't. But Eric has a bunch of glowing reviews in the *New York Times*, the *New Yorker*, the *Washington Post*, and elsewhere, and two plays with the Wooster Group. Sure beats serving tea in SoHo. And, for me, sure beats being part of an academic department in Buffalo that's long forgotten what made it interesting.

93. Will Creeley, Robert Creeley, and Penelope Creeley. Wilmington, North Carolina, 1984.

Bob Creeley was one of the reasons I came to Buffalo. The year I finished my Harvard Junior Fellowship, I had five job offers: Penn and UCLA said come and teach folklore; Alan Lomax, who had his Cantometrics project going at Columbia, said come and work with me; Lawrence Pierce, New York State Commissioner of Narcotics said come and be associate commissioner for communications (or something like that). Buffalo said: come and do whatever captures your interest; you'll be based in English, but you can teach in any department that wants you. Over the years, I've taught in Art, Media Study, Law, Architecture, Library Science, Sociology, and several other departments.

The main thing that drew me to Buffalo was the company: the English Department then was flush with writers: fiction, nonfiction, and poets. Some of them were hot in the moment; some of them had key connections to earlier times: Charles Olson, Lionel Abel, John Barth, Leslie Fiedler, Robert Creeley, and Dwight McDonald. For a young academic it was the promised land.

In those early Buffalo years, I'd see Bob Creeley only occasionally. He was often elsewhere, either on grants or in Bolinas. He had a deal: he taught a semester here and then he was on unpaid leave elsewhere.

We never really connected until we had a train wreck of a night together in fall 1972 or spring 1973. I'd come back from California and had moved in with Diane. She'd never encountered Creeley. He was one of the most famous people in our department. I said, "Let's invite him to dinner." Which we did. I was impressing her with our elder colleague.

Diane spent hours making something wonderful. It was totally wasted. Bob arrived three or four hours late, with a UB graduate student who had driven him from an event in Toronto, at which they had gotten drunk or which they had gotten drunk on the way from. The student deposited him and staggered away. At the table, Bob made a point by banging a crystal goblet against his skull. I said, "Stop that; it's going to break." He kept on, getting ever more enthusiastic. The goblet exploded. Then he got up, moved across the room, turned Diane's desk halfway over, and somehow landed on his feet. The desk and its contents were all over the room.

I don't remember how we got him out of the apartment. I do remember saying to Diane, "That motherfucker is never coming back to our place again."

So much for vows. Cut to three years later. Diane and I are in our present house. Bob calls. He's recently back from New Zealand; he met a woman there he really likes; she's here; might they come by for dinner?

They did. Bob and Pen were our first dinner guests in the Rumsey house. Since then, we watched one another's children grow up, hung out in various places, and attended funerals and weddings. Diane officiated at the wedding of Bob and Pen's daughter, Hannah. Pen was here last night and we told stories.

94. Skateboarder near Pier 11. New York, New York, 2016.

Diane and I were in New York for Wooster Group performances and meetings. After one of them, we were on our way to Margaret Kunstler's place in Red Hook, when, near the ferry that would take us to Red Hook from Wall Street, we came upon kids skateboarding under the FDR Drive. They'd get to the end of a raised rectangular concrete run, take to the air, and miraculously do a 180-degree turn, and continue.

95. Charles Neville (musician). Louisiana State Penitentiary (Angola), Tunica Trace, Angola, 2001.

I was invited to take part in a symposium on prison music, "Angola Bound," at the Louisiana State Prison. They were using some interview recordings I did in Cambridge with blues singer Robert Pete Williams years earlier, and I was on a panel with R&B and jazz musician Charles Neville, photographer Dick Waterman, NPR radio host Nick Spitzer ("American Routes"), and folklorist Kip Lornell. Charles and clarinetist Alvin Batiste gave illustrated musical talks, accompanied by drummer Herman Jackson and guitarist Harvey Knox.

During a lunch break, two convict bands performed outside. Nearly everybody at the symposium either stayed inside or under a tent off to the side, so the musicians played to a mostly empty parking lot. They didn't much care: they were having a good time playing. Charles, Batiste, and Knox joined in. One convict sax player had known Charles when he'd done three years there on a marijuana possession charge in the 1960s.

The black musicians performed first, then the white country band got angry: "When do *we* get to play?" one of them said. So Charles jammed with them for a while and then they all played together. I think it was the first time Angola's Black-and-white bands jammed as a single group.

After a while, everybody except the convict musicians went back inside to the symposium. Other than those musicians and the reporter from the prison newspaper, the *Angolite*, everyone in that parking lot was a free world visitor or a prison employee. Absent the ambiance, the event could have been held anywhere.

The talks at Angola were interesting, it was good seeing old friends Dick Waterman, Nick Spitzer, and Chris Strachwitz (Arhoolie Records), and the jamming in the parking lot at lunchtime was terrific. But the best part of the day for me was when I drove up early from Baton Rouge and met the others for breakfast at the St. Francisville Inn, and Charles and I wound up at a table together, telling each other stories for at least an hour.

We would have kept on, but the organizer of the program said, "We *have* to go to the prison now."

We kept saying, "In a minute," but she was persistent, so we got into cars and went off for the day at Angola prison farm. Charles and I promised to continue the conversation in Massachusetts, where he lived, Buffalo, or New Orleans, where he often performed and, with the other Neville Brothers, visited family. We exchanged emails now and then, but we never wound up at the same place at the same time. Charles died of pancreatic cancer in 2018.

96. Elders teaching traditional dance. Nome, Alaska, 1997.

For decades, the missionaries took the children to schools where they were forbidden to speak their own language or learn native ways. Now, elders teach a younger generation the words and dances that were denied to their parents.

97. Judith Spector Clancy (artist) and Diane Christian. San Francisco, California, 1977.

Judith, teenage model for Moses Soyer and wife of our friend Bud Johns, was a very good artist herself. Her drawings often appeared in the *New Yorker*, and she created a wonderful book, *Last Look at the Old Met* (1969). After her death, Bud curated several exhibits of her work, the last of them at the Corcoran in Washington, DC, after which he gave them her drawings and paintings except for a few, which he kept for himself and a few close friends. We have one of them.

Judith was what one of Diane's aunts called a "hairpin": she could fuss about anything to a point of distraction. The first time we stayed at their house on Sacramento Street, she showed me three times how to work the key in the front-door lock and at least three times how to keep hair from going down the shower drain. I think of her, and I immediately think of the wonderful Branford Marsalis album title, *I Heard You Twice the First Time.*

She could also be bitchy. At the 1978 Institute of the American West Conference in Sun Valley, the four of us were having lunch. She began talking about a wonderful art student who'd written her an appreciative letter. She pushed the letter across the table and smiled. But she was looking at Diane. I looked at the letter and recognized the handwriting immediately. It was from a woman I'd been friends with and had a brief involvement with before Diane.

"Ah," I said to Judith. To Diane, I said, "It's from Joan."

"Joan M?"

"Yes," Judith said.

"How is she?" Diane said. "Give her my best."

"You *know* about her?" Judith said.

"Sure," Diane said.

Judith took the letter back and shoved it into her bag. She was furious. She'd hoped to cause a row, or at least an embarrassing moment, and found out she was years too late.

I was even more furious. I spoke to her no more during that summer's conference. The next year, Bud said, "Will you please try to make up with Judith? I miss our hanging out."

I didn't want to, but I said, "Okay." Later that day, we encountered them coming across a small field. This time, I was the one who was bitchy. I said something I was sure would piss her off: "Judith, great to see you. And you brought your great tits with you."

Bud and Diane made eye contact with nobody. Judith, however, blushed, and burst into a smile and seemed delighted. The relationship picked up where it had been before the lunch with Joan's letter, with two differences. Judith and I were on a far friendlier basis than we'd ever been, and I realized I'd gotten two things wrong. The letter caper hadn't been directed at me: it was directed at Diane, because Bud was obviously very fond of her, and Judith didn't know how to deal with that. And Judith really liked me, and didn't know how to deal with that, either.

In 1992, when she was dying of pancreatic cancer, Judith went to Deauville in Normandy to paint. She'd started going there early in her career as an artist. During the years we knew Bud and Judith, she several times went off to paint in Deauville. She loved the light there, she said, it was like nowhere else. At the time, I thought it odd that she made that final trip when she knew she had only months to live, and I was puzzled at how comfortable Bud was with that trip. Why not stay in San Francisco, hang out with Bud, and tie up the loose ends. She was fifty-eight then and I was fifty-six. I'm eighty-five now and that final trip to visit the Normandy light makes a great deal of sense. Deauville for her was always a place of creative delight, of possibility, of a world without beginning or end. With only a few months left, fuck the loose ends. Someone else will tie them up, if they matter, which most don't.

98. Diane Christian. St.-Tropez, France, 1975.

The lavender dress Diane is wearing in this photo marks my most memorable trip to Europe.

The occasion was the publication by Plon of the French translation of my book *In the Life: Versions of the Criminal Experience* and an exhibit of my Arkansas prison photos at a gallery in Place Bastille. I've mentioned it several times in these notes.

Plon put us up in a small hotel on Place Saint-Sulpice, a short walk from their offices. The toilet was in the hall. The concierge referred to the room as a *"jolie chambre."* The room was so small, Diane and I could not both stand and dress or undress at the same time.

We met with Malaurie in his elegant eighteenth-century office at Écoles des hautes études en sciences sociales. Michel Foucault, who had written the introduction to the translation, came to the opening of the exhibit. The next night, he made dinner for us at his apartment on Rue Vaugirard. He arranged a visit for us to a French prison, Poissy. Diane wore an elegant Marimekko black-and-white pantsuit. She'd worn the same outfit once or twice when we'd been in Cummins prison in Arkansas the previous year. I never noticed the pattern until now, gathering and selecting these photos. She hadn't known when we'd packed for the trip that we'd spend a day at a French prison.

The day we left Paris, Diane bought a string bikini at a shop on Boulevard Saint-Germain. They were all the thing that year. We both thought it would be perfect for St.-Tropez, one of our planned stops on our drive to Rome.

Diane found one she liked. With string bikinis, there really wasn't much to like or not like: it was four triangular patches of cloth and strings. When she tried it on, the clerk put her hands together and said, "Ah, quelle belle poitrine."

I asked Diane what that meant. "Great tits," she said.

I loved the sound, rhyme and rhythm of the phrase. I kept saying it, "*Quelle belle poitrine. Quelle belle poitrine.*"

As we walked to where we were meeting Malaurie for lunch, I kept saying it to women we passed, young and old. "Quelle belle poitrine."

Diane was aghast. "You can't tell women that they have great tits."

"That's not what I'm saying," I said. "I'm saying *quelle belle poitrine.*" No one seemed to mind; everyone I said it to responded with a smile, some with a nod or wink. I'd get punched or jailed for that now.

When we told Malaurie we were driving to Rome, he said, "Then you must visit Vézelay. It has the most exquisite abbey in Europe, and there is a superb two-star restaurant next to it." Neither of us had ever heard of Vézelay. Malaurie was right on both counts. It was so beautiful I stood in the chairless, pewless nave and burst into tears.

We continued south. We decided to overnight in Lyon, France's silk city. Some of the hotels, the guidebook said, had silk sheets. "I've always wanted to have sex on silk sheets," Diane said.

We went to one of hotels a guidebook suggested. The concierge was turning away two Americans, saying the hotel was full. The two Americans left. Diane asked, in French, if she could suggest another hotel.

The concierge responded, in French, "We have a room. You can stay here."

We signed in and she gave us the key. Diane said, "Do you need to see our passports?"

"You're not French?" the concierge said. She looked at the American passports in Diane's hand and the smile evaporated. But we already had the key. The room had silk sheets.

"All we need now is bubble bath and champagne," I said. The bathroom had a large supply of bubble bath. I went out and got the champagne.

The next day we visited the Palace of the Popes in Avignon. A guide told us, in English, that it was too bad we hadn't come earlier; there had been a magnificent exhibit of late Picasso. He showed us a small door that would be an easier way back to the street. We stepped into a huge room, a basketball court on steroids. The walls were covered with hundreds of Picasso paintings and ceramics. The guide had meant to say it was fortunate we were there because the exhibit had been extended. It was like going through a door expecting to be pelted by rain only to find yourself bathed in sunlight.

From there we went to St.-Tropez. It was the only hotel in St.-Tropez with its own beach. The beach was perhaps fifteen paces from the door to our room. Diane put on the string bikini. And found herself incapable of leaving the room. "I can't go out there like this," she said. "I'm almost naked."

"We're in St.-Tropez," I said.

"You go out and find us a good place," she said. "I'll be out in a while."

I did just that. A long time later, Diane came out of the room. She was wearing a robe. She spotted me, came to where I was, took off the robe and sat down. She was stiffer than I'd ever seen her. She was looking at no one and nothing. It was like she was willing herself invisible.

"Look around," I said.

It was a topless beach. None of the women there, not even the very old ones, was wearing a top. Diane relaxed immediately. "So, I'm overdressed. That's my story: I finally get somewhere and everyone's already moved on."

That afternoon, walking along the quay, we spotted that lavender dress in a shop window. Diane wore it to dinner on the hotel patio that evening. This photo was just before we went to our table. Around us, were all the couples we'd seen on the beach that morning, fully clothed, as proper as could be.

After that, a drive along the coast then a turn north at Cannes for the visit with Legman. They invited us to stay overnight but we couldn't take any more, so we pushed on through Monte Carlo into Italy. We spent the night in a profoundly ugly Jolly Hotel in La Spezia. Early next morning, we drove to Florence.

Florence wasn't anything like it is now. There was no smog. The streets, bridges, and galleries weren't shoulder-to-shoulder tourists taking selfies. Diane knows far more about classical art than I, so I got wonderful tutorials as we walked through the galleries of the Uffizi and the Palazzo Pitti.

When we'd checked in to our hotel, which was located on the Arno between Ponte S. Trinita and Ponte All Carraia, I asked the concierge where I could park. "Anywhere on that side of the street," he said, pointing outside.

That day, the Communists won a regional election. The results came in about 10:00 p.m. For about two hours, a parade of three or four cars with honking horns and one huge red flag ran a circuit: they crossed Ponte S. Trinita, turned right onto Lungarno Guicciardini, turned right onto Ponte Alla Carraia, right again onto Lungarno Corsini, then began all over again with another right onto Pont S. Trinita. The entire time, a single police car pursued them, his version of a siren making noise and his blue light flashing. He chased them, but he assiduously managed never to catch them: when they were on one side of the Arno, he was always on the other side; when they crossed Ponte Alla Carraia, he was crossing Point S. Trinita. We sat on our balcony with a bottle of wine, watching it like a slapstick movie.

In the morning, our car was gone. Most of our luggage was in it. We went to the concierge in a panic. "Our car's been stolen."

He was calm. "Don't worry. The police probably stole it." We asked why they would do that. "Because it is not permitted to park on that street after midnight."

"You told us to park there! There are no parking signs there!"

He shrugged. "It doesn't need signs. Everybody knows you can't park there after midnight." He called for someone in the back to watch the desk. "I know where they hide them." He drove to what seemed a large public park. Cars were scattered everywhere. Not ours. He drove to another. Ours was there, next to a large tree. It had a parking ticket under the wiper. It said we owed Florence a hefty fine for the illegal parking and towing. The ticket said that if the car was rented, the Italian government would see that the fine was added to the rental fee. When we checked out, I gave the concierge our room key and the ticket. "These are both yours," I said. The fine never turned up on my Hertz bill.

Then on to Rome, where we stayed in a lovely hotel in Piazza Navona. We did the tourist things, then wound down and went back home.

When I was working on this book, I said to Diane, "I wonder whatever happened to that gorgeous lavender dress we got in St.-Tropez." She pointed to the middle drawer of a five-drawer cabinet in our bathroom. "It's in that drawer," she said.

99. David Felder (composer). Buffalo, New York, 2015.

David is an internationally known composer. He runs June in Buffalo, one of the major venues for new music. For years he and I, individually and jointly, ragged the University at Buffalo presidents and provosts about the declining number of creative artists on the faculty. In 2016, the provost asked us to come to a meeting. We went, and we delivered our usual jeremiad. When we were done, some people at the table were looking at us oddly.

One said, "Isn't the million dollars we just gave you enough to calm you down?"

"What million dollars?" David and I both said.

"The one in the memo." Someone held up a memo, waved it at us, then looked at it. "We forgot to copy David and Bruce on this," he said.

So, we set up the Creative Arts Initiative which, for four years, brought a lot of arts action to campus and to town. It was great fun and it resulted in a lot of great work, then a dean got wind of what we were up to and subsequent funding was deflected to a PR program.

100. Julia Jackson. Edison, New Jersey, 1972.

She was fiercely independent her entire life, which I didn't understand until very recently. I remember the last four things she said to me as she was dying.

The first was in response to my comment to Diane that, when I was young, she and my father spoke to one another in Yiddish so I wouldn't know what they were saying. "I didn't know Yiddish," she said. "Only your father knew Yiddish."

The second was, "Brucie, you know I don't get any pleasure out of pleasure." The third, as I was trying to get her to keep the oxygen feeds in place, was "Who invited you here?"

The fourth I'll never tell anyone.

101. Edna O'Brien in Just Buffalo's BABEL series, backstage at Kleinhans Music Hall. Buffalo, New York, 2017.

Her first three novels—*The Country Girls* (1960), *The Lonely Girl* (1962), and *Girls in Their Married Bliss* (1964)—were banned and burned in Ireland. Her home country wasn't ready to read about women's sexual concerns, desires, and frustrations. She is now considered Ireland's greatest living writer.

102. Jessica Jackson. Buffalo, New York, 1973.

Diane made that dress for Jessica, and a matching one for Rachel, in spring 1973, not long after I got back from California. Jessie is sitting in my father's rocker. Early in my first marriage in 1958, my parents said, "Anything you want for your new apartment, let us know."

"I'd like that rocker," I said.

"Anything but that rocker," my father said. "It was my father's. I got it when he died. You get it when I die."

When he died, my mother gave me the rocker.

103. Sarah and Emily Kunstler. Red Hook, Brooklyn, New York, 2015.

We've known Sarah and Emily since each was in utero. Both have children now. They've continued their parents' tradition of engaged, concerned political work. Sarah is a lawyer; she went to Columbia, same law school as Margaret and Bill. She and Emily make documentary films about political issues that light them up. Their most recent film, *Who We Are: A Chronicle of Racism in America*, which is based on the work of Jeffery Robinson, was featured at the 2021 SXSW Film Festival and is now being distributed by Sony.

104. Michael and Samuel Caico (actors). Buffalo, New York, 2021.

At 11:45 a.m., May 23, 2020, my grandson Sam, then nine, sent me a text message: "Hi bruce I would like to become a child actor. And I would like some help. Please."

I responded, "I have to give this some thought."

He replied immediately: "Ok."

At 8:46 p.m., I sent him this,

Here's what I think: Most people who try to be child actors don't get anywhere. There just aren't that many parts. And it's really a full-time job, for them and their parents. More important, it's got a built-in shutoff. Become a teenager and it's over. I can think of very few child actors who went on to become young adult actors, let alone career actors. The rest fell away. Why don't you think about being a film MAKER. That's a job you never outgrow. It's one you can get better and better at. Something else: actors are always dependent on other people's agendas: if nobody is producing a play or movie needing a 10-year-old kid, 10-year-old kids get no work. Filmmakers decide what they want to do and they do that. Give that some thought. We can talk about this.

He responded at 8:32 a.m., on June 3, three days later: "Ok."

Cut to a year later. Producer Jonathan Sanger (*Elephant Man, Vanilla Sky, Frances, Marshall*) decides to shoot a film about Mother Cabrini (directed by Alejandro

Monteverde) in Buffalo, because his shooting experience here during *Marshall* went so well. They build a shantytown like New York's Five Points in the late 1800s, and shoot there for several weeks. They shot in a few Buffalo mansions; an office building serves as New York City's City Hall; a hotel that was a hospital (the Hotel Henry, built in a former mental institution designed by Henry H. Richardson) serves as a hospital that used to be a hotel. And, for the Central Park scenes, they shot in the Olmsted Park across the street from our house.

The film hires 3,000 thousand extras, among them, 200 children to play orphans. Samuel gets a few days' work as one of the extras; his brother, Michael, who has blue eyes, gets none. Sam's few days expand, and expand again. He gets a speaking line, so his pay goes from $200 per day to $1,000. Michael accompanies him to the fittings. The dressers fit Michael with orphan clothes. He is in a few scenes. He is pulled into more and more scenes. Samuel and Michael wind up as two of the ten key orphans in this $35 million film about a nun and orphans. They even have singing parts, though their voices will be overdubbed by a professional choir in Italy.

This photo was one of the nights they were shooting in the Park. They stopped by here to hang out and get into costume.

I said to Sam, "So there's something important you learned here."

"What?" he said.

"When you want to do something, get all the good advice you can, and then just go do what you want."

"I've got what it takes, Bruce."

"Have you learned anything else?"

"Yes. To make movies, you need a lot of patience."

105. Sculpture. Palazzo Ducale, from Ponte della Paglia. Venice, Italy, 2016.

I stood in the middle of Ponte della Paglia on the Riva degli Schiavoni, and photographed this wonderful mélange of hands at the southeast corner of the Palazzo Ducale, then I leaned over the parapet to get a good shot of the Ponte dei Sospiri, the Bridge of Sighs, maybe fifty meters away along Rio de Palazzo. The bridge is only a few paces from the eastern entrance to Piazza San Marco, so it was, as almost always in the daylight hours, crowded.

While I concentrated on that legendary bridge of death, local pickpockets were concentrating on my wallet, which I had, foolishly, placed in my hip pocket. When we went to the Carabarini station to report the theft, the officer politely took the report and told me not to worry. "This happens all the time at that place. They just take the money and throw the wallet away."

106. Beggars. Church steps. Taxco, Mexico, 1970.

107. John Cleese (actor). Buffalo, New York, 2016.

He was performing in the University at Buffalo Distinguished Speakers Series. He sat in a chair and, for an hour or so, told hilarious and poignant stories about being young in England, being at university, and being one of the Monty Pythons.

But there was a glitch: the larger performance space in the University's Center for the Arts had been booked earlier for something that could be neither canceled nor moved. He had to perform in a room with half as many seats. "No problem," he said. "I'll do it twice."

And so he did, with not very much time between. The same hilarious and poignant stories, the same irony, range, nostalgia, and humor.

I realized the obvious: we hadn't been listening to and watching John Cleese talk. We had been listening to and watching John Cleese as he performed a character named John Cleese, one who told stories belonging to the nonperforming John Cleese. It was a dazzling thing see.

But—other than the proximity of his two performances—how much of what he did differs from what all of us who tell and retell family and personal experience stories do? The stories that, at family events, begin, "And remember the time . . ." Or, when someone new joins the table, gets to hear it afresh—but everyone else is hearing it again, maybe changed a bit to fit this occasion or because a detail was lost or remembered or slipped in from another story, but the same story, one more time.

What John Cleese did that day in the smaller theater at UB's Center for the Arts was terrific, and one reason it was terrific was because it was a consciously done narrative event of a kind the rest of us do all the time.

108. Amiri Baraka (writer). Buffalo, 2006.

Baraka was here for a May 20 memorial celebrating what would have been, the next day, the eightieth birthday of Robert Creeley, who had died March 30, 2005. The other poets on the program were Joanne Kyger and Tom Raworth. The program was organized by Hallwalls, a Buffalo arts group. When it was over, Ed Cardoni, director of Hallwalls, said to us, "Amiri didn't have time to eat before the program. It's too late for any of the decent restaurants. Any chance you and Diane could . . ."

"Sure," Diane said. "Bring him over and we'll put something together."

We took off to see what we had that could work. By the time they arrived thirty minutes or so later, the spread was ready. It was Baraka, Tom, Ed, a few other people I knew, and a young woman I hadn't met previously.

The conversation was like the small-reception-after-talk/performance conversations I've attended for decades. The guest listens to various riffs, responds to some, but knows that in a short time he or she will go back to the hotel or to the airport, never to meet or see most of those people again.

Baraka looked at me and said, "That's *Kind of Blue* you've got on. Too bad you don't have the vinyl. I wrote the liners for the vinyl. They're not in the CD."

"You're listening to the vinyl," I said.

He turned around and saw the record player on a shelf behind him.

I liked him, so I went upstairs to my study, got a copy of *Get Your Ass in the Water and Swim Like Me*, signed it to him, then went back down and handed him the book.

He took the book a moment, then handed it back. "I have that book," he said. "It's a good book. Rap comes out of those poems."

"Is your copy signed?" I said.

He looked at me oddly, took the book back, then said, "*You* wrote this book?"

"Yes."

In an instant, his entire relationship to the room changed. Instead of being a famous visiting writer putting up with the usual make-nice hour, he was part of the room. And Diane and I, instead of being professors with a big fancy house, were people he wanted to talk to. It turned out to be a great postevent evening.

As everyone was leaving, I asked the young woman what her connection to Creeley, Hallwalls, or the performers was.

"None," she said, smiling brightly. "I saw them leaving and getting into cars, so I got into one of the cars, too. I thought it would be interesting. Thanks for dinner."

109. Howard Lippes, MD. Buffalo, New York, 2016.

Howard is our Primary (as they say) and a dear friend. At one summer party, he walked from our dining room to our kitchen. Midway, in the pantry, he went down and out. When he came to, he said, "It's nothing. Just a syncope." *Syncope* is a physician's word for passing out. The word describes what happened but tells you nothing about what caused it. It is like saying, "There is a fire." Six other physicians who were at the party came into the pantry, whereupon they and Howard discussed what had happened. They agreed it was just a syncope and of no interest. I thought they were all nuts, but how can you argue with two endocrinologists, a cardiologist, a pediatrician, an oncologist, a vascular surgeon, and a general surgeon?

For years, Howard gently urged me to lose weight. I'd developed sleep apnea and type 2 diabetes. He would say, "Diabetes is really a lousy way to die," then we'd talk about where we'd been since our last encounter. Then, maybe fifteen years ago, I lost eighty-five pounds. The apnea and type 2 diabetes went away. Now, he says I'm one of the few people he knows who took the weight off and kept it off, then we talk about where we've been since our last encounter. His most recent trip was to Machu Picchu. That was before Covid.

Each time I go to my annual physical, he taps on the door, comes in with his laptop that has on it all my recent chemistry reports. A bit of blood, a bit of urine and they know almost everything going on in the soft parts of your body. Each time, since I lost the weight, he looks at the screen, smiles, and tells me they're all perfect. And, each time I wonder if this will be the time he doesn't smile and says something else.

110. Ronald "Candyman" Clark O'Brian and Raymond Riles (condemned prisoners). Texas Death Row recreation yard, Ellis Prison Farm, Huntsville, Texas, 1979.

O'Brian was, on the Row, known as "Candyman," because he poisoned his eight-year-old son with cyanide during Halloween 1974; he did it for the insurance money. He was executed in 1984. Riles lived on Death Row until 2021, when a court reversed his 1974 sentence and sent his case back down for resentencing. It took the courts forty-seven years to decide he should not have spent any of that time in solitary confinement on Death Row, fending off one execution date after another.

111. Jasper MacGruder (actor). Wooster Group rehearsal for The B-Side. Center for the Arts, University at Buffalo, Buffalo, New York, 2018.

112. Emile de Antonio (filmmaker). Buffalo, 1988.

Diane and I organized a symposium at the university, "Editing Reality." We invited some old friends: filmmaker Frederick Wiseman, sociologist Howard Becker, and historian Lawrence Levine. Our UB colleague Dennis Tedlock recommended Dan Rose, an ethnographer doing interesting work.

Bill Sloan, who ran the Circulating Film Library and documentary exhibition program at the Museum of Modern Art (MoMA), suggested filmmaker Emile de Antonio. Bill had shown two of our films at MoMA—*Death Row* and *Out of Order*.

We'd had conversations about documentary issues and, when we told him about the symposium, he immediately saw how de Antonio would fit. Jim Card suggested we invite Leni Reifenstahl (best known for her documentary of the 1934 Nazi Party rally in Nuremburg, *Triumph of the Will*). He'd gotten her to come to the first Telluride Film Festival in 1974. "She's fascinating and she'll spice things up." Bill and Jim made the connections.

Everyone we invited had produced books or films or other works based on fieldwork or on the fieldwork of other people. We asked each presenter: What happens between the decision to document something in the world and the release or distribution of the documentary object created for people who were not there—the book, the film, the report, the article, the radio or TV program, the LP (this was before CDs) or audiotape? How do you go about editing reality?

We had a great cast, a great topic, but just about everything that might have gone wrong did. The symposium could have been a comic academic novel written by Kingsley Amis.

At first Leni Riefenstahl said she would come to Buffalo, then wrote to say she couldn't. The date coincided with when she was doing an underwater film in the South Pacific. (She was then eighty-six.) Every email, letter, or postcard we sent her was from the two of us, sometimes "Bruce and Diane," sometimes "Diane and Bruce." All of her letters and postcards were to "Dear Bruce." She sent copies of two of her books—*People of Kau* and *Schönheit im Olympischen Kampf*—both with inscriptions beginning "For Bruce Jackson." She just subtracted Diane.

We began a phone and mail conversation with de Antonio. De (as he preferred to be addressed) was, at the time, America's most influential American political documentary filmmaker. He'd made ten films, nine of them about the Cold War. Three of those political documentaries are classics: *Point of Order* (1963), about the 1954 Army-McCarthy hearings; *In the Year of the Pig* (1968), the first important film to question and put into historical perspective America's involvement in Vietnam; and *Millhouse: A White Comedy* (1971), his hilarious examination of the career and character of Richard M. Nixon that seemed prescient several years later when Nixon's presidency disintegrated. He was also a close friend of, and important influence on, Andy Warhol.

Frederick Wiseman was and continues to be the consummate silent looker; he's the *Grey's Anatomy* of the last third of the 20th century in America and the first part of this one. Since *Titicut Follies* in 1967, he has made forty-seven films. A century hence, anyone wanting to know what key American institutions were like in the decades Fred worked, could do no better than watch every film he's made.

Diane and I were particularly excited about having the two of them in the same program. They were two of America's best-known and most-respected documentary filmmakers. Their styles and subjects were totally different. Wiseman immerses himself in an institution, shoots an enormous amount of film, then goes back to his studio and spends up to a year finding and forming the story in it. De Antonio would start with a political idea, then spend a huge amount of time doing archival or archeological work (finding film, photographs, audio recordings, and documents) and sometimes conducting interviews. Both relied entirely on the stuff of the world: Wiseman shot his film and de Antonio (mostly) found his shots. Neither used those ponderous and didactic narrators' voices and oleaginous musical tracks that provide the structure for most television documentaries. They wove their stories with the footage itself. We thought it would be great to bring them together in the public sessions and in the dinners and receptions we planned for the participants.

For Diane and me, each of their very different approaches to and uses of the documentary medium was equally valid. The films of Emile de Antonio and Frederick Wiseman were no more in competition than fish and squirrels were in competition.

Easy enough for us to say. From their points of view it wasn't a matter of competition, it was a matter of ontological legitimacy and personal style—and it turned out the two despised one another. We found this out from de Antonio shortly after he arrived Friday afternoon. He said he was really happy to be in Buffalo but he wasn't the least bit happy about being on a program with Frederick Wiseman. "He hates me," de Antonio said, "and he hates my work." He, Diane, and I talked in our kitchen for a few hours, then we moved to the living room. A dozen of our students and friends, as well as journalists had arrived to meet with him. He began holding court immediately. He was a great storyteller, so I began recording. I asked one student to tend to the cassette recorder: when it reached the end of the first side (45 minutes), turn the tape over and record on the second side. No problem, he said. Except one: he turned the tape over twice, thereby erasing the first forty-five minutes of De's riff, the sober part.

De had said to Diane, before we went to join the students, that he was on the wagon, so he would have no alcohol that night. Maybe ten minutes in, he beckoned her over, "A little Bombay on ice, please."

"But you said . . ."

"A little Bombay on ice—" He shrugged: "Nothing."

By the end of the evening, he had knocked off most of the bottle and was utterly drunk.

He was at his hotel by the time Fred arrived. Fred told us he disliked De profoundly. De had referred to his films as "a watery stew," for which he could not be forgiven.

The next morning, De arrived at the symposium room, not seeming at all hungover. He said he remembered our request that he sit on his Wiseman animus. I introduced the panel: Diane was first, then de Antonio, then Wiseman. In her talk, Diane said good things about the work done by both of them.

The title of de Antonio's talk was "Finding a New Form in Content," but that's all it was: a title. Many of the things he said were what the comic Lenny Bruce called "bits"—routines or riffs he'd done before and would do again. Some of them he'd said in our house the previous day, some he would say to our son Michael the next day on the road to Oneonta, some he'd said in other public and private events just like these. He began by telling the audience, "I never prepare. I like, in a sense, to be exposed to you, and I also solicit your interruptions as I speak," after which he rambled around some of his favorite subjects and anecdotes, then fielded questions. When he was done, I introduced Wiseman.

If you liked de Antonio, he was a man with interesting friends who figured in his professional life in interesting ways. If you didn't like him, he was a name-dropper who bragged about being close to the rich and famous. Wiseman didn't like de Antonio one bit. So Wiseman prefaced his presentation with a brief and brutal straight-faced parody of the remarks de Antonio had just made. He captured de Antonio's intonations and posture perfectly. I'd never known what a good mimic Wiseman was. This is what Wiseman said.

> I want to tell you a little bit about the origin of this short paper I'm going to read. I was sitting around one evening having a shrimp and drink with my friends Rupert Murdoch and John Wayne, and Rupert asked me to write an article for one of his English tabloids. So I did this little piece and it's very short and afterward I'll be glad to answer any questions or talk about any aspects of documentary filmmaking.

Then, without skipping a beat, Fred went into his own talk. De Antonio sat there, next to him, controlling his face. There was no Q&A because the session had gone on too long and it was time to break for lunch. Both took part in the Q&A following the afternoon presentations. Indeed, both asked critical questions of the same presenter, pointing to the presenter's inconsistency and self-indulgence. Ordinarily, two major figures in the same field homing in on the same errant performance by a third person would exchange looks and nods of agreement. So far as I could tell, neither de Antonio nor Wiseman ever included the other in his field of vision.

Barbara Tedlock, Dennis's wife and a UB anthropologist, was the final speaker in the day's second session. Like everyone else, she had a twenty-five-minute slot. She read for a full hour from a recent autobiographical book. She never looked up; she ignored suggestions that she cut it short. She went on and on and on. In the few minutes available for discussion, Fred said something like, "Did you know this conference is about *editing* reality?" She glowered at him, but said nothing.

We had a dinner at our house that night for all the participants in the symposium. We sent a graduate student to pick up de Antonio but he wouldn't get in her car. He told her that he would just order in because if he came to the house he'd surely get into a big fight with Wiseman and he didn't want to spoil the party. I phoned him and urged him to come anyway. "Come and get into a fight with Fred if you like," I said, "nobody will mind."

He said no, he was tired, he looked forward to the ride to Oneonta with Michael the next morning: they'd spend the five hours talking about politics, film, and Michael's clerking for civil rights attorney William Kunstler. He, Diane, and I would talk on the phone, he said. When we next got to NYC, we'd get together and talk into the night about everything.

The second panel of the second day was Dennis Tedlock, Dan Rose, and me. Dan began his talk by insisting that there was no such thing as reality, that "reality" was just a construct. I knew the place of that conceit in recent discourse, but I also know that the man who receives a bullet in his brain experiences an irreversible event that everyone who saw it would insist was real. Rose was standing at a lectern, and I sat at a table to his right while he was saying these things. I got more and more annoyed with the way he seemed to be dismissing the premise of our symposium without even suggesting that it was at least a discussible notion. The nonexistence of reality was, he said, a given. I couldn't interrupt him right after Diane had just introduced him and said how smart he was, so I took my water glass and, the next time he said "There is no such thing as reality," I emptied the entire glass of water onto his right foot. When the audience quieted down, he said, "I suppose you think you've made a point." I shrugged. "Well, you haven't," he said. I refilled my water glass. When Rose saw me drink from it, he went on with his presentation.

At the end of the day, the technician from University IT gave me the recordings of the presentations and audience comments. They hadn't bothered to take a feed from the audience microphones, so the comments and questions were inaudible.

That night's dinner at the Tedlock's was a fitting end to the symposium. Dan Rose didn't talk to me; perhaps his shoe was still wet. Barbara was in a foul mood all evening. At dinners at our house, she'd often get drunk after only a few glasses of wine. I never knew if she was someone who got drunk very easily or if she had a head start before she arrived. I didn't get a chance to find out that night, either, because she knocked back several filled glasses in rapid succession. Wiseman's name came up and we learned the source of her mood: "That little Jew," she muttered. She was enraged because he'd called out her boring performance the previous day. There was a stunned silence. Barbara then took a swan dive over a couch, and passed out cold on the floor. Dennis paid it no mind, as if it were an ordinary occurrence. With that bit of reality, the "Editing Reality" symposium ended.

The subsequent meeting with De never happened. We just kept not getting down to New York City and then, a year later, De died.

Three things came out of the "Editing Reality" symposium: the books and postcards Leni Riefenstahl sent me (but not Diane); a small annotated book of the recordings of De at our house, in the symposium, and the drive to Oneonta with Michael (*Emile De Antonio in Buffalo*, Center Working Papers, 2003—annotated because, as Fred noted in his parody, De's talk was full of names); and the story I just told you.

113. Two hands. First Resurrection City town meeting. Washington, DC, 1968.

Index

Notes: page numbers in *italics* refer to photographs.